A LIFE HALF LIVED

SURVIVING THE WORLD'S EMERGENCY ZONES

ANDREW MACLEOD

NEW HOLLAND

*This book is dedicated to two people whose lives were cut short:
My mother Gabrielle did not live long enough to see her children
achieve adulthood. Maria, a small refugee child, did not live long
enough to see hope.*

First published 2013 by
New Holland Publishers Pty Ltd
London • Sydney • Cape Town • Auckland

Garfield House 86–88 Edgware Road London W2 2EA United Kingdom
Wembley Square First Floor Solan Road Gardens Cape Town 8001 South Africa
1/66 Gibbes Street Chatswood NSW 2067 Australia
218 Lake Road Northcote Auckland New Zealand

www.newhollandpublishers.com

A record of this book is held at the British Library and the National Library of Australia

ISBN 9781742572529

Managing director: Fiona Schultz
Publisher: Linda Williams
Publishing director: Lliane Clarke
Designer: Keisha Galbraith
Project editor: Simona Hill
Production director: Olga Dementiev
Printer: Toppan Leefung Printing Limited (China)
10 9 8 7 6 5 4 3 2 1

Keep up with New Holland Publishers on Facebook
http://www.facebook.com/NewHollandPublishers

Cover photograph: Sarajevo, 1996.

Disclaimer
The views expressed in this book are solely those of the author and do not necessarily reflect the views
of his employers past and present, or the publisher.

Contents

∞

Preface

Life gains a new meaning once you have stood outside a church in Ntarama, Rwanda, where the stench of thousands of rotting human corpses permeates the air. The smell never leaves you.

When a small refugee girl from the war zone of Bosnia, completely shuts down emotionally and chooses your shoulder to cry on, you can never look at refugees without sympathy. It is for this reason that the fear and hatred perpetrated by political parties in their discussions around refugees so disgusts me. When you share a beer with a man named Michael Fry, who saved thousands of people by standing in front of an advancing tank in Bosnia, you will count yourself lucky for the rest of your life for having known him. Today he has found his peace living in a Buddhist monastery in southern Brazil.

It was a great privilege to work for two and half years with General Nadeem Ahmed, the Vice Chief of General Staff of the Pakistan Army. During the hours 'chewing the fat' with him, or in a helicopter flying over the Himalayas, he taught me about the futility of the war on terror and the real value of love and of family.

The journey I have been on has taken me through every emotion. I have experienced joy and exhilaration like never before. At other times I've found myself crying in frustration. I have memories that make me smile, and there are others that still sicken me many years later.

It is, however, a journey that has filled me with resolute conviction that the advice I was given as a young student by Senator Michael Tate should be broadened to include: "If you have the good fortune to be born in a country with freedom and education, then you must hone your skills and use them as best you can for the betterment of other people."

I dream that one day humanitarian and developmental aid will not be needed, that conflict is reduced and economic development is more even across the globe. But until that day I dream of a world where collaboration between public and private aid exists to improve emergency humanitarian response and economic development. I wish for a world where private and public sector roles are accepted by all.

We often hear the saying 'Give a person a fish and they will go hungry tomorrow. Teach a person to fish and we beat hunger'. The private sector 'teaches a person to fish' whereas the public sector-based aid and development industry still spends considerable time 'giving fish' instead of teaching to fish. Unless the public sector changes its way of thinking and unless the private sector is accepted as a leading partner in aid and development then poverty will not be defeated. I recognise that private/public collaboration, together with the rehabilitation of profit as an accepted incentive is a revolution in thinking. Let the revolution begin.

Useful Acronyms

AETVP Australia East Timor Volunteer Project
BCPR Bureau for Crisis Prevention and Recovery
BRC British Red Cross
DRC Democratic Republic of Congo
EMA Emergency Management Australia
ERRA Earthquake Reconstruction and Rehabilitation Authority
FAO Food and Agricultural Organisation
FATA Federally Administered Tribal Areas
FRC Federal Relief Commission
FRY Federal Republic of Yugoslavia
HDZ Hrvatska Demokratski Zajednica
HRR Humanitarian Response Review
IASC Inter-Agency Standing Committee
ICRC International Committee of the Red Cross
IDP Internally Displaced Persons
IFRC International Federation of Red Cross and Red Crescent Societies
IHL International Humanitarian Law
INSARAG International Search and Rescue Advisory Group
IOM International Organisation for Migration
MSF Médecines sans Frontières
NGO Non-government Organisation
NWFP North West Frontier Province
OCHA Office for the Coordination of Humanitarian Affairs
OSOCC On-site Coordination Centre

POW Prisoner of War
RC Resident Coordinator
RPA Rwandan Patriotic Army
SADU Small Arms and Disarmament Unit
SALW Small Arms and Light Weapons
SOG Strategic Oversight Group
TRC Transitional Relief Cell
UNAMIR United Nations Assistance Mission for Rwanda
UNDAC United Nations Disaster Assessment and Coordination
UNDP United Nations Development Program
UNHCR United Nations High Commission for Refugees
UNICEF United Nations Childrens Fund
UNMET United Nations Mission in East Timor
UNPROFOR United Nations Protection Force
WHO World Health Organisation
WFP World Food Program
YRC Yugoslav Red Cross

"Each time a man stands up for an ideal, or acts to improve the lot of the rest or strikes out against injustice, he sends forth a tiny ripple of hope, and crossing each other from millions of centres of energy and daring, those ripples build a current that can sweep down the mightiest walls of oppression and resistance...

Few are willing to brave the disapproval of their fellows, the censure of their colleagues, the wrath of their society. Moral courage is a rarer commodity than bravery in battle or great intelligence. Yet it is the one essential, vital quality for those who seek to change a world that yields most painfully to change."

Robert Kennedy, 1966

1.

Why Aid?

I was just 21 when I was in a lecture on constitutional law. Halfway through the lecturer stopped and said, "I don't want to talk about constitutional law today. I prefer to talk about meaning.

"...Having a law degree does not grant you a happy life and a wealthy existence; it imposes upon you an obligation to use your skills for the betterment of other people."

That counsel (the lecturer was Australian Minister for Justice Michael Tate) resonated with me. My mother's premature death the year before at the age of only 45 had caused me to struggle with the big questions: What is the meaning of life? Why are we here? What is the big picture? Michael Tate gave me an answer that I refined into the 'do' or 'be' question.

"Do you want to be a doctor, a teacher, a lawyer?", a parent may ask a child. Concentrating on 'be' is a flaw. Here's an alternative question: What do you want to do? Do you want to do good, do you want to make squillions of dollars, do you want to rape and pillage? For me the 'do' is the more important question; it's about philosophical being. If you get your 'do' right, then you can 'be' different things in life. If you stay consistent with your 'do' and are not focused on the 'be', then you are more likely to be fulfilled. My focus was now to 'do' good work, and inspire others to do good work. This has remained resolute throughout my career. I have had success and sometimes failure – but my objective has stayed the same.

When asked fundamental questions such as, why am I here? the response of many people is to say "I want to provide a good start and a good future for my children." While people wishing a better future for their children is understandable, for me it has never seemed quite enough, because of what happened to my mother. For me, if we are simply producing children who themselves have a better future, who in turn produce more children having the best, surely someone along the line needs to do something to justify not only their existence, but the existence of all the people along the chain? Rightly or wrongly, within my decision-making process following that lecturer's counsel was the belief that I needed to achieve something that not only justified my life, but justified the fact that my mother never got to live as long as she should have. A self-imposed double obligation was formed, firstly to use my skills for the betterment of other people, and secondly to justify the existence of my mother. I was beginning to put shape on my future.

My first goal was to work for organisations that helped on a global level and assisted those who were most in difficulty. To my mind either the International Committee of the Red Cross (ICRC) or the United Nations High Commission for Refugees (UNHCR) seemed logical organisations that fitted the bill. One might as well aim global to try and make some sort of impact. But first I had to finish my studies and learn.

It's fair to say though that most of my learning at university came outside of the academic curriculum. I held various positions within the student union and off-campus I became Vice President of the local branch of the Labor Party, and president of various policy committees. I was a competitive swimmer, played water polo, and founded the university swimming and water polo club. I also trained to become an officer in the Australian Army through the part-time Army Reserve scheme. Each of those aspects of learning became critically important in the jobs that I later did – the least important was that academic study of law, as important as it was. Army Reserve training would unfold to be the most important aspect early on and later in Rwanda and Pakistan particularly. I could never have predicted just how important the experience became in my future career.

At university I began to rejig my law degree to focus on international subjects. While I didn't know exactly how to get into the organisation that I wanted to work for, my subject choice was designed to give me the widest range of options. One evening, a friend and fellow law student, David Bushby asked if I had heard of shipping and transportation law.

"No, what's that?", I replied.

Shipping and transportation law is an unusual area. To understand, think of the following analogy. If you crash your car into someone else's car you'll be sued by the owner of that car for damages. But if you crash your ship into someone else's ship the owner of that ship may sue you or they may sue the owner of your ship. It's a weird provision of international law that ships have 'legal personality' to bring or defend legal actions independent of that of their owners. Shipping and transportation law is some of the most widely accepted private international law in the world, deriving from two major treaties, the Hamburg Rules and the Hague Rules.

In wanting to work for the ICRC or UNHCR I needed to develop an expertise in the Geneva Conventions, which is the most widely accepted public international law in the world. There is an intellectual consistency between a specialisation in shipping and transportation law, and a specialisation in War Crimes, Crimes against Humanity and Genocide. They offer different subject matters but very similar legal structures govern them. The most important thing about these two areas of law is that they are 'non-jurisdictionally isolatable'.

Both shipping law on one hand, and war crimes, crimes against humanity and genocide, on the other are the same law all over the world and are based on an international convention. Criminal law does not provide as many options as Shipping and Transportation Law does because of the jurisdictional mobility of the subject matter. It became a clear choice to specialise.

Training with the Army

In the late 1980s the Australian Army ran an experiment in Tasmania called the 'Brighton model'. The theory was to take university students and put them through military training in the college holidays. For university students it was a guaranteed holiday job. For the army it was an experiment to determine if a closer connection could be made between university campuses and the regular military. The Ready Reserve scheme derived from this model and lasted in Australia for more than a decade.

The military is a good training ground for a number of life skills. It taught me resilience, leadership, how to give a presentation, how to handle weapons, and the skill that became most useful, how to deal with senior officers. One of the most potent lessons was provided by Brigadier Rowe, Commander Ninth Brigade during one of his visits to Tasmania. As the president of the Officer Cadet Mess it was my responsibility to host the Brigadier around Brighton Army Camp.

"What's the worst thing about being a Brigadier?" I asked the commander.

"Everyone wants to kiss my arse. No one wants to tell me when I'm wrong," he said. This was one of the most important lessons I've learned. A poor leader surrounds him or herself with sycophants.

The Next Step: A Lawyer Defending Paedophiles

With my law degree behind me, my next focus was to secure the one-year post-university training at a law firm, which was prerequisite in order to be formally admitted as a legal practitioner to the court system. While the lawyer's life would not be my entire career, failing to find such an apprenticeship and therefore failing to gain formal admission to practise as a lawyer, would be foolish. Besides, I figured the easiest place to look for work in the ICRC or UNHCR, my ultimate aim, would be while working for a law firm in London.

At this point my focus was to be a shipping and maritime lawyer. As luck would have it, David Nathan at the law firm Dunhill Madden Butler, was hoping to expand their practice in shipping and maritime law to the Melbourne office. Being the only student who had expressed an interest in that area, I was hired.

One of the earliest cases I worked on involved the Catholic Church. Dunhill Madden Butler acted for Catholic Church Insurance and we found ourselves in the position of providing legal services to defend priests against the civil claims made against them for sexual harassment, abuse and rape of young boys.

Dunhill Madden Butler did not have a criminal law practice, and did not defend the priests of their criminal actions. However, once found guilty civil claims for compensation would follow. While visiting the priests in prison, I found that many of the crimes that they had committed were greater than those that they had been accused of in court. It was shocking. Often the priests described in disgusting detail the actions that they had perpetrated. The complete lack of guilt because their 'sins' had been 'confessed' and 'forgiven' was staggering. It was the first of several events that made me sceptical of institutionalised religion, to question the existence of God and ultimately to come to the conclusion that I believe God does not exist.

Dunhill Madden Butler had a shipping practice led by partner Rod Withnell. It became acutely clear that Rod was a man who cared deeply about his clients and was fastidious in checking every detail, and working as hard as he could in the best interest of those people. When he left Dunhill Madden Butler, he reduced the incentive for me to remain as a lawyer. My desire to work for the ICRC or UNHCR remained strong. I volunteered with the International Humanitarian Law (IHL) Committee of the Victorian branch of the Australian Red Cross. This experience was useful later. The partners at Dunhill Madden Butler were aware of this and a couple of them also joined the IHL Committee. Following my Articles year, with the support of Dunhill Madden Butler, the next step was to head to the UK to study for a Masters Degree in both Shipping and Human Rights Laws. This, I hoped, would help me enter the aid world.

Studying in the UK

Inter-Varsity debating in the United Kingdom was fun and provided the opportunity to win prize money which, for a university student, is always a good thing. There were some interesting characters involved in the debating union at the University of Southampton, principal among them being Donal Blaney, Paul Osborne and Sarkis Zeronian. Donal Blaney was very right wing in his political outlook and has gone on to run the Young Britons Foundation, a think-tank aimed at getting 16 to 19-year-olds involved in the Conservative Party. Despite our political differences, we all remain friends today. Paul has a sharp brain and a dry British wit. He became my regular debating partner. The two of us were never defeated when we debated together. I brought to the partnership a laconic Australian style, which matched well with Paul's keen intellect. Because we were so successful in debating, we were invited to the United States to give lectures to the Americans on how to undertake parliamentary-style debating, together with the top debater from Oxford University, Rufus Black. Rufus also knew Michael Tate. So as we sat one night in a pizza shop in Princeton, New Jersey and chewed the fat over what it was we wanted to do in life. I told him I wanted to join the ICRC or UNHCR.

"Why don't you want to work in Australia?" asked Rufus.

"Because Rufus, at the end of the day, I have inherent faith that the Australian people get it right."

Rufus agreed that Australia was lucky but did say, "Remember, there are also talented people there who will try and destroy that."

Maritime Law: A Boatload of Russians and a Suitcase of Cash

By mid-1995 I'd finished my Masters Degree and had organised to work with the law firm Watson Farley Williams. Watson Farley Williams acted for CIT, a capital investment company based in New York. CIT was owed multi-millions of dollars by Adriatic Tankers, and under the terms of the mortgage agreement could take possession of the vessels that Adriatic owned. The problem was that Adriatic Tankers owed a lot of money to a lot of people. Since maritime vessels have their own legal personality, they can be arrested, and this is what happened with Adriatic's ships – many were under arrest in ports all around the world.

In order to arrest a ship, a person owed a debt by that ship would go to a local court to seek payment of that debt. The court would order that the ship be 'arrested' and not leave port until the debt is paid. Port authorities would be obliged to prevent the vessel from leaving port. Once a ship is arrested, anyone owed money would register their claim. The arrest cannot be lifted until all debts are settled. Where a corporation owns multiple ships, it's usual for that organisation to set up individual ship-owning companies to try and protect the ships with no debt from other in-debt vessels.

Watson Farley Williams was looking for different Adriatic Tankers arrested around the world to have CIT's debt recognised as part of the local court proceedings. In most cases CIT was the largest creditor and would try and negotiate an assignment of other people's debts for a reduced payment, then go to court with the combination of all debts requesting a court order for the ship's ownership to transfer from Adriatic Tankers to CIT. CIT would then on-sell the vessel. Early on, CIT had determined that the vessel *Rokko San* was a 'scrapper', meaning that it would be sold for scrap metal. In order to transfer ownership in this way, someone has to fly to whichever jurisdiction the vessel is in and do deals with everyone who is owed money by the vessel, which often would include the ship's agent, the local chandler, port authorities and the crew.

The MV *Rokko San* was a 300-metre, 150,000 deadweight tonne bulk ore carrier with twenty-five crew on board that had been stuck in Varna, Bulgaria for two years. Watson Farley Williams sent me to Varna to find out if it was possible to do deals with the various creditors. I ascertained that the shipyard had a claim for US$150,000, the agent for about US$20,000, the Bulgarian Register of Shipping for about US$43,000, Navigation Maritime Bulgare for about US$16,000, and the crew for more than US$600,000, rising at a daily rate of about US$1,000. I also met with all the creditors to determine the level of settlements that were achievable with all, except for the crew.

The crew were effectively prisoners on board the vessel, for if they left the ship they would lose their claim, but every day that they stayed on the ship their claim grew larger. In the two years they had been on board many had suffered tragedy in their families back home but had been unable to return there. They were demanding 100 per cent of their back pay. Part of my role was to negotiate the minimum possible because, after all, CIT was not the bad boy in this. After tough negotiations the crew agreed to accept 70 per cent of their claim but with two very interesting conditions. One was that they wanted to be paid in cash in Bulgaria, and the other was that they wanted to meet the client, a guy named Bob DiMarsico.

In the mid-1990s there simply wasn't half a million US dollars in cash in Bulgaria to pay the crew. The crew pointed out that as they all came from Vladivostok, and hadn't been back there for two years, they had no idea which banks still existed, so a bank transfer was out of the question. There was also no chance that any sane person would be going to be walking around Bulgaria with 70 per cent of $600,000 stuffed into a suitcase. The solution was to fly half the crew to an intermediary port where they would be paid in cash, and then return to Bulgaria to pick up the remaining crew. The crew were rightly very suspicious and also aware that once they left the vessel they would lose their claim. By doing it in two halves the crew knew that at least half of them would get their pay as the second half would be insurance back on the vessel. But for the second half of the crew to get paid once they left the ship, they needed to trust me and trust the client, hence their demand to meet Bob. They also asked for US$1,000 each in cash before they would leave the vessel. I returned to London and telephoned Bob, the client.

"G'day Bob. The crew will settle for 70 per cent."

"Great job, you've done well."

"There are two conditions." A worried DiMarsico asked what they would be. "They want $1,000 cash each upfront."

"No problem", he said.

"And they want to meet you."

I explained to Bob that this was a deal-breaker and that we would have to go back to Bulgaria together. But we had another problem. Which intermediary port could we use between Varna, Bulgaria and Vladivostok in Russia, where we could pay two lots of approximately US$300,000 in cash, and where the Russians would be accepted with expired passports?

As it turned out, Gatwick airport in London was the easiest intermediary port, but it took some organising! Bob DiMarsico flew to London and then we flew together with $28,000 cash in a suitcase to Varna, Bulgaria via Sofia; the first leg with British Airways and the second with Antonov. In retrospect, while on board we were at the mercy of the Russian crew. If they or even a few of them had decided to become violent, we were in trouble. The picture of Bob with a black suitcase balanced on his knees handing out wads of cash still brings a smile to my face. It was no small feat getting the first half of the crew to disembark and follow us to England, and Bob put this down to my ability 'at the Blarney' as he calls it. But this was only the first part of the journey.

The plan was to take half the crew to Gatwick airport and pay them their due. Bob would fly back to New York; I would fly back to Varna and pick up the second half of the crew. Part of the British Airways business is called Special Services. It usually deals with rock stars and the like so when told of my challenge in needing to pay two lots of $300,000 to 25 Russians with expired passports, they said they could quite cheerfully assist, as long as the money was organised with Thomas Cook. We had to trust them.

We reversed the route from Varna to Sofia and headed towards Gatwick. As the plane touched down at the airport we were surprised when the plane stopped before reaching the gate and an announcement was made, "Could Mr MacLeod make himself known to the airline staff?"

A set of stairs was pulled to the side of the plane and on came two machine-gun armed policemen saying, "Mr MacLeod please come with us." The police escorted me across the tarmac, out through customs and into Thomas Cook on the land side of the airport. Thomas Cook had pre-packaged the first half of the $300,000 into the individual bundles for the crew and insisted on a count. After we were satisfied that the cash count was correct, the money was placed inside a metal suitcase, attached to my wrist with a handcuff, and I was escorted back through the air-side of the airport.

As we walked through the metal detectors they squealed like scalded children. Everyone froze in the departure lounge and stood agape as we passed by with the metal suitcase handcuffed to my wrist, two machine-gun-armed escorts, making our way to the British Airways first-class lounge. British Airways had gently told the first-class passengers that they would have to share with business class. The entire lounge was turned over to the Russians, including free food and drinks. Clearly British Airways staff had some sympathy for the plight of the crew.

Bob re-counted and handed out cash to the first group of Russians who were then trans-shipped home for the first time in two years. I returned to Varna and the entire exercise was repeated before we got the rest of the crew home. Justice was done for the crew.

The Problems of Finding Work in Aid

When I arrived in the UK in 1994 I started my search for aid work while completing my master's degree and working for the law firm. My initial focus was on UNHCR. At that time, the UN was going bankrupt, partly due to the refusal of the US to pay their dues, and partly because of an 'outbreak of peace'. The UN had increased operations in a number of countries such as 'Operation Restore Hope' in Somalia, dealing with the Rwandan crisis and peacekeepers in Bosnia. All of these operations were now in relatively stable periods, yet the UN had given permanent roles to people dealing with these countries and couldn't downscale those permanent postings. The organisation therefore was cutting staff by 10 per cent across the board – with job losses falling mainly on non-permanent employees, but also severely restricting new employment. The result was that the UN was overstaffed.

Compounding my problem of finding employment within the UN was their system of quotas. The UN and its associated agencies hire people on a geographical quota basis as well as on ability, and it had an over-supply of Australians. As a general rule, for any job that is advertised in the United Nations, female candidates from the developing world are considered first. If a suitable candidate cannot be found then they look for male candidates from the developing world. Following that, female candidates from the developed world are considered, and only if no one is found in the previous three categories does the organisation look at males from the developed world. The worst thing to be if you wish to get a job in the United Nations is a white Anglo-Saxon male.

Australia's Ambassador to the UN informed me that he would love to help me get into Aid, but as he hadn't been able to help an Australian female lawyer with 10 years' experience with the UN General Assembly who had the direct backing of the Australian government to find work, then he saw little hope for my chances. It was disillusioning. After 12 months of hammering on doors, meeting people and asking for jobs, the same message kept coming back: "There isn't anything here! When we do start looking again you'll need to have had some Africa experience."

Recruiting organisations wanted people with experience – Oxfam and other agencies wanted people with African experience – but how do you get experience? It was a classic example of 'catch 22'. Many people would like to be aid workers. Yet it is a surprisingly difficult world to access and many who find the system too hard to break into simply give up. In desperation I went into small aid organisations in London and said, "I'll do anything! I'll dig ditches or drive trucks – I need experience!"

Finally, I was given some really good advice: "If we wanted to hire ditch diggers or truck drivers then we would hire local staff," an aid worker told me. "You cost us US$100,000 in training, accommodation, transport and insurance, not to mention your salary, before you even arrive in the country. You need to understand what your professional skill is and sell that professional skill. Being motivated is not enough."

And that was when I met Thomas Riess.

My Lucky Break

I was sent to Amsterdam from the London law firm in the early part of 1996 to attend a shipping law conference. As I cast my eyes down the attendance lists my eyes settled on one name: Thomas Riess, deputy head of the transport division of the International Committee of the Red Cross. Taking my chance, I introduced myself to him.

"What are you doing here, Thomas, we're all lawyers and insurance companies screwing money from each other, but you are the ICRC?" I said.

"We are the biggest shippers in the world of cargo to war zones and we have a problem with a Bill of Lading," said Thomas. A Bill of Lading is the legal contractual document involving cargo and ships. This was right in my area of speciality.

"Let me take a look," I ventured. With the help of others in the firm we rewrote the ICRC Bill of Lading overnight and gave it to Thomas the next day.

"How much?" he asked.

I told him it was free, and gave him my CV. Thomas asked me what I wanted to do with the ICRC, to which I suggested that if he had anything in his division I'd take it.

"No," he replied. "As a lawyer you want something like inspection of POW camps and dissemination of the Geneva Conventions in war zones. I'll see what I can do."

Coincidentally at that precise moment in Belgrade, the Dissemination Delegate, Pierre Townsend, the person who had responsibility for International Humanitarian Law and relations with the armed forces for the ICRC office, quit. It was good timing for me. The day after my chance meeting with him, Thomas returned to Geneva. He went into a meeting held by the dissemination division just as they were asking where they would find another English-speaking lawyer who understood the law, the military and was ready immediately to replace the delegate who quit in Belgrade. Thomas called to ask if I would be interested. Was I interested? At last, my dream was beginning to materialise.

Thomas sent my CV to the dissemination people at the ICRC who sent it to the recruitment section who wrote informing me that they could do nothing as I was not a Swiss citizen. In those days the ICRC hired few non-Swiss. The ICRC was founded by a Swiss, based in Switzerland and firmly believed that only Swiss could be neutral. The recruitment section did say that perhaps I could be 'loaned' to them by a National Red Cross Society and that I should speak to them. I rang Thomas for an explanation. This was the official line, he said, but we could try some unofficial stuff. He put me in contact with Vivian Mattay of the recruitment section at the ICRC. Vivian said that she would send my CV to the British Red Cross (BRC), expressing an interest on my behalf; and then hopefully BRC selection would be a formality. It wasn't.

The theory went like this: I would first have to be pre-selected by the BRC, then do a selection day with them and if accepted be placed on the list of approved delegates. Every two weeks or so the ICRC would send a list of positions that they need filling, leaving National Red Cross Societies to nominate the people that they think are acceptable. Once I was on the approved list I could advise Vivian, who would then ask, innocently, "What about Andrew MacLeod?" If the BRC then said, "Well, he may be okay," I would have to go to Geneva for a formal ICRC interview. If accepted by them then the file would return to the BRC for funding approval. The Desk Officer responsible for the geographical area that the ICRC wanted filling would then decide if he could afford the funds to have me do that job. It was overly complex, bureaucratic and entirely normal for the aid world.

So much reliance was placed on events and people beyond my influence. There was an awful lot of "if this, then that" had to be got through. So many things could go wrong, but I had to play my role and hope. With Vivian's pushing there came an invitation for a BRC selection day in early July 1996. Vivian intimated that the ICRC had a position that they needed filling urgently. After a week's wait, the BRC let me know that I had succeeded at step one, subject to them receiving urgent references. I told Vivian who then called the BRC "out of the blue" to see how things were going. The BRC then called me back with the "surprising news" that the ICRC wanted to see me the next Wednesday. Could I make it? they asked.

Of course I could. Nervous, excited and scared, I was getting closer to my goal. The day with the ICRC went well with relatively simple questions about the application of International Humanitarian Law and the relationship with the military, the first time my military experience became clearly relevant. We also spoke of my military training and legal background. The head of dissemination finished the day saying that he wanted to send me to Yugoslavia to fill the position that Thomas had advised me about.

Yugoslavia is a country in which the operational language is English. In most other countries it is French. The ability to speak French is usually compulsory to work with the ICRC, but as Yugoslavia was a non-francophone mission, no one remembered to ask whether I could speak French.

There was still another hurdle, though. Funding. I returned to England and waited another week. Vivian unofficially called to say that the ICRC was serious about the position, and would ask the BRC if they would pay for my posting.

I called my voicemail to check the messages. My knees buckled and I sank to the floor. I became oblivious to all around me as it seemed finally to be happening. Yes, my selection was successful and the British Red Cross would approve my posting should the ICRC have one! There was no absolute certainty, however, as it was all subject to a successful completion of a basic training course. Another hurdle.

The basic training course was held with the Austrian Red Cross. With a little bit of good fortune, that which I'd strived for and set my mind to seven and a half years earlier was about to come true. It had taken a lot of planning and persistence, and a tactful sense of when to push or sit back and hope. I'd fought so hard and for so long to get a role with one of these organisations, and hoped not to be disappointed.

2.

Understanding Yugoslavia

Like many war zones, Yugoslavia is deeply misunderstood by people in the West. Opinions formed on the basis of 30-second sound bites are rarely well informed. Few people take the time to learn the history and try and understand why it is that others engage in something as horrific as war.

The Berlin Wall dividing Germany came down in 1989 and many of us remember the spread of cheer across the world as the Cold War ended. Good cheer was short lived. The 'New World Order' was tested in August 1990 by Saddam Hussein when he invaded Kuwait. Russian president Gorbachev faced a coup in August 1991, and somehow a war had started in Europe, in Yugoslavia, by August 1992.

Yugoslavia's story is complicated by the fact that there was not one war, but four. Yugoslavia had been made up of six republics (Slovenia, Croatia, Bosnia, Serbia, Montenegro and Macedonia) and two autonomous areas (Vojvodina and Kosovo). The first war was the 10-day long breakaway of Slovenia in 1991, the republic that bordered Italy and Austria. The second was in Croatia starting in 1991. The third, the war in Bosnia starting in 1992 and the fourth, in Kosovo, which was capped by the NATO-led bombing in 1999. Each of these conflicts had their roots in post-World War II country borders and alliances and pre-existing ethnic tensions that had been held in check by Yugoslavia's dictator, Josip Tito during his 1945–1980 rule.

In the ten years after Tito's death, ethnic tensions slowly rose, and somewhat ironically it was the end of the Berlin Wall and the hope of peace following the Cold War, that brought war to Yugoslavia. Understanding ethnicity helps the understanding of conflict.

Slovenia was the most 'ethnically pure' of the republics, being more than 90 per cent Slovene. Croatia had distinct parts that were mainly ethnically Croatian, as well as some areas that were ethnic Serbian enclaves. Bosnia was an area ethnically mixed largely between Serbs, Croats and the Muslim communities. Macedonia had a mixed population of around 70 per cent Macedonian and 30 per cent ethnic Albanian. Montenegro, the smallest republic, was mainly Montenegrin, although the sense of self identity was split between those who thought to be Montenegrin was really to be Serbian, and those who believed Montenegro to be truly separate from Serbia.

In Serbia the ethnic mix was even more complicated given the two 'semi-autonomous' provinces, Kosovo and Vojvodina. Kosovo was mainly ethnic Albanian, Vojvodina had large Hungarian minorities, and Serbia proper had several nationalities represented.

When Tito died he was succeeded not by one president, but by a collective presidency of eight men, one from each of the six republics and two autonomous areas. The power balance was split between the ethnic groups and no one group had absolute control. This was to change as the Berlin Wall fell and new elections drew near.

The Rise of Nationalism and the Role of Elections

On a superficial level, elections are a sign of democracy. But if a country does not foster the creation of a civil society that has healthy public debate, and a party-political system that represents the people rather than elites, then elections held too early in that country's history will hinder and not help democracy. Early elections allow extremists in society to rally around a manifesto loaded with fear and hatred of other ethnic groups. This happened in former Yugoslavia.

The insistence on early elections became a magnet for nationalists in each of Yugoslavia's republics. Nationalists were able to create emotional arguments around 'greater Serbia', or the birth of an independent Croatia, and balanced and less emotional views did not gain air time. Half a century of repression under Tito ensured that civil society had not yet developed healthy public and democratic debate. By insisting on elections too early, the West inadvertently gave life and stage to the nationalists – with disastrous consequences in each of the republics.

It was this interface between nationalism and early elections that provided the spark that lit the fire of war in the Balkans.

The Rise of Nationalism in Serbia

Serb nationalism was revived in 1989 when on June 28 of that year one million Serbs went to the site of the 'Battlefield of the Blackbirds' at Gazimestan to hear Slobodan Milosevic speak. The date of the speech was significant as it marked the 600th anniversary of the founding of nationhood for the Serbs.

Milosevic was at that time trying to take control of the Serbian Communist Party. While he gave his speech, he had plain clothes policemen, dressed fraudulently as ethnic Albanians, throw stones at the Serbian onlookers. The action was deliberately intended to inspire hatred and fear and created an opportunity for Milosevic to proclaim that the 'Serbs were under attack' and he, Milosevic, would never allow Serbs to be beaten again!

This was master political manipulation at its best – using manufactured fear as a political tool. Milosevic well understood the political maxim 'If you have a choice between preaching fear, hatred and intolerance on one hand, or compassion, understanding and togetherness on the other, fear wins every time'. Milosevic was elected president of Serbia and immediately unilaterally removed the autonomy of both Vojvodina and Kosovo. Removing the autonomy gave Serbia three out of eight votes on the collective Yugoslav presidency (Serbia's vote, plus that of Kosovo and Vojvodina). Montenegro, long seen as a puppet of Serbia due to the ethnic bonds between Montenegrins and Serbians, would in effect give Serbia the fourth out of eight votes. With Serbia's political power growing and threatening control over the presidency, it was natural that the other four republics became nervous.

The Rise of Nationalism in Croatia

In the lead up to the first Croatian multi-party elections in 1990, nationalist parties began to emerge in Croatia. The Croatian Democratic Union (Hrvatska Demokratski Zajednica or HDZ) piloted the Croatian Nationalist charge under the lead of a former General and historian, Franjo Tudjman. The Croatian-based Serb nationalists were first led by the moderate Jovan Raskovic, who was usurped by the more radical Milan Babic.

Raskovic's demand for recognition of a Serbian nation as part of a Croatian state undermined the Croatian leader Tudjman's view of a united and ethnically pure Croatia. When Tudjman failed to recognise the Serbs as a constituent minority in the new draft Croatian constitution, alarm bells rang in the Serbian radical community, ultimately leading to the demise of Raskovic and the rise of Babic.

Babic first sought to unify the various Serb-led regions of Croatia and one by one brought the moderate Serb areas into his Association of Serbian Municipalities. By July 1990 his association had gathered enough strength to plan a referendum on Serbian sovereignty within Croatia, planned for that August. Two days before the planned referendum on August 17 Tudjman acted and sent his police to 'regain control' of 'secessionist' municipalities. Croatians armed for the upcoming battle with Serbia for independence, and the Croatian Serbs armed for what was to become their battle for independence from Croatia.

March 1991 was a critical month. The people of Yugoslavia become aware that the nation was on the verge of tearing apart and took to the streets of Belgrade to protest about rising nationalism. Pacifism was suppressed by state-sanctioned violence. Milosevic called on the army to fulfil its constitutional role as protector of the nation by forcing it to stay together. Milosevic, at that time, was leader of only one republic (Serbia) and not yet President of all of Yugoslavia. "They [the Croatians] are trying to force Serbia to forego Yugoslavia and accept a diktat about the disassociation of Yugoslavia into as many states as there are republics. Serbia would then have to abandon the political ideal with which it entered into the creation of Yugoslavia," Milosevic had said. Many viewed Milosevic's statement as nothing more than confirmation of Serbian desires for domination.

Slovenia – The First War (June/July 1991)

In the republic of Slovenia (often confused with the Croatian region of Slavonia for the similarity of the name), calls for secession had begun quietly, but grew louder as fear of 'Serbian domination' grew along with Serb and Croat nationalism. Nationalist voices scared the Slovenes. On June 25, 1991 Slovenia, in part fearing Serb domination and in part seeking its own national autonomy, unilaterally declared itself an independent state. What followed was a 10-day war in which hardly a shot was fired. Many in the Yugoslav military thought that Slovenia was bluffing, so the tanks that were sent from Belgrade carried no ammunition.

Slovenia, fought one of the shortest and bloodless wars in history, and from it gained independence. The immediate consequence would be the reduction of the rotating presidency from eight to seven members. Serbia retained four votes, and would have the majority.

Slovenia's population was almost entirely ethnic Slovenian. That republic's breakaway would have little impact on ethnic tensions and nationalist dreams in other republics, but politically it was a time bomb.

Macedonia too, quietly slipped off into secession almost unnoticed. Macedonia was well placed to boom economically after a split but instead became mired in controversy with Greece about the historical traditions of Alexander the Great, the name Macedonia, and the flag. This prevented a rapid accession to the European Union through a Greek boycott, and decades of economic stagnation.

The four remaining republics, Croatia, Serbia, Bosnia and Herzegovina, and Montenegro, remained with the difficult and volatile problem of mixed ethnicity in their own territory, and with the issue of Serb political domination. There were now four republics and two autonomous areas. Six votes, of which Serbia effectively controlled four.

Western governments seemed oblivious to the rapid unravelling of a nation in the heart of Europe. The European Union didn't know how to take a consolidated approach to this political dilemma, and didn't want US intervention. The break-up of Yugoslavia was to be the first test of European collective foreign policy, and by their own admission, they failed. Indeed western action inflamed, not calmed tensions.

Croatia – The Second War (August 1991, ceasefire January 1992, ended 1995)

More than one-third of the territory of Croatia was ethnic Serb. Croatia is roughly crescent-shaped with the Serb minority in Croatia centred in three main areas. The inside apex of the crescent (later known as the Serb Krajina) bordering Bosnia, the far north-eastern section (known as Eastern Slavonia) and finally, a small section in the western part of Slavonia, near Zagreb. Having seen the republic of Slovenia slip away from Yugoslavia, there was little interest from Serbia in allowing Croatia an easy exit. If Croatia were to secede and become a separate republic, then many within the nationalist movements of Croatia wanted an ethnically pure country. The Serbs, to their thinking, had no future in an independent Croatia and therefore wanted Croatia, or at least, the ethnic Serbian parts of Croatia to stay part of a greater Serbia Conflict began, initially just between the different ethnic groups mainly in the Serb Krajina and the Eastern and Western Slavonia regions (not to be confused with the now independent Slovenia).

As the European summer of 1991 drew to a close, the war heated up. Croatia declared independence. The Serb Krajina fought to a stalemate;. Western Slavonia had also battled to a stalemate. In the Eastern Slavonia near the town of Vukovar, the flames were fanned and burned strong. The fighting was brutal.

The Yugoslav Army was given the order by the Serb-dominated Yugoslav government to clear Vukovar of 'rebel' Croats. Of the 40,000 people that lived in Vukovar before the war, only 15,000 now remained; the rest had fled or been killed. The Army was told most of those remaining were Croatian fighters and not civilians. In August 1991 the shelling of Vukovar began. Three months later the town fell. At the same time, the Yugoslav Army sought to assert control in the south and began the siege and shelling of Dubrovnik, on Croatia's Dalmatian coast. The shelling achieved little of military benefit, but ensured the world would turn against the Serbian people. Of all things Milosevic underestimated, and Tudjman understood, nothing was more important to the long-term perception of their people and their cause, than the power of the international media.

On October 8, 1991, the Croatian Parliament, with the strong backing of the Germans, severed all ties with the former Yugoslavia. Their independence was born. British PM Margaret Thatcher had opposed the dissolution of Yugoslavia, however, German Chancellor Helmut Kohl asserted enormous pressure even threatening to leave the EU.

By the end of 1991 the former Yugoslavia was in ruins. Slovenia and Macedonia had gone, stalemates had been fought in brutal conflict in the Serb Krajina, and Eastern and Western Slavonia. Bosnia looked on nervously. The Europeans were cocky in their approach to foreign affairs, saying that at the end of the Cold War the world no longer needed 'Uncle Sam' as a policeman. The Americans left peace creation to the Europeans – who failed miserably.

The Devils' Pact Towards a New War

At the end of 1991 and start of 1992 both Milosevic and Tudjman had other cards to play. Tudjman wanted the Croatians in Bosnia to merge with Croatia to from a 'Greater Croatia'. Milosevic needed a land bridge to the Krajina via the Serbian areas of Bosnia for a 'Greater Serbia'. For each man achieving independence for all of their ethnic brothers would see them remembered as fathers of their nations. The problem was what to do with Bosnia.

A series of secret meetings between Milosevic and Tudjman took place at Karadjordjevo, Tito's old hunting lodge. The subject of the discussion was Bosnia. So, while Croats and Serbs fought brutally in the streets of Vukovar, their own leaders secretly met to carve a deal around the division of Bosnia.

Milosevic and Tudjman shared one critical view – Serbia and Croatia were 'nations' but Bosnia was not. To them Bosnia was an artificial creation formed in 1974 by Tito to placate the Islamic minority. This Islamic minority did not deserve the nation status that Tito gave them believed Milosevic and Tudjman, who decided the Muslims were either Croats or Serbs who had changed religion. To them, Bosnia should not exist so they agree to divide that republic between Croatia and Serbia. The Bosnian Serbs would join a greater Serbia and the Bosnian Croats would join a greater Croatia. Milosevic and Tudjman may have agreed, but they underestimated the Muslim community.

To tame the Muslims, the Croats and Serbs first needed to stop fighting each other. The secret Karadjordjevo agreement between Milosevic and

Above: Me (on the left) aged 3 with my brother.

Left: Me at Carlton Kindergarten, aged 4.

Below: My great mate Chris Hewison, and his father Tony Hewison, my life mentor until his death.

Above: With my mother, a few months before she died, 1987.

Below: Andrew Farquhar (left) and me after the last field exercise and before our qualification as an Officer in the Australian Army, 1990.

Below: With Michael Tate when he was Ambassador to the Netherlands (right), circa 1995.

Above: Michael Fry (front left) me (front right) with Red Cross youth at Sutamore in Montenegro. Michael is an unsung hero from Kladusa in the Bosnian war.

Above: The first beach rescue training in Montenegro.

Above: With Gordana in Sombor. An amazing woman, she trained every villager to register and receive refugees. She ran the orphanage where I met Maria.

Above: A family reunion in Rwanda 1998; the mother had no idea her child was still alive four years after the genocide. The uncertainty in her body language shows how difficult reunions are after long periods.

Above: Ntarama Catholic Church, Kigali, Rwanda, 1999. The stench of death.

Above: A skull on a bible set on an altar. Ntarama Catholic Church, Rwanda.

Above: Kilele, left, leading the 'hear no evil' joke. He is a great guy with a good sense of humour.

Above: Kilele, me and Bertilde, with Leopold behind – a great team.

Above: At the source of the River Nile, Rwanda 1999.

Above: Four local boys waited for me each day, Rwanda 1998.

Above: Janelle Saffin with her escort. An amazingly brave woman. Timor, 1999.

Far left: Outside a polling station. Referendum Day, East Timor, 1999.

Left: Signing the 'all clear' Referendum Day, East Timor, 1999.

Below: Helio (left), Ericho and me. Ericho headed the Aitarak Militia and wanted us dead, but he didn't know what we looked like, 1999.

Right: With Abel Gutteres (right) just before the Aitarak Militia tried to kill him, 1999.

Left: With soon-to-be President Gusmao in East Timor leading up to the presidential elections, 2000.

Above: Lining up to vote for the future of their country for the first time. Referendum Day, East Timor, 1999.

Above: Campaign trail, 2001.

Above: During electioneering in 2001 with Julia Gillard (left), who then became Prime Minister of Australia, and Craig Emerson on the right.

Tudjman was cooked up to have internationally monitored ceasefires. They would invite peace-keepers in in order to keep the two groups separate. in the Krajina and Slavonia and at the same time the Serbs and the Croats would tame the Muslims.,

The Europeans naively came to help sending peace monitors. With European peace monitors in place in Vukovar and Krajina the war in Croatia was put on hold and the war in Bosnia could begin.

Bosnia – The Third War (March 1992 – December 1995

Many people thought of Bosnia as a mixed society made up of many groups. This is not strictly true. It was multi ethnic, but never mixed. Few individual villages were mixed. Some towns did mix to a degree, most notably Sarajevo, but even in this town the suburbs were often divided into Serb, and non-Serb.

Bosnia too fell to the desires of nationalists. In the lead up to European/ US pressured, post-Cold War multi-party elections, various ethnic and nationalist parties formed. Croats calling for autonomy for Croats, Serbs calling for autonomy for Serbs. The only group opposing the spread of nationalism was the reformed communists.

But what of the Muslims who made up 44 per cent of the population? Would they agree to carve up their community and calmly join with a Greater Croatia or a Greater Serbia?

Alija Izetbegovic rose to become one of the leading intellectuals within the Muslim community. He fought for a united Bosnia to include Muslim, Serb and Croat. Izetbegovic did so not because of over-riding desires for a multi-ethnic haven, but under the realisation that if the Croatian and Serbian communities split, then the Muslims as a 'nation' would be split between Croatian control and Serbian control and would cease to exist.

Alija became president of Bosnia under its complicated seven-member presidency. Two members would represent each of the ethnic groups (Muslim, Serb and Croat), and one represented the 'nation' of Bosnia.

The Independence of Croatia sealed the fate of Bosnia. Bosnia had to declare itself independent, or agree to split and join Croatia and Serbia. Serbs, Croats and Muslims of Bosnia could not agree.

Izetbegovic and the Muslim-dominated parliament argued for independence, with Serb nationalist leader Radovan Karadzic declared that the country would be 'dead at birth'. The Muslim-dominated parliament declared independence and on April 6, 1992, Bosnia was recognised as a separate state. On April 8, two days into nationhood Karadzic's prediction came true when the notorious Serb paramilitary leader Zeljko Raznatovic, alias 'Arkan' began to shell the predominantly Muslim border town of Zvornik from inside Serbia. By April 10 the town had fallen and the ethnic cleansing began. The war in Bosnia had started, the country was stillborn.

Ethnic-based self-fulfilling prophesies became the norm. As more and more propaganda permeated through of ethnic groups claiming 'kill before they kill you' spread from village to village, state-sponsored militias, ad hoc village-based militias and everyday citizens armed themselves to 'shoot and ask questions later'. People actually did kill before being killed. Village after village purged any minority. Serb villages wiped out their Croat neighbours. Croats wiped out Muslims, Muslims wiped out Serbs. Large villages purged small.

Initially the Muslim and Croat forces were united against the Serbs as both had suffered at the hands of the largely Serbian Yugoslav Army remnants. But this was to change.

The Muslims were fighting for survival. They based their government in Sarajevo, the capital of Bosnia and Herzegovina. The Croats had formed the central Bosnian Republic of Herceg-Bosna, based in Mostar, but had never defined the boundaries of this state. The Serbs centred their territory 'The Republic of Srpska' around the tiny mountain hamlet of Pale.

The town of Mostar in Bosnia and Herzegovina is central to the Croat/ Muslim story. The Croat forces, led by Mate Boban, pushed the Serbs out of Mostar early on in the conflict, but had to live uncomfortably with the Muslim 'allies' in the town, strictly divided into different areas. The western media was quick to blame the Serbs. In fact, the fighting In Mostar was between Muslim and Croat, but the misunderstanding of the international media was normal in such a complicated conflict. Unfortunately international policy makers often listened to the erroneous media reports.

Years of slaughter followed with at least 100,000 people dead and millions displaced. Hundreds of thousands of refugees had their lives destroyed forever.

The US became involved and negotiated a new pact between the Croats and the Muslims, in order for them to develop a united front. In August 1995, the Croatians launched Operation Storm and pushed the Serbs out of the Serb Krajina. The Muslim Fifth Corp led a parallel push called Operation Flash, toward the Serb stronghold of Banja Luka. Both were supported by the United States. Suddenly the Serbs wanted to negotiate.

The parties met at Dayton in Ohio, USA, and after long negotiations agreed on the plan that stopped the war but fell well short of peace. The resulting agreement is still in place. It may have lasted since 1995 but many simply look at Bosnia as a frozen war. Without the on-going international forces in the country, few believe Bosnia could exist, even today.

All sides perpetrated huge crimes, leading to the creation of an International Criminal Tribunal set up in The Hague to hear the crimes of genocide and ethnic cleansing. Radovan Karadzic is on trial today. Izetbegovic and Tudjman both died in their countries, and Milosevic died during his trial.

My Role in the Former Yugoslavia in 1996: First Mission

Yugoslavia was to be my first mission as a Dissemination and Co-operation Delegate for the International Committee of the Red Cross. November 16, 1996, marked my arrival in Belgrade as a wet-behind-the-ears delegate. I was enormously curious about some very simple things such as what would an ICRC Delegation look like? What would Belgrade be like to live in? Being a fan of history, I wanted to know the city's background.

Belgrade is a city that has had strategic importance for more than 5000 years. It sits at the meeting of the Sava and Danube rivers on the southern part of the Central European plain that extends through Hungary, Bulgaria, Romania and the former Yugoslavia. Its geographical importance, at the crossroads between Europe and Asia, between Christendom and Islam, is obvious from a strategic look at any map. Perhaps that is why it's a city that claims, as part of its culture, to be the city destroyed and rebuilt more times than any other in human history. As the capital of what was then the remains of Yugoslavia, Belgrade was not a city recovering from war. Rather it was one that tried hard to pretend the war never happened. It was and is a lively city, with parks, gardens and people going about their daily business without much hindrance. Its buildings have more architectural beauty than you may expect.

The city is blessed with a number of sporting facilities. One statistic that appealed to me was the number of Olympic-sized swimming pools. Being a swimmer and water polo player, this would be good for me.

My job would range from discussions with relevant authorities about protection of the Red Cross symbol; responsibility for coordinating a program with the Yugoslav Army for incorporation of Law of War training into existing military training structures; negotiations with the army about protection of Red Cross workers, co-operation with the Yugoslav Red Cross to ensure that it could undertake its tasks; and to liaise with the International Federation of Red Cross and Red Crescent Societies Delegation in Belgrade. Working with the Yugoslav Red Cross, I attended many of their activities in order to better understand their operations.

If I had any hope of understanding my job, then an early trip to Bosnia to learn as much as I could was needed. The drive to Bosnia tested my belief in reality. One heads northwest out of Belgrade in the direction of Croatia along a highway that Tito called 'The Highway of Brotherhood and Unity'. After 100 km or so, a left turn leads straight into Bosnia-Herzegovina, and here the world slowly changes. At first there were occasional signs of war. Soon, however, pock-marked buildings gave way to small amounts of destruction until eventually entire villages and valleys of ruin lay ahead. On the road, traffic jams were created not by civilian traffic, but by the international peacekeeping vehicles clogging the roads: Russian BMPs, American Hummvies, assorted bits of military hardware driven by Canadians, Poles, Turks, Greeks, Italians, French and more. Almost every country that is in NATO, and those that want to be, had some force in Bosnia – even the Romanians.

Out of the land cruiser's windows all I could see were the remains of people's lives; what was left of their properties and way of life. My senses were tested as the beautiful landscape was dotted by the devastation caused by landmines, on the journey toward Sarajevo. Villages that would once have been full of farmers oblivious to the larger events going on around them, are now 'cleansed', empty, or slowly being repopulated by refugees and those displaced from other cleansed areas. Their presence is given away by the abundance of plastic sheeting that bears the trademark 'UNHCR'.

In these villages children learned too late the motto, 'If you don't know, don't go' – a reference to the abundance of mines that would go on killing the innocent and unsuspecting, mostly children, for years after a conflict had ended. These were the days before the campaign for which Princess Diana was a figurehead and the anti-landmine treaty. ICRC staff knew very well the threat that these hidden killers posed, having been told quite clearly that during the drive to Sarajevo, if we needed to urinate, we should get out of the car and do it on the bitumen. A walk across a stream to find privacy behind a tree presented a risk of leaving you without a leg. Those landmines inevitably attracted the attention of curious children, who by merely playing lost an arm, leg or their life.

Five hours after leaving Belgrade, I entered Sarajevo. The old town had a Muslim charm, with its winding alleyways dotted with little shops, restaurants and cafes. It was and still is a legacy from centuries ago when that part of the world was ruled as part of the greater Ottoman Empire. In Sarajevo, a linguistic and cultural line divides Cultural Europe from Cultural Asia, much like the Bosporus Strait divides the two continents geographically. The minarets of the many mosques dot the old and new parts of the town, standing very close to synagogues as well as Orthodox and Catholic churches, reminding passers-by of the multicultural nature of this city. It was the multicultural mix, once a source of great pride for the city that, during the 1990s, proved its most tragic downfall.

I arrived in Sarajevo to hear of the death of her people and of the lifestyles now gone. Evidence screamed from every burnt shop, destroyed house, every bullet hole and every one of the thousands of booby-traps and mines. Most of all, the failing humanity of the destroyed city made its cry from the thousands of new graves, and the hundreds of souls that must still be lying unknown and buried among the myriad fallen structures. The soccer fields, having seen their last game years earlier, had become ad hoc graveyards for the city during the siege as access to graveyards outside the city was blocked.

Sarajevo's airport was the focus of much world attention during the war. All but a small part of it was controlled by the Serb forces that encircled the city. A small corridor was given over to the UN to allow humanitarian flights, so long as none of the city's inhabitants used that part of the airport as their escape route from the city. Citizens found that if they tried to flee across the UN-controlled section of the airport, UN soldiers would have to honour the agreement not to allow them to pass. At night this was done by shining a floodlight on those fleeing, which turned them into targets for surrounding snipers. The residents of Sarajevo became so desperate to flee that at one point they tunnelled right under the airport. I can't help wondering how the UN soldiers may have felt to be unintentionally helping snipers kill innocent people. Many peacekeepers who served in Bosnia have never recovered from the psychological trauma of standing by and watching the catastrophe unfold in front of them and yet had the power, but no authority, to stop it. The tunnel is now a tourist attraction. Many in Sarajevo still hold a special place in their hearts for the United Nations, but for them there is no association of that organisation with kindness.

In the ICRC Delegation there was a photograph of a little boy, perhaps seven years old. Most of his life's memories must be of war, or of hell. In the photograph he is squatting while propped up against a faded brown wall. He is holding a little toy rifle, for he is just taking a break from the game he is playing with his friends. The photograph made me wonder if the war he has seen makes him want to play his games for real. He reminds me of why it is that an organisation such as the Red Cross needs to exist.

So How Does the Red Cross Work?

The International Committee of the Red Cross is a strange organisation. Many people simply associate the Red Cross with first aid or medicine, and although that is partly true, it is not completely accurate. The ICRC is an organisation far more comfortable working in a war-related environment than in peace. It was formed in war and through the Geneva Conventions it is integrally linked with war.

On June 24, 1859 the Austrian and French armies clashed at Solferino, a town in northern Italy. After 16 hours of fighting, the battlefield was strewn with 40,000 dead and wounded men. That same evening Henry Dunant, a Swiss citizen, arrived in the area on business. He was horrified by what he saw: for want of adequate medical services in both armies, thousands of wounded soldiers were left to suffer untended, abandoned to their fate. Without discrimination, Dunant immediately set about organising care for them, helped by civilians from neighbouring villages. To prevent any recurrence of the situation he had observed, Dunant proposed two ideas: the establishment of societies for providing relief to the wounded, and the adoption of a convention to protect wounded soldiers and medical personnel on the battlefield. He wrote: "Would it not be possible, in time of peace and quiet, to form relief societies for the purpose of having care given to the wounded in wartime by zealous, devoted and thoroughly qualified volunteers?

"On certain special occasions, as, for example, when princes of the military art belonging to different nationalities meet – would it not be desirable that they should take advantage of this sort of congress to formulate some international principle, sanctioned by a Convention inviolate in character, which, once agreed upon and ratified, might constitute the basis for societies for the relief of the wounded?"

The first of these ideas led to the creation of the National Red Cross (and, later, Red Crescent) Societies, and the second to the development of modern International Humanitarian Law, which first found written expression in the Geneva Convention of 1864.

Very early in their career, each employee of the Red Cross learns the seven fundamental principles of the Red Cross movement – Humanity, Impartiality, Neutrality, Independence, Voluntary Service, Unity and Universality – from which all of the operations are derived. Only with these basic principles can a mosaic of almost 170 national societies, the International Federation of Red Cross and Red Crescent Societies (ICRC), and the IFRC, have any hope at all of working closely together.

The Geneva Conventions, and International Humanitarian Law contained within them, are under the guardianship of the International Committee for the Red Cross, the only major international conventions not overseen by the United Nations. International Humanitarian Law, also known as the 'law of armed conflicts' or the 'law of war', is the body of rules that in wartime protect persons who are not, or are no longer participating in the hostilities, and limits methods and means of warfare.

The four Geneva Conventions of 1949 and their two Additional Protocols of 1977 are the principal instruments of International Humanitarian Law. Other humanitarian texts do exist, such as the 1925 Geneva Protocol banning the use of gas and the 1980 Weapons Convention adopted under the auspices of the United Nations.

As the promoter of International Humanitarian Law, the ICRC contributes to its development and, to that end, prepares for the work of diplomatic conferences empowered to adopt new texts. At each stage in the codification of humanitarian law, it prepares drafts that form the basis of the texts adopted by states. This is how the four Geneva Conventions of 1949 and their two Additional Protocols of 1977 came into being.

As the custodian of International Humanitarian Law, the ICRC has been mandated by the international community to monitor its application by the parties to a conflict. It does this through its delegates in the field. The Red Cross works to ensure:

- The civilian population is properly respected, that is, protected against hostilities.
- Prisoners of war are treated in accordance with the provisions of the Third Geneva Convention.
- The population of occupied territory receives adequate supplies. Where this is not the case, the ICRC reminds the belligerents of their obligations under the Conventions.

In this capacity, the ICRC encourages states to take practical steps in peacetime to ensure that the rules of humanitarian law will be applied in the event of war, for instance:

- Adoption of provisions for the prosecution of war criminals.
- Adoption of legislation to protect the emblem. It also reminds States of their obligation to disseminate International Humanitarian Law and supports their efforts in that direction.

Finally, the ICRC itself strives to spread knowledge of humanitarian law, particularly among the armed forces, and organises a large number of seminars on the subject.

The International Red Cross and Red Crescent Movement is made up of three components: the ICRC, the national societies (for example the British, American, and other Red Cross Societies) and the IFRC. The ICRC has the mandate to operate in conflict. Each national society has the mandate to operate in its own country and the IFRC has the mandate to facilitate exchange between national societies. Independent from the others, each is governed ultimately by the statutes of the Red Cross and Red Crescent Movement, created by an international conference made up of one representative of each state party to the Geneva Conventions and one representative of each national Red Cross Society. As a result, the Red Cross Movement is partly an international governmental organisation and partly an international non-governmental organisation. It has a distinct and separate legal personality recognised under international law and has permanent observer status at the United Nations.

The ICRC sees itself as the 'Custodian of the Fundamental Principles of the Red Cross Movement'. It is the ICRC's responsibility to verify that future national Red Cross or Red Crescent Societies are able to conduct their activities in accordance with those principles and to grant them official recognition and to ensure that the national Red Cross Society is acting as a humanitarian organisation, not as a puppet of government. In its own country, every national Red Cross Society serves as an auxiliary to the public authorities in humanitarian matters, and its primary task is to back up the army medical services in time of conflict. To do that, a national Red Cross Society has to prepare itself in peacetime. In addition, each national society may carry out specific peacetime activities such as blood collecting, training first-aid workers and nurses, running dispensaries or hospitals, and providing aid to the disabled, young and the elderly.

The IFRC provides support for the humanitarian activities carried out by the national societies on behalf of vulnerable groups. By coordinating international relief operations in disaster situations and encouraging development aid, it endeavours to prevent and alleviate human suffering.

I was to learn quickly that co-operation between the different branches of the Red Cross was not as easy as one should hope. Indeed, in many circumstances, co-operation and liaison with the military was often easier than co-operation with colleagues in the Red Cross Movement.

Collaborating with the Military in Serbia and Bosnia

One of my critical roles as the Dissemination Delegate was to oversee the relationship with the Armed Forces for all aspects of International Humanitarian Law training. It may seem strange that a humanitarian organisation like the ICRC develops close relationships with the military around the world. But consider this: in any conflict area we now think it is natural that humanitarian organisations deliver aid and supplies to vulnerable people.

We often see peacekeepers within many of these conflicts. The fact is, in modern warfare, belligerent parties, neutral peacekeeping forces and humanitarian workers all have legitimate roles within the battlefield and they all need to know how to work together.

In the midst of a war or crisis, civilians must be given the means to stay alive today and to survive tomorrow. Combatants (soldiers) and non-combatants (civilians) must be kept separate and the life and livelihoods of aid workers and the people they are trying to help need to be protected. This is what IHL aims to do and why ICRC delegates train soldiers in IHL around the world; aid workers do have a legitimate role to play in the battlefield and that role must be respected.

One may wonder if this is naïve. Many people naturally question how, in the context of an on-going armed conflict, one can hope to have all of these principles, laws and humanitarian objectives, complied with. There is little likelihood of a body of law being observed unless soldiers are familiar with it. The dissemination delegate has to figure out how to adapt the basic teaching of IHL into local settings so that soldiers do become familiar with it. The delegate must learn local cultural values very quickly and think of ways to incorporate teaching in a way that is seen as appropriate within that culture.

I often liken it to speeding laws. Everyone agrees that speeding laws should exist, and we all agree that many people, ourselves included, often break speeding laws. However, we don't say that speeding laws should be abandoned just because most people, at some time in their lives, break these laws. Instead, we continue education around the laws of speeding and by doing so, hope to reduce the amount of times that people speed and in the process kill and injure people.

IHL is the same. By spreading the knowledge and mechanisms to comply with IHL, the ICRC hopes that the breaches and contraventions of the law, and the humanitarian catastrophe that follows as a result, are reduced. Ideally those breaches would be eliminated, but pragmatically it is about reduction.

One of the difficult things to understand about the laws of armed conflict is that in international law soldiers are allowed to fight and are allowed to kill opposing soldiers. The Geneva Conventions and International Humanitarian Law prohibit soldiers from such actions as rape, pillage and murder, but do set out the laws by which soldiers, when following lawful military commands within an organised military structure, can 'participate directly in hostilities'. The Geneva Conventions allow soldiers to fight, so long as they are doing so within the agreed rules.

This is the context of the law, but what of the facts on the ground?

In 1997 there were 10,000 non-military expatriate staff in Sarajevo alone, apart from the rest of Bosnia. At this time, other than the ICRC, and perhaps Médecins sans Frontières (MSF), most non-government organisation humanitarian staff had a deep scepticism of dealing with any military organisation. Likewise, many in the military were sceptical about co-operation with humanitarian Non-government Organisation (NGO) staff.

One of my roles supported by Regional Armed Forces Delegates was to build bridges between the two worlds of humanitarian and military. Today, most of the world's leading military forces and NGOs have civil military coordination offices to ease that process and build those relationships. Back in 1997 this was new.

Paul Muggleton, the Regional Armed Forces Delegate and I made a number of trips with the Yugoslav senior officer corps. We also visited the Cela-Kula Monument. Cela-Kula was built in 1809 when the Serbs, then under Turkish rule, rebelled. The Turks won and built a grizzly monument of 959 severed heads to warn Serbs against uprising. The Serbs have preserved the monument as a warning, somewhat ironically given events in Bosnia, of the dangers of extremism.

On another evening of the IHL course we were conducting, the army were our hosts on a visit to a former German concentration camp in Nis. There we heard stories of Nazi atrocities during World War II. I couldn't help but get angry, not only at the Nazis, who deserve the anger, but at the Serbs. At this site, Paul Muggleton gave a speech about how we must remember the history and hope it is not repeated, a subtle reference to current activities in Bosnia. Yet the atrocities had been repeated.

Many elements of the Bosnian war can validly be compared to that of the Nazis. In this region, history had not become a lesson from which the people learnt in order that they might avoid future mistakes. Instead, the history had become a reason for the hate that leads to the future mistakes. It is said that he who forgets the past is condemned to repeat it. That may sometimes be true. But here, those who remember the past use it to justify its repetition. In this region things would improve if all traces of the past from the year 900 onwards (after the first Slavic nation state) were ploughed into the earth and forgotten. Only then may we not repeat history here again.

Even in the military though, we could find people with their own tragic story. My main liaison officer, Colonel Memisevic's own son emigrated to South Africa as he had married a Croat. He often expressed sorrow that the break-up of his country had also broken up his family.

Colonel Spasiovic, our other liaison officer, introduced me to Milosevic. In doing so he asked "MacLeod, so you want to meet our President?"

"Honestly, Colonel Spasiovic," I said, "no".

"Don't worry, I hate him too", said the Colonel.

In April 1997 Paul Muggleton, Bruce Oswald and I, conducted an IHL course with the Yugoslav First Army led by the chief of operations General-Major Georgi Churchin. The course was held in Belgrade, in the old residence of the King, later converted to the barracks of the headquarters of Yugoslavia's First Army. I sat next to General-Major Churchin, toasting to his good health, while in the room next door a plaque on the wall reminds the visitor that this was the room that Tito and Kruschev signed the Yugoslav – USSR Normalisation Agreement.

Paul Muggleton and Bruce Oswald conducted most of the course with their usual flair. We were to later find out that every one of the officers that participated in a training session refused the orders of Milosevic to ethnically cleanse the Albanian population in Kosovo in 1999. Our work sometimes had impact.

The Protection of the Red Cross Emblem

One of my roles was to spread an understanding of the meaning of the Red Cross Emblem. The Red Cross is a non-religious organisation and the emblem of the cross is merely the reversal of the Swiss national flag, a white cross on a red background. The use of the Red Cross emblem is often mistaken as being one of first aid or a hospital. This is not true. The meaning of the Red Cross is much more powerful. Under international law it acts as a protective symbol to recognise those 'out of combat' in conflict zones and requiring protection. Protection applies to doctors, medical workers, members of the ICRC or victims and civilians outside of military forces.

Misuse of the emblem in a time of peace undermines that organisation's ability to work as a protective device in times of war, therefore one of the most important roles for a Dissemination Delegate is to expand the understanding of the role of the Red Cross symbol and ensure that it is not misused in times of peace.

The emblem is a critical component in the protection of aid workers. When the law is breached this may be horrifically recognised.

I returned to Belgrade from Bosnia in the early hours of December, 17 1996, to the news that six delegates of the International Committee of the Red Cross were assassinated in a brutal attack by gunmen at the ICRC hospital in Novye Atagi, near Grozny, Chechnya. Speculation and strong evidence pointed to the murder being perpetrated by the Russian special forces as the field hospital was not seen by them as neutral. Earlier in 1996 three delegates had been targeted and killed in an ambush in Burundi. They were also not seen as neutral. In late summer 1996, the ICRC had decided to open a field hospital in Chechnya because the main hospitals in Grozny had been seriously damaged, leaving large numbers of war-wounded without adequate care. This perception of non-neutrality started in the 1990s, and grew.

But why kill aid workers?

In simple military terms, one attacks an enemy where the enemy is most vulnerable. Take Iraq and Afghanistan. Disorder and disruption to aid supplies increases disquiet within the civilian populations. If the aid agencies scale back or pull out as a result of their employees being attacked, it puts the pressure on the military forces to deliver the aid needed by the population. Aid delivery stretches scarce military resources and requires the force to move bulky cargo in strategically vulnerable convoys open to easy attack.

Anti-coalition forces may think that attacks on the UN and the Red Cross disrupt aid supply, increase disquiet in the community, enhance the opportunity for recruitment to their cause, and increase the number of vulnerable soft military targets on the road. Not a bad result, from their perspective. A more frightening way of looking at this is to say that the more efficient and effective a humanitarian organisation is, the more important a target it is in the eyes of the belligerents. The effective delivery of humanitarian supplies is what makes the UN a target, precisely because the delivery undermines one side of the conflict and helps the other. So what do we do?

Do we ask humanitarian workers to do their work, knowing that they are unarmed and undefended targets? In short, the answer is yes. And this is why the protection of the emblem is so important.

It is the emblem that protects the true heroes, heroes like Michael Fry. His story explains why Red Cross delegates must be pedantic in their protection of the emblem.

A Hero in the Middle of War

My counterpoint in Zagreb, Bruce Biber, organised a dinner of ICRC national staff from Serbia, Croatia and Bosnia. It was a night to celebrate heroes and humanity. It was on that night that I came to understand one of the many heroes and one of the many horrific stories that came from the Bosnian war.

During the closing days of the Bosnian war, operations 'Flash' and 'Storm' marked the final cleansing of Serbian civilians in the western parts of Bosnia and the Serbian Krajina in Croatia. At its heart was a town called Kladusa, and in its centre was a Swiss-German ICRC delegate named Michael Fry. On August 8, 1995, Mike wrote an urgent message to headquarters. Kladusa was about to fall and soldiers had stolen everything of use, including his bicycle. Mike stood in the Kladusa Delegation, staring at his message knowing that the town was caught up in one hell of a storm. As a Swiss-German, Mike had a sense of humour uncharacteristic of his countrymen. He worked hard on it in the belief that his good humour could raise the spirits of those around him. Now, in the heat of a battle, he looked at the faces in front of him, and realised they needed every ounce of good humour they could get. His dark hair and brown eyes stood out on a face that could light a room. Those who knew him would always remember Mike's regular 'good-good-good morning'. Afraid, but scared to show it, he reflected on the recent events that had placed him in this position.

Kladusa was more or less the capital of the 'Republic of Western Bosnia', as it became known. This little known enclave-within-an enclave was surrounded by lush green hills more like those of central England than the rough mountains further south. Kladusa and the Western Bosnian Republic were bordered to the north and west by the predominantly Serb areas of Croatia. To the southeast was the 'Bihac Pocket' – a Muslim enclave inside

Serbian Bosnia. The self-proclaimed Muslim republic was run by Fikret Abdic, who, after his split with Izetbegovic to create the Republic of Western Bosnia and his separation from the rest of Muslim-controlled Bosnia, found himself in a pocket within a pocket.

To the local Serbs, Abdic and his Muslim colleagues were respected due to the fact that the Muslims of this region fought against the Croats in World War II, and also for simple monetary reasons. Abdic employed the local Serbs, and as the war in Bosnia dragged on, and money and jobs were harder to find, loyalty to Abdic became greater. In addition, Abdic, although watching the war closely for business opportunities, stayed fairly clear of the fighting, at least initially. After he formed his Republic of Western Bosnia, Abdic had to defend his town and often brutally as it pitted Muslim against Muslim – often brother against brother – and father against son, eyeing each other across the frontline and over the gun barrels. With the support of the Serbs in the Serb Krajina however, Abdic could hold his town.

On May 1, 1995, the Croatian forces launched Operation 'Flash' against Sector West in Croatia, forcing all Serbs to leave.

Known as the Republic of Serb Krajina, these sectors bordered Abdic's Western Bosnia. 'Krajina' means 'military frontier' and in the 16th and 17th centuries, the Austrian Emperor invited Serbs to settle the region to defend the empire from the Turks. The area forming the Krajina enjoyed special self-governing status within the empire. It was large, stretching from the Dalmatian coast, along the Una and the Danube rivers and into Transylvania. To the Serbs of the region this was their home, and they considered themselves special.

The Serbs in Sectors North and South should have prepared for an attack against them, but for some reason preparations remained small. On August 4, 1995 the attack came with ruthless brutality. The Croatians then launched Operation 'Storm'. On Sunday August 6, 1995, two days after the launch of the Croatian Operation 'Storm' in the Serb Krajina, the Muslim Fifth Corps did indeed push for their 'brothers' in Kladusa.

That morning Mike had sent a message to his headquarters saying that things were tense, but calm. Power and water in the town had been cut at 8.10 am and medical staff had been evacuated. Others residents had begun to flee, but the 'storm' had not yet broken. Writing his message to headquarters, Mike remembered feeling hopefully optimistic and fatefully pessimistic. On the morning of the August 7 Mike noted the defences hastily being reinforced around the town. All the reservists had been called up and frontline troops withdrawn to the town. It seemed all were preparing for the onslaught of the Fifth Corps. No one seemed to think that the town would survive. The Republic of Western Bosnia would soon die and the town would be surrounded.

Mike was relieved that the Fifth Corps had been informed of the ICRC Delegation's position. Relying on the ICRC's neutrality for protection, Mike would not evacuate. By afternoon, Mike's message revealed a quickly deteriorating situation. His message read...

"Fifth corps troops appear to be moving close, a belt of tanks has been set up by WB [Western Bosnian] forces south of the town in order to secure the mass exodus of the population out of Kladusa to the North. Some 20,000 to 30,000 people are on the move, perhaps more, some are walking out with crutches, others are bare footed, children hanging from shoulders of frantic mothers, just all are running for their life, tractors, horses and carts are used for transport of belongings and food, cattle is being moved out, massive panic has broken out, it is a terrible picture to describe....

A little girl living in the house adjoining the delegation was heard screaming, as she dragged her two-year-old sister into the street, and her mother was still nowhere to be found. Others were crying and running around, confusion is all over the place, in particular nobody knowing where they were going. Some military persons were clearly angry at the situation and were pointing guns at everyone; persons from the LRC [local Red Cross] and from the authorities came to say bye to us, some sporadic shooting can be heard, there is definitely another humanitarian disaster taking place here...

... Soldiers of WB have come to the delegation. They requested something we did not understand. We brought the keys of the car, but they shot around in anger, and also at the tyres of our cars. We faced some violent talks with some nervous soldiers barely in control of their anger. They forced the Red Cross field officers to leave with them. We do not know what will happen to them...

...The situation is difficult to describe, sporadic shelling and shooting

can be heard, a lot of soldiers are moving closer to our house as we are on the main road of Kladusa. ...This will probably be the last message for a while...."

What Mike was describing was the fall of Kladusa. Hidden in his basement with his colleagues he could not know of the chaos outside. He didn't know of the brutal hand-to-hand fighting taking place a few hundred yards away. Blood flowed down the streets and anyone who had remained behind truly fled for their lives.

Mike was significantly worried about the immediate future of local staff. Local staff are always the key to the ICRC operation. The risks they take are greater than those of foreign staff since in the heat of a conflict a soldier may believe a foreigner when he says he is a neutral observer, but may be more reluctant to believe that information from local people. Mike feared for their lives, his only consolation being that they left with the soldiers who were fleeing, not those arriving.

By Tuesday August 8, the town had fallen and the Fifth Corps moved in. The brutal attack of the town and the view that the inhabitants were traitors ensured that those who remained would be harshly dealt with. For Mike, the morning, though tense, brought relief that the town had fallen quickly. He guessed, correctly, that the Muslims fleeing Kladusa into the Serb Krajina would run right into the Croatian troops storming up from the regional town of Knin in Croatia. Mike could only wonder what might happen in the impending conflict.

As his report showed, the arrival of the Fifth Corps did bring problems. Aside from the shooting and shelling in the morning, the visiting soldiers had taken personal belongings and communications equipment from the delegation including the last car. Soldiers arriving later took the bicycles.

Mike had a number of priorities now. He had to register the new POWs in accordance with the Geneva Conventions. He had to make a medical assessment of the Kladusa hospital, which had been hit by shells during the day. And he had to try and find 20,000–30,000 fleeing refugees, all without a car.

An amazing series of radio communications began to the ICRC office in Bihac, a few hours' drive away, which had three spare cars – although that office was reluctant to release one. His frustration and rage, followed by various communications going higher and higher up the ICRC chain of command, finally secured a vehicle for Mike by the morning of the 9th – five days after 'Storm' and nearly three days after the exodus of people had begun.

Mike guessed that the refugees would be somewhere between Vojnic and Tusilovic, the main road to Zagreb and he could think of no other place the Muslims of Kladusa could go. Then again, he was fairly sure they would not be welcome there either. The Muslims of Kladusa were now everybody's enemy. Mike feared for them. Wherever they were, they were under the control of the Croats – who had their blood lust at full charge. He wrote... "Concerning these thousands of refugees, urgent steps have to be taken in order to understand the fate of these people who most probably are just leaving and sleeping under trees as they had left in panic without taking clothes and food with them. We need urgently steps be taken towards getting access to these people..."

Mike knew his move would have to be drastic. He left Kladusa, heading northwest towards the areas of confrontation. His borrowed vehicle grumbled along the highway toward Vojnic although he only got as far as Kristinja a little over 30 minutes away. Here Mike was met, as he had feared, by Croatian forces. This 30 km of road began in Bosnia in a Muslim enclave, continued into the Serb Krajina and ended up in front of the advancing Croatian troops. The problem for Mike was that in this short distance, which covered two confrontation lines, he had not yet seen those that had fled Kladusa.

His urgent requests for access to the area beyond the troops where he thought the refugees must be were prevented for 'military reasons'; a euphemism usually reserved by warring factions for situations when the slaughter of civilian populations is imminent. Now Mike really had cause to fear. The area was controlled by Croatians, was being purged of Serbs, and the Muslims were stuck in the middle, unsupported. Reluctantly Mike turned back towards Kladusa, convinced that the ICRC had to make urgent requests in Zagreb for access to this area, so he would need to hurry. He hadn't gone far when, coming in the opposite direction was a Croatian troop-carrying truck heading towards where he assumed the refugees were. On instinct, Mike swung his land cruiser around and followed the truck, driving so close that his vehicle could not be seen in the side mirrors of the troop carrier. With its rear flap down, those inside could not see him either. His hunch was that the vehicle would not be stopped at the checkpoint and that he could sneak through on its coat tails. Mike hoped that those on the checkpoint would not fire on him, or care, either.

As he sped along the road hugging the rear bumper of the truck Mike hoped that he would be right. As the truck and the ICRC cruiser neared the checkpoint Mike's nerves increased. Instinctively he wound down the windows to minimise the risk of flying glass fragments should they hit him. He would have prayed if he had not lost faith in a god many years before.

At the checkpoint the soldiers saw the speeding truck from a distance and raised the temporary boom to allow it through. His assumption was correct; once he'd passed the checkpoint the guards just assumed he had gained permission. Why else would he drive so close to one of their trucks? Mike then overtook the truck, the driver of which must have assumed he had permission to be there.

Only a short distance down the road near the small village of Kuplensko, a few kilometres short of Vojnic, 20,000 or more women, children and men were huddled on an exposed valley road. The chain they formed stretched for more than seven kilometres along the roadside, surrounded almost completely by Croatian tanks.

Mike did not slow down at the next checkpoint. He drove right into the middle of the crowd allowing the soldiers to assume he should be there. How else, they reasoned, could he have got this far? He did not give them time to think how strange it was that a foreigner had been allowed in, given the orders they had just received. Mike stopped his car and exhaled deeply, appalled by what confronted him. All these people in such a small place! They were drinking water from a small stream and from puddles formed by rain. They defecated where they could as the risk of land mines prevented them seeking privacy behind a tree. Cattle that had been taken had been slaughtered and were being torn apart by desperate and hungry people. And the Army just waited, silent, like a cat watching its prey.

With no food, sanitation or shelter, a humanitarian disaster was quickly unfolding. People would die of exposure, and disease would very soon spread – if the Army let them live that long. Mike noticed tanks on the move, their turrets swinging in getting ready to shoot. Horrified, he realised what was about to happen, and he was in the middle of it.

In desperation he took the only course open to him and climbed out of his vehicle, onto the roof and simply shouted at the soldiers. "I have authority to speak to your commander." Tank turrets froze for a moment as armed soldiers made their way down the road, while Mike quickly put in a radio report to Zagreb, seeking urgent clearance for humanitarian help.

An enraged Croatian soldier, with a strong US accent, demanded proof of Mike's authorisation. Mike could only reply that his commanders could be called to confirm it, hoping to hell that the ICRC in Zagreb had got through to the high command. The ICRC was negotiating in Zagreb but authorisation had not been granted. However, now that an 'international' was present, any thoughts of mass execution by the soldiers had to be tempered by the certain knowledge that someone would know. The soldiers feared later reprisals from the international community, and were thankfully unaware that the ICRC delegates cannot give evidence in War Crimes Tribunals.

While the ICRC negotiated, Mike stayed put, knowing that his presence in what became known as 'Kuplensko camp' was the only protection these people had while the ICRC negotiated. He stayed put for three days, drinking the cesspool waters, eating torn cattle, dirty grass and anything else he could get his hands on – just as the others did. Along with them, he fell ill with dysentery, went hungry and was cold. Mike was one of the thousands, but he could escape. After three days of negotiating, the ICRC was allowed to bring in emergency shelter, water and food and Mike could leave.

On the last day the rain came down. Drizzle marked the onset of autumn and temperatures began to drop. Mike left via the same route as he'd arrived, taking with him the cold stares of disappointed soldiers robbed of their prize. He is an unsung hero, a brave man and an example of the Red Cross at its best.

In the days leading up to the attack his national Red Cross staff fled Kladusa in the last of the ICRC vehicles. Mike told them to choose whichever direction they thought was the least dangerous. They would have to risk choosing which army to run into: the advancing Croatian army, the retreating Serbian army or the advancing Muslim army. When Mike's people left they honestly had no idea whether they would live or die that day. If they approached a Croatian military unit, they would use their ICRC radios to contact the Delegation in Zagreb and have them contact the Croatian army to give them access. If they approached a Serbian unit they would call Belgrade, and if they approached a Muslim unit they would call Sarajevo. Their lives were literally in the hands of people they had never met, connected only by a common bond of being staff of the ICRC.

The night in Zagreb was the night Bruce Biber and I decided to bring the entire ex Kladusa ICRC national staff from Serbia, Croatia and Bosnia together for dinner, to meet for the first time. In 1996 it was a brave attempt to bring Serbs and Muslims to Zagreb, but we brought everyone together and had a meal. The evening started with the individual groups of Croats, Serbs and Muslims only speaking to each other, clearly nervous about interacting across the ethnic groups.

Eventually one man, Dusan, told the story of his escape from Kladusa. An ethnic Croat, he had eventually made his way back to Zagreb, but en route he had run into the advancing Muslim army. Dusan told the story of how he radioed Sarajevo and how the operator in that city had saved his life, but he had never met the person. Slowly a hand at the other end of the table went up. "That was me," a voice said. For the first time, saved and saviour met. Another told her story of approaching the advancing Croatian forces and calling the operator in Zagreb. Another hand rose, "That was me." Another saved and saviour met. The stories were repeated around the table until everybody met the person they had saved or were saved by. As these brave people got to know each other, Bruce and I sat back and watched them interact for the first time, reflecting that if only people got on like this in the first place, they would never have needed a war.

Maria – The Real Cost of War

Maria was a girl who was barely into her second decade of life. She had fled across the border from Bosnia into Serbia in late 1995 during operations 'Flash' and 'Storm' in what some commentators said was the largest human movement of refugees recorded to that time. Maria arrived in Sombor, a village in the Vojvodina region of northern Serbia. Each villager had been trained to register and receive refugees by Gordana, an heroic woman who ran the local Red Cross unit and who could fill you with joy and enthusiasm merely by being in her presence. Her energy and passionate focus to do the best she could for some extraordinarily beaten children was amazing.

Gordana was also a sanctions breaker. The village in which she lived was well-known for its Naive School of Art. Gordana would smuggle art from Serbia into Switzerland, where she would auction it, then smuggle the money from the sales back into Serbia, against all sanctions imposed on former Yugoslavia. The money she raised was used to set up an orphanage for children who arrived unaccompanied, one of whom was Maria.

Gordana had a vision to build a summer camp in addition to the orphanage for these children and given that this was a Yugoslav Red Cross camp, I was invited to attend as the delegate of the ICRC. In my role I had been able to secure from the ICRC 100,000 deutsche marks to support Gordana's aim. During several visits to Sombor while the summer camp was being built, I came to know several of the children.

I returned to Sombor for the opening of the summer camp and had intended to visit briefly, but I was besieged by emotion. I was overwhelmed by the state of the children and to this day that night sits uncomfortably in my memory. The children laughed and cried, fought and played, danced around the campfire and cooked camp bread, just as they would in any similar camp. All of these children were different and they all had something to hide, or be fearful of. Some were refugees; the parents of others had died in Bosnia, although they lived in Serbia. Some were what the humanitarian 'industry' calls 'social cases' – a euphemism for children thrown out of home as the parents had no money or desire left to look after them, or were in prison.

One of the children named Susanna took my hand in hers and led me to Lilian Tobler, a Swiss volunteer and one of 10 from Care Concern at the camp to assist the volunteers. Susanna took Lilian's hand and formed the link between the three of us. She then looked up at Lily and me and said simply, "Mummy and Daddy". To this day I still don't know if this was meant as a statement or a question. What became apparent to me was that for just a few short minutes we gave Susanna what she didn't have – a family, attention and a little bit of love.

Maria, a little girl, sat silently beneath the canopy of a tree isolated from the rest of the children by her refusal to speak and join in. Her demeanour saddened me most. Whatever had happened to Maria in Bosnia, whatever she had seen and suffered, resulted in her being reduced to a shell of a human who did not communicate in speech. She didn't laugh or cry and she showed no emotion. No one could imagine the tragedy and the horror that she'd witnessed in the conflict or what had made her shut down. Yet she stood up, and came to sit next to me. She placed her arms around my waist with the soft touch of a shy, young girl. Her pale face had a strong, dimpled chin and she had hardened eyes that didn't look directly at me. Instead, she snuggled her head on my shoulder and gently hugged me as her mind wandered to some lonely part of her history, oblivious to the campfire and the other children around it. In the moonlight I saw a tear making its way down her pretty face. Then she cried a silent flood of tears, then a sniffle and a sob that convulsed through her body.

I wondered what role I was playing in Maria's mind. Who in her past was I replacing for that short moment? Where was her imagination taking her and what did she wish for? What caused this child to behave in this way? Why did she choose this moment to let the emotional floodgates open? And why did she choose my shoulder? Each of these children tugged at my heart, but the greatest pull came from Maria, letting escape part of the pain she held inside. As I write, the memory of that day floods back.

I later found out a lot more about Maria. She was probably the small girl that Michael Fry had heard screaming when the Fifth entered Kladusa. Maria's story is a tragic reminder that war has an impact on people in the worst possible ways.

When I think of Maria, I know why we must fight to end futile war. It is why Kosovo was so important for the Red Cross, in 1996. We could see a new war coming, and we wanted to stop it.

Kosovo 1996: A Ticking Time Bomb

Many people have heard of Kosovo. Some may recall stories from the media about how Albanians were struggling for independence from Serbia. It seems a simple story of independence. But like all such stories, the truth is far from simple. In 1996 and 1997 Kosovo was central to our conflict-prevention work.

Following the fall of the Roman Empire, the southern Slavs (including those now considered Croats and Serbs) first settled what is now the Balkans. The Serbian nationhood established itself in what is now Kosovo. The southern Slavs were not independent though. For most of their history the Serbians were ruled brutally by the Turks with many marking the Serb defeat by the Turks at the 'Battle of the Blackbirds' in Kosovo in 1389 as the foundation of their nation.

For the Serbs, Kosovo held and still holds a special place in their national psyche. Serbs maintained a majority population in Kosovo right up until World War II. With the assistance of some forced migration of ethnic Islamic Albanians by Hitler's occupying forces, and by the sheer force of demographics (the average Kosovan family has two more children than the average Serbian family), by 1996 Kosovo was 90 per cent Albanian.

Additionally, Kosovo contains within its borders, the Field of the Blackbirds, the site of the defeat of the Kingdom of Serbia by the Turks on June 28, 1389, an event still commemorated with a Serbian national holiday. The Battle of the Blackbirds is so important that it is historically ironic that on that same day in 1914 a Bosnian Serb nationalist, Gavrilo Princip, shot Franz Ferdinand at a protest for the independence for Yugoslavia. Some claim Princip to be ethnic Albanian, although the weight of evidence suggests he was Serb. Franz Ferdinand had foolishly but deliberately chosen the day to show his empire's power.

Kosovo also contains many churches and monasteries central to the Serbian Orthodox faith. It is considered the heart of Serbian nationality by many, with some historical validity.

The vast majority of the Kosovo population at that time was neither supportive of the Serb authorities or Serb. Milosevic controlled the territory through fear and brutality, not through acceptance.

Around the time of my being selected to join the ICRC, the principles of democracy and political tolerance were far from accepted in the institutional framework in Serbia and Montenegro, which were then the last two republics that made up the Federal Republic of Yugoslavia (FRY). Milosevic was still dictator. Political unrest between ethnic Albanian and Serbian authorities continued in Kosovo, and grew until the later breakaway of Kosovo in 1999.

In 1996 the leaders of the Kosovo Albanian population supported boycotts of programs that were run by Serbian authorities, and set up parallel organisations including health and education programs – and even claimed an independent Red Cross Society.

This was a problem for me on my arrival since a country may have only

one Red Cross Society and the ICRC could not recognise multiple societies within one internationally recognised state. There was continual unrest
within the Albanian population, and large refugee populations from Bosnia
created areas of political instability in parts of Serbia.

The ICRC presence in Yugoslavia in 1996 was reshaping itself in the transition from a situation of conflict to post-conflict. The Federation's presence
was tainted by difficulties, particularly in Kosovo, where the ethnic Albanian population allegedly linked their activities with those of the Serbian
authorities and has supposedly encouraged a boycott of Federation and
Yugoslav Red Cross programs.

The Yugoslav Red Cross (YRC), during the time of the former Yugoslavia,
was recognised as one of the best 10 national societies in the world, having run a very strong international program. Assumptions of 'Balkan pride'
created difficulties in confronting the Yugoslav Red Cross with the reality of
their situation, now trailing at least the Croatian Red Cross in restructuring
and development. The YRC was 'confirmed' as the legitimate Red Cross Society for the Federal Republic of Yugoslavia at the same time as the Croatian
and Slovenian Red Cross Societies were recognised, clearly remaining a
point of contention in Kosovo.

The scope of ICRC activities in 1996 was quite wide in its attempt to
disseminate humanitarian values as well as humanitarian law; however, diplomatic and political problems prevented their full application.

Plans for an ICRC/YRC schools' program, primarily aimed at recruiting
youth into the YRC while also encouraging values of tolerance, had been
delayed due to problems of access to the Albanian population of Kosovo,
although it became obvious that the problem was more one of institutional
arrogance of the ICRC.

Early on, it became clear my role would be just as much an internal diplomat within the different branches of the Red Cross Movement, as it would
be as an external diplomat. The biggest challenges, problems and dangers
were internal not external. In the post-conflict environment there was a
danger of forgetting that the most important thing was the people affected
by conflict and hostility.

Changing Cultures in the Red Cross

The Delegation in Belgrade was never a truly operational Delegation as the ICRC would understand it. To put it simply: the war was never in Belgrade (although it supported the Delegations that were in the war). The mainly Swiss delegates of the ICRC who worked with the organisation in those days were used to being in an environment that was considerably poorer than Geneva and considerably less educated than Geneva. They were also used to being in places where people were of a different skin colour and educational background. The plain truth however, is that the ICRC was founded by a European largely due to a European war and was formed to deal with Europeans. Most of its history is tied up in European conflict, and its involvement in Asia and Africa is relatively recent in its history.

The wars in former Yugoslavia took the ICRC back to its roots in Europe. However, by this time it was no longer used to dealing with people from a relatively wealthy country (Yugoslavia was the wealthiest of the former communist countries). The ICRC was unused to hiring local staff who were as well educated, and often better educated than the expatriate staff. As a result of prejudice or perhaps thinly-veiled racism local staff were subsequently treated, in general, with far less respect than they deserved. The generality was more pronounced among the Swiss-born delegates.

Until the 1990s the ICRC was entirely Swiss. The hiring of non-Swiss was, in 1996, still considered an experiment (and indeed hiring a non-Swiss who doesn't speak French is almost unheard of). Before I was deployed to Belgrade I joined a dissemination course largely made up of non-Swiss citizens. One of the directors of the ICRC found it necessary to tell us that the ICRC hired non-Swiss because of donor pressure and that it was "an experiment that would fail".

In those days a non-Swiss person was left in no doubt that they were not considered by the organisation to be of equal standing to the Swiss. However, by opening up to the 'outside', the pool of talent that the ICRC could hire from was larger and therefore, with proper recruiting, the level of expertise and skill must rise. A non-Swiss person joins the ICRC for a belief, rather than a career, unlike many of the Swiss.

The same theme played out in many other countries. Within the humanitarian world the lowest in the hierarchy was a locally employed national staff member, who may have been grossly over-qualified for their role. In the 1990s the treatment of non-Swiss expats was tolerable, but the treatment of the local staff was very close to intolerable, only saved by the notion that no matter how badly they were treated, they were still employed.

It is a difficult factor within many developing economies, that comparatively rich NGOs and aid agencies pay higher salaries than many of the local governments or organisations. This is sometimes called 'capacity stealing' in that many of the best and brightest will take menial jobs in a high-paying international NGO, rather than substantive but low-paying jobs in their own government. As a result, many NGOs inadvertently upset the economies in which they operate and can actually do more harm than good by taking from a local economy its best intellectual capacity.

The very strong 'Swiss-centric' way of thinking permeated everything and I had to keep that factor in the back of my mind. In a report on the context of Yugoslav operations in December 1996 I wrote:

"Plans for an ICRC/Yugoslav Red Cross schools program, primarily aimed at recruiting youth into the YRC and secondarily aimed at encouraging values of tolerance, have been delayed due to problems of access to the Albanian population of Kosovo."

It is possible for a whole program to be delayed because access to one part of the population was blocked. Equally and undoubtedly the Kosovo issue was part of the problem. The ICRC attempted to bring a program into schools to disseminate humanitarian principles to youth, and to help heal the psychological effects of the war – admirable stuff. A nationwide campaign would naturally need the permission of the Education Ministry, which was originally given, but later withdrawn when the ICRC insisted that the program could not operate in Kosovo because of the perceived lack of neutrality. On the surface, given the political environment, the ICRC's belief on why the program failed seems sound.

But, when one looks closer, the first stages of any effective planning process include: gathering information, identifying a potential need, ascertaining if the need is being met, and if not, formulating an aim for a program to meet the need (then go on to plan the program). In my opinion, this is where the school program really failed. I visited a number of local YRC branches and found that they already had localised school programs. No national permission is needed for these as each is local to its own community. If we assumed there was a need for a school program, why didn't we know or think that the need was being partly met by the Yugoslav Red Cross?

When asked why the ICRC didn't just improve the local programs rather than invent new ones, the Head of Delegation, François Bellon said "you don't understand. You are new. You are not Swiss and will take some time to understand". The truth is, the Delegation was completely unaware of what the Yugoslav Red Cross was already doing and that it was one of the most admired Red Cross organisations for its capacity and ability around school-based programs.

The ICRC was not blocked because of 'Kosovo', but because of institutional arrogance and the lack of an ability to accept that a local program, run by a Red Cross for many years, could be better than the program envisaged by the ICRC which, up until that point, had very little experience in running school-based children's programs. An outsider would think it surprising that the two branches of the Red Cross cannot co-operate. Early in 1997 I learned one of my tough lessons about the 'co-operation' side of my mandate. François Bellon, my Head of Delegation at the ICRC had said to me, "You may co-operate with anyone except the IFRC."

The ICRC must be neutral and be seen to be neutral. It is also better funded than the IFRC. The IFRC works very closely with national Red Cross societies, which are often bound up with national politics. The Australian ambassador Christopher Lamb (who has remained a friend) hosted a drinks party at the Australian Embassy, and it was here that I met the head of the IFRC Delegation, Hannes Hauksson. He was also trying to strengthen the Yugoslav Red Cross children-in-school programs but had no funding to do so. Ambassador Lamb organised for Hannes and me to meet in secret in order for us to coordinate our programs without François knowing.

We were able to gain funding from the ICRC for the IFRC and Yugoslav Red Cross together with the ICRC to run combined youth and children's programs in Sutomore that year. Sutomore is a town on the Montenegrin coast that the Yugoslav Red Cross used for youth summer camps. It was also the place where we decided to run a beach rescue program. One of my mandates was to run programs that would encourage 'humanitarian values' in youth. On arrival in Belgrade, I found and joined the Partisan Swimming Club, which had within it many of Yugoslav's national swimming team. At one of our training sessions the coach mentioned that he would like to set up a beach rescue program because nearly 800 people a year drowned in Yugoslavia I told him of the Australian surf lifesaving movement and my time at my home swimming club in Point Lonsdale. He asked if we could set up something similar in Yugoslavia. We managed to get some equipment from Australia, some trainers from Italy, and had the Yugoslav Red Cross recognised by the World Lifesaving Federation as a training organisation sponsored by McDonald's, the hamburger chain, which was just setting up for the first time in Belgrade, post sanctions.

The captain of the Partisan swimming team, Vladislav Chale, selected a number of his colleagues to become the first volunteer lifeguards in Yugoslavia. Over the summer of 1997 we trained this first group and I'm proud to say that our program runs today, still saving many lives each year. All of this had to be done in secret because the Head of Delegation would not have approved, even though I could think of no better humanitarian value than to volunteer your time to save the lives of others.

In May 1997 the Head of Delegation left. Thomas Merkelbach, as new Head of Delegation, proved to be a breath of fresh air that was desperately needed. Thomas is a tall and wiry Swiss-German who has, he says in his self-deprecating way, a habit of making things worse – a reference to the fact that every time he has started a mission the political situation in that region has deteriorated.

When he arrived, Thomas looked and listened and in his words, "very quickly realised something was wrong". He had to undertake a radical shift in the position of the ICRC delegation. Thomas was also open to the idea that the Yugoslav Red Cross did have a capacity in dissemination and youth programs – even considering its problems in Kosovo. The ICRC school program was canned, and replaced with support for those already existing within the Yugoslav Red Cross. Thomas also loved the idea of the beach rescue program, so finally we could now continue publicly. Hannes and Thomas became firm friends. Another good side of Thomas is his treatment of local staff, welcoming and encouraging a sense of true equality with national staff. The relations with the Federation improved radically, and I really enjoyed working with Thomas, but my time in Belgrade was coming to an end.

Understanding Deep-seated Hatred

My assistant was Jelica, a Serb, who spent most of the war in Belgrade, watching Serbian TV, and whose understanding of the political situation was shaped by the Serbian TV that she watched. I wanted Jelica to see what the Serbs did. If she saw what the Croats did she would just have another reason to hate them – she knew what they did was wrong, but to encounter what your own people did is confronting. The Serbian Serbs destroyed Vukovar and the Bosnian Serbs bombarded Sarajevo. A rehabilitation of the Serbian population needed to begin with recognition of their own errors. Jelica hadn't been to Sarajevo since the Winter Olympics. On this visit she saw that the apartment block in which she had stayed for that visit had been destroyed. Instead of flowers and life, Sarajevo had rusted barbed wire, bullet holes and death. Jelica cried as we drove by the buildings.

We attended a Bosnian field officers' meeting, which allowed Jelica to meet Muslim, Croat and Serb people whom she had spoken to on the telephone during the war. Although all these people work for the Red Cross it was the first time many of them had met. At this time, things were still extremely tense between the ethnic groups. Even though our national staff all worked for the same humanitarian organisation and they knew that they could not blame each other for all the wrongs, the Serb contingent stayed overnight in the Serbian capital of Bosnia, and the Muslims in Sarajevo.

In Sarajevo, once she had established they were still alive, Jelica was able to meet some of her pre-war friends. She came back with stories of how much heat can be gained from a burning shoe when there is no wood, and how her friends had boiled shoes to eat during the siege because there was no food. Jelica had arrived in Sarajevo and gained an understanding of the Serbs' role in the city's destruction and left with stories of how much pain nationalism had caused to her friends.

During this time I continued to enjoy work with the summer camps and the Red Cross Youth. It became clear to me that 14–18-year-olds were well worth spending time with. They were old enough to understand what was happening in their country, but too young to realise that politics would demand that they lie about it.

There was one other depressing note that came from the camps. At the youth camp hosted by the Novi Sad Red Cross (from Vojvodina, Serbia) I was able to meet many teenagers with 'good Red Cross spirit'. They were at the camp to learn skills to take back to their communities. Jelena was an 18-year-old from Banja Luka, a Serb town in Bosnia and Herzegovina. The Bosnian Serbs often attended Serbian Red Cross camps in Serbia. After the camp she came to Belgrade and we met one afternoon for a walk and a chat. At one point, as we overlooked the Sava and Danube rivers from the Kalamegdan Fortress, we began to talk of politics, refugees and Bosnia.

Jelena began speaking about a former Muslim neighbour in Banja Luka. The Muslims were cleansed from Banja Luka fairly early on in the conflict, but the neighbour now wished to return home. Jelena told me that a Serb refugee was now living in the house of the Muslim, so it would not be possible for the Muslim to return. The Serb, she said, should not have to move.

"But," I replied, "the Muslim is currently a refugee and he wants to return to his house. Why can't he return home?" Her answer was simple. "Because he is Muslim – don't you understand? The Serb should stay."

"But they were your friends before the war?"

"Oh yes, good friends."

"Would you be friends now?"

"Well, no, I can't. After all, they are Muslims."

I was dumbfounded.

I looked out over Zemun, once a small town just outside of Belgrade and now more or less a suburb of that city.

"What do you think about Seselj?" I asked.

Seselj is the Mayor of Zemun and also the leader of one of the more ruthless state-sanctioned paramilitary organisations. His criminals were responsible for some of the worst atrocities in Bosnia. Now, as Mayor of Zemun he was forcing any ethnic Croat that stayed during the war to leave – a Croat who had got on so well in the town that they stayed for the entire war was only now being 'cleansed'. Additionally, Seselj was head of the Serbian Radical Party and running for Serbian President in the up-coming elections.

"What do you think of Seselj?" was Jelena's reply.

"I think he is a criminal," was my simple answer.

Jelena then stunned me by saying that she would vote for him. I asked her why and what she thought of the cleansing of the Croats.

"We are doing them a favour," she said.

Now I was lost. How could forcing someone out of their home be a favour?

"Well," she said, "at least we are not killing them. In Zagreb they killed the Serbs. Here we will let them live, so we are doing them a favour."

I really was surprised. She used unconfirmed stories of atrocities committed by the 'other side' (many of which were true, however) to justify atrocities of their own. The logic was not that two wrongs make a right, but that one wrong justified that another could be committed. Perverse, barbaric and backward in my view, but here they are still proud of it. Jelena is not typical either. She has a humanitarian heart, otherwise she would not be spending her time taking care of the elderly and doing the other good work that the Red Cross Youth in Banja Luka do. A product of the 'hate' years, Jelena is now a member of the 'hate generation'. She is an excellent example of what is meant when people say, 'Bosnia used to be multi-ethnic. They used to live together. Now they can't. The hate is too great.'

I had a similar discussion with one of her Red Cross youth colleagues, this time a teenage boy.

"What nationality are you?" He asked me.

"I am Australian", I said.

"No, you misunderstood my question. What nationality are you?"

"No, you misunderstood my answer. I am Australian."

"But you can't be," he said, "Australia is not old enough to be a nation."

"Does your nation have to be older than 200 years?"

"200 years is not enough" he said.

"500 years?" I asked.

"No" he said.

"Thousand years?"

"Still not enough", he said.

"Well the Serbs have only been here 800 years," I said.

He had no answer to this. These discussions reinforced my view that 'you cannot win an emotional argument with logic or logical argument with emotion'. Jelena's view and that of her colleague were based on emotional logic and no amount of rational logic would change their minds.

Under Tito, Yugoslavia was in the process of creating a 'Yugoslavian' identity, that over time could have supplanted individual ethnic origins. The war destroyed any hope of a unified self-image.

Reflections on My Time in the Former Yugoslavia

In my last letter home from Yugoslavia I wrote the following about the people:

I dislike the way the people blame everyone else for their problems. It wasn't, they tell you, the people of former Yugoslavia that started the war – it was the EU, the US, NATO, UNPROFOR, Germany – for all they care it could be grandma blogs and her pet dog 'Spot' – but it was not them. They didn't mean to pull the triggers, they didn't mean to stand by and watch the slaughter – it was all someone else's fault. This is why they will do it all again.

And what of their future? The country is crumbling. Political assassinations have commenced. In the election campaign for the Montenegrin President both candidates accused each other of criminality, smuggling and profiteering. As a result, I get the feeling that people are beginning to lose confidence in the fabric of society.

I am often asked if I will return to Yugoslavia. If I think of the nature or the friends I have made, the genuinely good people I have met, then I might be tempted. But then I think of the people as a whole. The 'nation' they are so proud of. The history they are so proud of. The denial they are so good at. Then I think 'no I won't come back'...and I can hear some of the Serbs say, "Good riddance you Ustaše bastard – it was all your fault anyway.'

Yugoslavia is a beautiful country. It is a shame it has been ruined by its people. I have never felt so much bitterness about a place I enjoyed living in. The temptation to stand on a street corner and yell, "Can't you see,? don't you know what has happened? It was your fault," is just too strong.

Given that my letter was written only a year before the full invasion by Serbia of Kosovo, it seems prophetic. I just hope that the people of the Balkans have learned now, yet somehow I doubt it.

The Yugoslav Red Cross threw a going-away party for me. A huge variety of people turned up, including Red Cross youth, the Partisan Swimming Club, people from ICRC and IFRC, which showed that you can get all parts of the Red Cross Movement in the same room. General Churchin also turned up, and being respectful of the Red Cross, he came in civilian rather than military uniform. Churchin presented me with a formal gift from the Yugoslav Army. It was an old artillery shell polished and mounted with an emblem of the Yugoslavs on the casing. He also presented me with a small cap badge from Yugoslav Special Forces. It was a badge that he had worn. In military circles it is the small gifts like that which mean the most. They provide subtle messages of friendship, and complicated circumstances.

The shell casing provided an amusing anecdote. On shipping my personal effects back to London I asked an old Irish friend if he would clear my goods through customs.

"Is there anything in the baggage I need to know about?" he asked me.

"No," I said. "Oh, wait a minute, there is a shell casing from the Yugoslav Army."

"Andrew," he said to me in his very heavy Irish brogue, "I am from Ireland, I cannot very well turn up to customs at Heathrow airport saying I am here to collect that wee shell from the Yugoslav Army!"

3.

Rwanda: Aid and Genocide

If fireworks reminded you of death, would you still watch them? I don't like fireworks. The sharp cracks of the shells and the loud booms of the larger pyrotechnics take me back to a steamy equatorial night when thousands of men in gumboots and green fatigues marched across an international border. Many would be dead by morning. With the sounds of AK-47 rifles cracking like small fireworks and artillery whistling overhead, on the night of August 2, 1998, Rwandan armed forces invaded the Democratic Republic of the Congo, kicking off what became known as 'Africa's First World War'. The war that began that night was to last a decade; it involved at least eight countries and killed approximately eight million people throughout the central African region – almost as much as the entire population of Rwanda. On that one night in the remote central African town of Gisenyi, I witnessed an invasion and dread filled my soul.

I had been given four weeks' notice of that night's invasion, and the story of how this came to be is a story of trust; one that offered one of the largest moral dilemmas a person could ever face. Do you prepare for an inevitable conflict, or do you try and stop it?

In early 1998, following the conclusion of my mission in the former Yugoslavia, I was deployed to Africa to be the Communications Coordinator for the International Committee of the Red Cross Delegation in Rwanda.

Four years after the 1994 genocide the repercussions of the aftermath still reverberated. I was overseeing military-based International Humanitarian Law and also overseeing all external communications. I had a detailed briefing from several people in Geneva, but it was Yves Daccord, then Head of the Dissemination Division of the ICRC who gave me the simplest instruction: "Whatever else you do, you must re-establish contact and trust with General Paul Kagame."

Paul Kagame was then Rwandan Vice President, Chief of the Defence Force, Head of Military Intelligence and an ethnic Tutsi. President Pasteur Bizimungu was a puppet president and ethnic Hutu, in the position partly for his outspokenness against Hutu extremists, and also to give a show of ethnic unity at the start of Rwanda's journey to post-genocidal reconciliation. It was Kagame who was the real power in the country.

The West is still trying to come to terms with the events surrounding the 1994 genocide in Rwanda. Why did the 85-per-cent majority Hutu massacre up to a million minority Tutsis in 100 days? How was it that the West did not know that 1994 was not Rwanda's first genocide? In fact, there had been three that century – 1959, 1972 and 1994. Why did the West not understand the on-going genocidal attacks from eastern Congo would be seen as a threat to Rwanda? Why didn't the West see that failure to preserve Rwanda's border security would mean that Rwanda, led by a Tutsi general, would have to respond?

To begin to understand the events that led to the invasion on that steamy night in Gisenyi and the importance of Kagame's role in the rescue of the country, one needs a quick revision of Rwandan history.

Rwanda has three ethnic groups, roughly divided into 85 per cent Hutu, 14 per cent Tutsi, and 1 per cent central African Twa Pygmies. The Tutsis were said to descend from the cattle-herding nomads of Somalia, and shared the same tall, slim Somali characteristics. Hutus descended from Central African Bantu farmers and shared the shorter and more robust physical appearance. In reality things were not that simple and the Hutu/Tutsi differentiation is a strange mix of ethnic background and wealth.

Like many areas of Africa today, in pre-colonial Rwanda wealth was measured in livestock. A generalisation, I was once told, is that if you had ten cows, tradition said you were Tutsi, and if you did not have ten cows you were Hutu. It was possible to be born into one group, but through acquiring or losing wealth, you could die as a member of the other group. In many ways the Hutu/Tutsi differentiation was part ethnic and part economic.

Pre-colonial Rwanda had a monarchy and the kings were Tutsi. Known as the Land of a Thousand Hills (*Pays des Mille Collines*) Rwanda's society was organised around each hill. The cattle-owning Tutsi gentry of each hill ruled over that hill's Hutu farmers.

At the Brussels conference of 1890, the European powers gave Germany colonial authority over Rwanda but Germany took little real interest. Following World War I, Germany lost her colonial territories and Rwanda was added to the territory of the Belgian Congo as part of the political and diplomatic post-war manoeuvrings. The Belgians, seeking to expand their interests in Africa, took a much more hands-on approach to Rwanda, ruling through Tutsi elites. One early decision of the Belgians was to issue identity cards, and critically, these cards listed each person's ethnic group. Two things resulted from this decision. Firstly, the fluid ethnic group now became fixed, at least as far as the identity card was concerned. Secondly, as the Tutsis were responsible for implementing the card system it was in their interest to keep the Tutsi grouping as small as possible to limit the power of the ruling class to the smallest possible elite. Some people who could lay claim to being Tutsi under the partly flexible pre-colonial system now found themselves defined as Hutu.

When people now talk of 800,000 ethnic Tutsis and moderate Hutus being killed in the 1994 genocide, what is really meant is 800,000 ethnic Tutsis and others who had Hutu written on their identity card, but who were really Tutsi, died.

In 1959, as African countries began their push for independence, Rwandan ethnic tensions broke out, resulting in around 100,000 Tutsis being killed (the first genocide), with many surviving Tutsi families fleeing to neighbouring countries – particularly Uganda. Hutus now took control of Rwanda. As an infant, the two-year-old Paul Kagame was part of the exodus into Uganda. The 1959 refugees grew up to become the backbone of Yoweri Museveni's rebel army that eventually took power in Uganda in the mid-1980s, bringing relative stability to Uganda in the post-Idi Amin days. Growing up in a former British colony, these largely anglophone Tutsis spoke no French (the governing language of their former Belgian colonial homeland) and often struggled with their native ethic tongue: Kinyarwanda.

In 1990, descendants of the 1959 refugees invaded Rwanda to attempt to re-take the country for the Tutsis. A civil war followed. Around half to one million Tutsis still lived outside Rwanda at this time. Ruling upper-class Hutus spoke French and the less educated spoke Kinyarwanda. Tutsi invaders from Uganda spoke English with little or poor Kinyarwanda, and Tutsi returnees from Burundi and Congo spoke a mix of Kinyarwanda and French. To add to the complication of war, there was no common language to unite all Rwandans.

A UN-monitored ceasefire held Rwanda in a stalemate in the early 1990s, until President Habyarimana's plane was shot down in 1994, which was taken as the signal for Hutu extremists, who had formed into genocidal gangs, led by the 'Interahamwe militia', to start 100 days of genocide. To this day there remains doubt as to who actually shot down the plane. What followed was brutal in its ruthlessness. Bodies littered the streets and choked the Akagera River as machetes provided by the UN under an agricultural reform program were wielded by everyday people to butcher their neighbours.

Control of this massacre was simple. In a mix of pre- and post-colonial command regimes, one representative of the government (be it pre-colonial tutsi-led, colonial Belgian-led or post-colonial Hutu-led government) was assigned to every 10 households: the *Chef du dix maisons*. It remained a constant aspect of Rwandan culture that there was a government representative right down to the most local of levels. In a stroke of ruthless organisation the Chef du dix maisons would deliver to each household the list of people that the household was to kill, and householders largely complied. People complied because local cultural norms, built over centuries, required one to do what one is told – particularly if it is by a representative of government. It took me some time to understand this phenomenon. It wasn't until I visited Gitarama prison in central Rwanda that I really understood. Part of the ICRC's role was to conduct on-going prison censuses, leading us to spend plenty of time in these hellholes. Originally built for 1500 prisoners, this prison held more than 10,000 people and recorded high rates of death from malnutrition, suffocation, beatings and rape in an environment that was heavily infected with HIV. Yet here there were only two guards at the front 'gate' and that gate was merely a string of rope.

"Why don't people escape?" I asked.

"Because they are told not to," was the answer. They were told this by the other ex-government Hutu prisoners held on suspicion of perpetrating the genocide. The aspect of control by government was replicated in informal structures in the prison system led by the prisoners themselves. This may seem strange until you realise that in a country like Rwanda, where every person on a hill knew all others, there would be no place to hide and you would be subject to reprisal attacks if you were to escape back to your home village anyway. If someone escaped and went to another village, they would immediately be suspected as an interloper. In other words, you couldn't escape prison because there was nowhere to escape to.

I wasn't completely convinced of this until, during the census at Gitarama prison, a prisoner, named Andrew, was allocated to me as one of the few people who could translate from Kinyarwanda to English as opposed to French.

Andrew and I got on well, and joked and chatted freely during the routine census. "Why are you in here?" I asked.

"Because I killed 10 children," he answered. When I asked why, he simply replied, matter-of-factly, "Because I was told to." The longer I stayed in Rwanda, the more I realised that the more you learned, the less you understood.

The culture of Rwanda had evolved so that people simply did what they were told. So when the Chef du dix masons delivered instructions to kill then those instructions were followed. If they weren't, then the Interahamwe would pay a visit. It was kill or be killed.

To this day, many in Rwanda believe that the French Foreign Legion actively participated in the genocide of 1994 speculating on the on-going desire by the French to continue to dominate foreign influence in central Africa. UN Peace-keeping Commander Canadian General Roméo Dallaire had, as early as January 1994, uncovered the plot to launch the genocide and requested additional support to stop the killing. The French had, as a Permanent Member of the Security Council, made it clear that the French government would veto any attempt to expand the size and mandate of the UN forces in the country. An expansion of the mandate would very well have stopped the genocide from taking place. Dallaire's request was refused by the UN Department of Peace-keeping Operations, then headed by Under Secretary General, and later Secretary General Kofi Annan.

What would you have done if you were Annan, a career UN staffer?

Would you have defied a Permanent Member of the Security Council and risked your job? Annan later conceded that this was his greatest regret in life.

Gerard Prunier, the adviser to French President Mitterrand at the time, suggested in his book *History of a Genocide*, that the one main reason the French continued to back the Hutus, even during the genocide, was to protect French linguistic influence in Africa. The Hutus spoke French, the invading Tutsis spoke English. For some in the Élysée Palace, genocide was bad, speaking English was worse. Indeed, the plane that the former Hutu President had been shot down in was a gift from the family of President Mitterrand. Prunier's book was initially banned in France and was originally published in English.

It is a big call to say the French were involved, but in my 18 months in Rwanda, I found no evidence to disagree with the presumption that the French played an active role.

It is worth noting that geopolitical events also influenced the decision of the international community to keep out of Rwanda. In the late 1980s and beginning of the 1990s the world saw the end of Communism, the fall of the Berlin Wall and the hope for a New World Order. The United States reaffirmed its claim to be the 'world policeman', a notion that many Europeans, particularly the French and Germans, found discomforting. In 1991 Operation 'Restore Hope' (the US operation against Somali warlords, went terribly wrong, ending with the bodies of US marines being dragged through the streets of Mogadishu. In addition, at this time the wars in Yugoslavia began with European powers insisting to the United States that this was a 'European problem that Europeans could fix'.

By the time the 1994 genocide began in Rwanda the US had little appetite to be involved in Africa, the Europeans were shown to be inconsistent and dysfunctional when it came to dealing with the Yugoslav wars, which is why no-one really argued with the French not to expand peace operations in Rwanda. If the French wanted to solve the problem, who else would intervene in that climate?

In terms of casualties, the failure to intervene in Rwanda cost far more lives than the 2003 intervention in Iraq and the 2002 intervention in Afghanistan combined. The genocide of 1994 could have been prevented, but was not. The failure to intervene is perhaps the greatest foreign policy failing of the last 60 years. General Dallaire never emotionally recovered and to this day a large amount of bitterness and resentment is felt in Rwanda for both the French and the UN. He ultimately wrote; "I know God exists as in Rwanda I came face to face with the Devil".

In 2010, during a visit to Rwanda, French President Nicolas Sarkozy acknowledged that France made "mistakes" during the genocide, although, according to a BBC report, he "stopped short of offering a full apology". Many people often say that if only the world had better intelligence services that uncovered plots we could stop some of the world's atrocities. The truth is, the political community has almost always known in advance of such plots. Rwanda was just the best example. Darfur in 2002 was another. I wrote a UN report in 2003 naming Darfur as 'Genocide'. What stops the world preventing atrocity is not a lack of knowledge; it is a lack of will.

The 1994 genocide was halted, not by the international community, but by the Paul Kagame-led Rwandan Patriotic Front. With the commencement of the genocide and the clear breakdown of the ceasefire in the 1990–94 war, the Tutsi-led Rwandan Patriotic Front, somewhat understandably, took up arms again to stop the genocide and also to take power in the country. Upon victory in late 1994, Kagame quickly realised that to secure long-term peace, there had to be reconciliation between the ethnic groups, and one of his first acts was to remove the ethnic designation from identity cards.

Unfortunately, immediate post-genocide policy of the West was no better than the pre-genocide policy. BBC journalist Nik Gowing, in his 1998 conference paper, 'Dispatches from Disaster Zones', reported that the arrival of the international media in Rwanda came one news cycle too late, and created flawed foreign policy decisions through 1996 and 1997, which ultimately contributed to the 1998 invasion of the Congo, which I witnessed that evening in Gisenyi. In his paper Gowing said:

...given the trends...neither the Humanitarian Agencies (HAs) nor the Non-Governmental Organisations emerge with much credit. Too often what they said, reported or claimed was simply wrong. Their reporting was unreliable. So were many of their assumptions and hypotheses. They were caught out by the issue of information and how to handle it well.

The poor handling of information by the humanitarian community and media was exacerbated by a complacency and arrogance based on assumptions that they knew best and had the technology to outsmart fighters wrongly portrayed as a "rag-tag force of African rebel" in a "tin-pot war". Instead the political and military strategists showed great cunning and ingenuity. They wrong-footed the international community.

The culture of information control was first developed earlier through the Habyarimana regime before April 1994, and then by those who committed the mass genocide. Evidence amassed in the refugee camps of Eastern Zaire confirms that like Rwandan and Alliance forces, the Interahamwe and Hutu soldiers also had a well-developed I-warfare strategy (information warfare – control over public relations) that relied extensively on infiltration of the UNHCR and humanitarian community.

Gowing had grasped the essential impact of information control in the Great Lakes Refugee Crisis. The warring factions, far from being "semi-literate rag-tag military forces" had very sophisticated information strategies and set out to, and succeeded in, deceiving the West, the aid agencies and the media. White man's arrogance is a theme that still lives in Africa. Gowing again:

Through the later stages of war in former Yugoslavia and right up to the last stage of the Great Lakes [refugee] crisis, most large media organisations – especially the technology-rich international TV news organisations – believed they had the upper hand on information.

They assumed a new level of omnipotence. They believed that increasingly the lightweight satellite technology for telephone, text and video transmission had created a new information transparency in zones of conflict. Experience showed how technology was helping news organisations and the humanitarian community defy the instincts of governments, the military, warring factions and war lords to impose controls on information.

However, in the Great Lakes, both the humanitarian community and media were deceived comprehensively. By and large they did not perceive accurately the hidden military campaign that was unfolding beyond their reach. As a result they never gained the usual upper hand on information that they had come to assume in recent years. They were outsmarted.

When the journalists arrived in 1994, they often reported about many refugees "fleeing the violence into Zaire" (now Democratic Republic of the

Congo). What was not well understood by the journalists was that many of those fleeing were ethnic Hutus, and within them were a large number of the perpetrators of the genocide, including the feared Interahamwe militia. Consequently, the refugee camps established in Eastern Zaire on the border with Rwanda contained not only genuine refugees, but many militia groups that used the refugee camps as bases, fed by the international community, to continue genocidal attacks into Rwanda for years to come.

To understand the wars in central Africa, it is necessary to understand the driving demand for Rwandan border security and the need to stop on-going ethnic tensions and genocidal attacks launched from refugee camps in Congo into Rwanda's western regions. Kagame had called on the international community to control borders and close refugee camps from 1994 through to 1998. In part, the 1998 invasion of Congo by Rwanda on that August 1998 evening, was to deal with the camps as the West had completely failed to address Rwanda's legitimate concerns on border security.

By the time I arrived at the start of 1998, the death toll recorded in cross-border genocidal attacks measured hundreds per week. The Rwandan Patriotic Front had restyled itself the Rwandan Patriotic Army (RPA) and was, by its own admission, a guerrilla army in the process of becoming more professional. There was no functioning police force, no judicial system, but there were 110,000 prisoners awaiting trial on suspicion of taking part in the genocide, housed in a prison system built for 10,000. The major cause of death in the prisons was suffocation overnight, as the air quality dropped so low that people simply died.

There was no real functioning economy or trade to speak of and half the country was still off-limits for security reasons. White people were hated by many as a result of the blame attributed to the French. Small children threw stones at passing land cruisers while yelling 'mzungu' – a word that can have similar connotations, positive and negative, to 'nigger' – but used against white people. It is strange to be in a minority and suffer violent racial-based vitriol.

My job was to ensure that the role of the Red Cross, as well as the 'rich white guys in their big white land cruisers,' as many local people perceive foreign aid workers, were accepted by the general community, that we would somehow create Law of Armed Conflict-training programs in the military, and create programs to 're-instil humanitarian values' in a post-genocidal country. Kagame had refused to meet with all but the most senior of ICRC representatives for some time, due to the perceived (rightly in my view) racial arrogance of some Swiss delegates. It was my job to try and fix that. My French was poor, the Head of Delegation hated Anglophones, so delegation meetings were conducted in French.

My predecessor, Glenn O'Neil, had done a very good job before me in difficult circumstances, but still the contact list with the Rwandan Patriotic Army and government was small. I was introduced to a man described to me as our key contact: the military Prosecutor General Lieutenant-Colonel Andrew Rwigamba. He was to be my main contact point, and through him I had to try and re-establish relations with Kagame.

Like many in Rwanda, Andrew Rwigamba was a softly spoken man. He seems quite gentle and reasonable, although at the rank of colonel in a guerrilla army he certainly had the ability to be firm when necessary. Rwigamba was a refugee child of 1959 and like many of that generation, was schooled all his life in the need to return to Rwanda and 'rescue' the country. He was patient and highly intellectual, with a Masters Degree in Law from the London School of Economics. A good and intelligent man, he was initially a 'stonewall'. He was the interlocutor designated to block deeper access into the army. His clear instructions had been to be diplomatic, but to keep the ICRC at arm's length as far as possible. While the ICRC was allowed into civilian prisons to visit the genocide suspects, and to pay for the food to feed them, it was not allowed into military prisons or to have too much interaction with the RPA – the ICRC was simply not trusted.

Diplomatically, the Rwandans controlled how much access they allowed to key people. They would provide enough access to rebut potential diplomatic criticism, but not enough to provide a full understanding of how Rwanda worked. Full understanding would require trust – a trust that was hard to build with a government who in part blamed the West for allowing the genocide to take place. They were shrewd and smart enough to get that balance right.

The more I came to know the Rwandans, the more I realised that, unlike preconceptions, they were far from naïve. In fact, they were intensely intelligent. This was to become strikingly apparent many years later when Rwanda re-established diplomatic ties with the French, and joined the British-derived Commonwealth as a non-former colony – on the same day. The clear diplomatic message from Rwanda was, and remains, "We are in charge of our country".

Rwigamba wanted to write the first Rwandan Army Discipline code, instil Law of Armed Conflict programs around the rules of the Geneva Conventions, and re-create a police force for Rwanda. As two British-trained lawyers (me and Rwigamba) with passions around International Humanitarian Law, we should have been able to make progress, but for three months we didn't move beyond the situation that I'd inherited. I am not a patient person by nature. I wanted to implement the instructions given by Yves, but it would have been possible to spend the entire 12–18 month mission going nowhere unless the status-quo changed. In sheer frustration I entered Rwigamba's office one day and opened the meeting with my feelings.

"Sir, can I be frank?" I asked.

"Sure," he said.

"If you have been given the instructions to be diplomatically nice, but to block us from doing things, then just let me know and let's stop wasting each other's time. Let's can the meetings, I'll stop coming, I'll write the nice reports saying we met, but instead, let me go off and play tennis and no one need know the truth. But if you want to actually do something, you know my skills, you know which ones you can use, just tell me which ones you want, which ones you don't, and let's get on with it. Your call."

He laughed, looked at me and said, "I have been waiting three months for you to say something like that. Now let's get to work."

Australians, coming from a nation free from a colonist's legacy that insists one's culture can and should dominate the world, bring a different approach to that of others. Australians come to a country to learn, whereas many Europeans come to a country to teach.

I learned this in the 1992–93 Christmas-New Year period when travelling with Amanda de Luca, a Brazilian girl, on a trip around Europe. We were arguing on a train to Rome about my claim that one could just 'pick' Australians out of a crowd. Given Australia is a multi-ethnic nation, Amanda didn't believe me. On arrival in Rome railway station, we sat and I started to nominate people as Australian. She then went and verified. I was right every time. We sat for a while, people watching, and trying to figure out what made the Australians different. We finally observed two factors that, if both existed, were likely to indicate an Australian. Firstly, Australian tourists dress badly, Europeans don't. Secondly, in railway stations most people look for the exit, head straight for it, and get out of there as fast as they can. Australians, on first arrival, gaze around, meander, absorb and learn.

Later, on the isle of Capri, we ignored a 'do not enter' sign to climb down a very dodgy set of stairs to a secluded beach only to find eight other Australians there.

Amanda said to me, "You know, I have finally figured out you Australians."

"How so?" I asked.

"You are always on the other side of a 'Do Not Enter' sign asking, Why not?"

I laughed, but she was spot on.

Rwigamba and I became good friends. He had an extremely ambitious set of goals for his country.

Rwigamba would say the RPA were a guerrilla army in the process of becoming professional. So we set to work on one part of the professionalisation: drafting the Defence Force Discipline Code for the RPA, unapologetically using the Australian Defence Force Discipline Act as a basis for our work. This was the starting point, but we had bigger fish to fry – compliance with the law.

I asked Rwigamba about an Army-wide program for International Humanitarian Law. "This would take the permission of Colonel Patrick Nyamvumba and General Kagame," he said. Colonel Patrick Nyamvumba was the Chief of Operations, Plans and Training for the Rwandan Patriotic Army, and in the years since has risen to the rank of Lieutenant-general and commanded UN Peace Operations in Darfur. In almost any other army in the world, both Patrick Nyamvumba and Andrew Rwigamba would have been generals with the roles they were filling.

To visit Nyamvumba at army headquarters, ICRC delegates had to park across the street, go through security and request an appointment. Rwigamba changed that for me. After we started work, and after we made the personal breakthrough, he announced one day "Andrew, you are a former Army Officer, maybe we should allow you to drink in the Officers' Mess. Join me tonight. The guards will know you are coming and you will be allowed in the car park." The invitation to the Mess was not only the cementing of a friendship, it was a professional breakthrough. To be allowed into an Army

Officers' Mess, where men relax and let their guard down is an honour, and symptomatic of trust for either you or your institution. ICRC had not been allowed there before. It later led to a breakthrough with Kagame.

A Church Where God Does Not Exist

At Ntarama church, about 45 km south of Kigali, from April to May 1994, killers brutally massacred an estimated 5000 ethnic Tutsis. The compound is no bigger than a convenience store, yet body after body was piled in. To this day the government of Rwanda has left around 3500 rotting bodies in place as a reminder. My team insisted that we visit this small church so that I could begin to learn what genocide really means.

Genocide is a misused word today, and its misuse degrades the force and revolution of the crime. Having been in the former Yugoslavia, I knew the horrors of ethnic cleansing and mass murder, but they are not the same as genocide. Genocide is a tool used to forcibly move a population. Ethnic cleansing is killing a few of an ethnic group to encourage the others to move to areas where the perpetrators of the crime wish them to live. Ethnic cleansing is like saying, 'You can't live here – but you can live way over there, and we will kill as many of you as we need to in order to convince the rest to leave'. It's a despicable crime, but genocide is worse. Genocide is defined as killing with the intent to destroy an ethnic group. In other words it is like saying, 'You, and everyone like you, cannot live here, cannot live there, indeed cannot live anywhere. We are going to find you, everyone like you, and kill all of you. No exceptions.'

The first thing that struck me about Ntarama was my guilt about being a voyeur. Yet this guilt was outweighed by the urge to see, learn, accept and to lament. The second thing was the smell. The smell of love and death are so close. The church had a musk-like odour of rotting flesh and death. The smell of death, being very musky, is so close to that sweet smell of love and sex, except it burns your nostrils with an acrid after-smell that never – and I mean never – leaves you. The third thing was the eye sockets in the head of a baby. Not the entire body, just the head. The baby's head balanced on the pile of bones, staring lifelessly at me, accusing me endlessly: "Why did you let this happen to me?"

It was then that I realised God failed the 'logical test'. Theologians tell us that God, from whichever monotheist religion, is an all-powerful and benevolent being. But if God were all-powerful, and let this happen, then he is not benevolent. If he is benevolent and this happened, then he is not all-powerful. While a theologian may then say "God in his wisdom gave man free will", my response is quite simply this: no one gave that baby any free will or choice, and there is no benevolence in what happened to that small child.

Walking into Ntarama church is confronting. It is the place that haunts my soul and where I moved from agnostic to atheist with a positive disbelief in God.

Within our being we know what is right and wrong. We do not need the existence of a great outside power to direct us, or to tell us what happened in Rwanda was wrong. To me, the mere existence of life is enough of a reason for a life, and the desire to do good is enough of a purposeful life for me not to need God. There were times in my life that I did not believe this, but any doubts about the non-existence of God were expunged inside that church in Rwanda.

While Dallaire said; "I know God exists as in Rwanda I came face to face with the Devil", I take a different view. The Devil may exist locked inside all of us, but God does not exist. To my mind, the existence of god fails the 'logical test'.

Reuniting Families is a Good Thing?

One of the very good things that the ICRC does is to reunite families in post-conflict and natural disaster settings. Instinctively, one would feel a family reunion would be an unequivocally good thing. Sadly, this is not the case.

One of the tragedies I witnessed was a family reunion. In 1998 four years after the Rwandan genocide, many parents had assumed that their children were dead. In most cases they were correct. The ICRC had created a book of orphans, photographing each and listing the orphanage in which they were held. Many of those orphans had lost their parents in the genocide. However, many were merely separated and unable to find each other.

In today's mobile-phone age it's difficult to comprehend that if a child is split from his or her parents, there's no way to reconnect if that child doesn't know where he or she lives. It may be the case if a child is 13 or 14 at the time of the conflict he or she would know where they live. But what if the child is two, three or four years old when separated from the parents? In this case, often the child's photograph would end up in a booklet and some time down the track a parent would claim that child. Or at times perhaps, an extended family member would let the ICRC know where the parent was. Sometimes during a family reunion when the child was brought back to the parents there was nothing but happiness on people's faces. But sometimes the case was different.

In some developing countries parents have many children, assuming that a large family size is in effect a superannuation for the parents when they get old. There is an assumption that a family of eight would naturally lose two children in childbirth, two in early years and maybe one or two in the middle years, leaving two or three children to support parents in their old age. In the absence of a national superannuation scheme, the one guarantee of a good old age is to have lots of children. This is the reason why economic development is such an important aspect of bringing global population growth under control.

But imagine this: you are a poor family stuck in the middle of the genocide in Rwanda in 1994. During the fighting you lose one of your children. After a couple of years the child has not been found and you assume that child died during the genocide. There are no national records for births and deaths so you have nowhere to go to check. You therefore have another child.

That additional child often extended the resources of a family to the limit. Then imagine one day you're contacted by someone in authority from the village who tells you the ICRC has found your original child and is bringing him or her back to you. Two emotions would cross your mind: firstly, you're filled with excitement that the child you thought was dead is, in fact, alive. Conversely however, you also recognise that your family does not have the resources to feed the additional mouth that you had assumed was dead. I will never forget the look on a mother's face when we brought a child back to her, a child who was in his early teens at the time of reunion but who would have been no more than eight years old at the time of the genocide. He had assumed his parents died. They had assumed he died, and had another child. The ICRC was fully aware of the problem of bringing a child back to a family when the family had limited resources and brought with the child support in the form of non-food items such as plates, cups, and other household items that would help the family accept the addition. On a designated point on a red clay road, banana palms on one side and eucalyptus trees on the other, we met up with the mother and reunited her with her child. Clear, conflicting emotions showed on her face – unabashed love for her child, but also concern for the rest of her family. There are few things in life more heart-breaking than a mother who is not sure that she should accept her lost son because she does not know how to choose which mouth to feed.

Law and a Guerrilla Army: A New Challenge

While Rwigamba was becoming more confident of a working relationship, and while his gentle coaching of me on how to behave in the Rwandan Army Officers' Mess was starting to create trust, Patrick Nyamvumba was still not totally convinced.

"Andrew", Rwigamba once said to me, "What else can we do to establish trust? I need you to meet Colonel Kalimba, the head of our medical service. Can you help us in first-aid training in our army, for example?"

Colonel Kalimba had banned all interaction between troops under his command and the ICRC since early 1994. He had done so as he had felt the approach by ICRC delegates had been neo-colonialist and insulting. He didn't like foreign people telling him what he 'must and must not do', in his own country. This was not an uncommon story. A new bridge of trust had to be built with Kalimba. There was some logic to his concerns. For years the ICRC had concentrated less of its effort on soldiers and more on civilians. This was partly due to how the nature of conflict had changed. At the time of the first Geneva Convention in the mid-1800s, 90 per cent of casualties in conflict were soldiers and 10 per cent civilian. In World War I it was about 50:50. Post World War II, civilian casualties in conflict is close to 90 per cent and combatants 10 per cent. Naturally, as the victims of armed conflict became more civilian, so the work of the Red Cross changed. The root of the organisation though is the provision of service to wounded soldiers. A request for first-aid kits and first-aid training made a lot of sense.

I ran the idea by Yves Daccord in Geneva before approaching Dominique. Yves got the link right away, but counselled me "not to forget how much this departs from our recent practice. Some people will not like it and some people will question our neutrality. Remember, neutrality is not the same inaction to everyone, it is the same action to everyone, and stress to the Rwandans that we would offer the same service to the other side." Yves asked headquarters to identify a suitable trainer and a budget, and not long after Paule Rousseau, an ambitious Frenchwoman in her mid-60s, and a powerhouse of energy, arrived to start a massive military-wide training program in first aid, while I made it clear that we would do the same for the other side of the conflict. We were getting closer to the goal of an army-wide training program.

Trust was continuing to build, and a critical component of this was the Officers' Mess. Tradition in the officers' mess is consistent across different cultures and armies. One tradition dictates that visiting members present their home unit plaque to decorate the walls of the mess they visit. Before I left Rwanda, I had an ICRC plaque made in military style and presented it to the mess. "With this plaque, every ICRC head will be welcome here," the Mess President said when I presented it. In 1998 only two white guys had permission to drink off-duty in the Mess. One was Lieutenant-colonel Richard (Rick) Orth, who had a 'liaison' role with the US Forces. The second was me. Rick and I became good friends over beers in the Mess, as I did with his successor Rick Skow.

The Officers' Mess had a small billiard table, and like billiard tables everywhere the winner gets to stay on the table. I enjoyed the odd game here and there, won some and lost some, and in the process slowly gained the trust of more of the officer corps. General Kagame would come in some nights. He was and remains an unusual guy. Tall, but physically slight and softly spoken, sometimes he would quietly sneak in and be unobserved for a short while. Many in his past have misjudged him and not seen the true strength and leadership he commands by using his sharp intellect and a forward vision. Few hold these skills. He would always win at billiards and I guessed he was allowed to. I also guessed he hated it. Brigadier Rowe's complaint came back to me. Good leaders want people to confront and challenge them – albeit in the right way. Kagame had a track record as a good leader.

Having not actually met Kagame yet, I asked Rwigamba if it would be possible to play the General in a game. The next day Rwigamba told me that a game would be organised. Things like that need checking out in advance. Not being the world's best eight-ball player I nevertheless backed my ability against someone who had always been allowed to win. The game commenced. Cues were chalked. Balls broke. All the officers watched intrigued as the General took on the 'mzungu'. I started to pot a ball or two, making it very clear that it would be no walk-over. Mind you, he was not laying down either. The game moved on and the tension in the room started to build. More and more officers were offering their commander more and more advice: 'Sir, pot the five-ball'. "Sir, careful of putting the white down near his ball." "Sir, try the six."

"What, is it me against everyone?" I asked. The silent but strong return stares gave me my answer. Not only was it me against the world, it might just have been my last night in the Officers' Mess. Perhaps I had underestimated the power of protocol around the boss winning. The game came near to its close. I looked down my cue lining the white, the black and a pocket. This was the call to make. Pot the ball and win? Miss and let the General take a shot? Try to win, or let him? I took the shot, potted the ball, looked up and saw a sea of silent black faces looking from me then to the General.

Kagame quietly handed his cue to a major. "Your turn," Kagame said.

Game on now, with me against the major and everyone else – bar one – Kagame. While all the other officers gave words of encouragement to my opponent, Kagame put his arm over my shoulder, and suggested the shot at the nine-ball. Rarely did anyone deliberately lose to Kagame again. Over the coming months we played several times with our game score tied by the time I left the country. The game of billiards worked.

Colonel Nyamvumba smiled as we met the next day, "It's all very well to talk about the Law of Armed Conflict, Andrew, but let me explain the real world." He started moving some things around on his desk. "We have a defensive position here," he said pointing at a cup, "and the Interahamwe attack us from over here, forcing the civilian population to act as human shields. Tell me, what alternative does the law give to simply shooting at the advancing group, or should our soldiers just wait to die?"

"Fire control orders," I said, my military training kicking in. "You train the sub-unit commanders to control the soldiers to target the weapon carriers, and leave the non-weapon carriers untargeted."

Fire control orders are pretty basic parts of any sub-unit infantry operation. I was never sure when Patrick was testing me, and when things I said were genuinely new to him. Without doubt the RPA was an effective military force, after all they did stop the genocide, but they were a guerrilla army in the process of professionalising and were only beginning to implement training programs. Perhaps this stuff was new to him? Two of the basic principles of war are 'Economy of Effort' and 'Concentration of Force'. This basically means focus your fire power on the enemy, and don't waste bullets on someone who is not the enemy. If you have carried a whole bunch of bullets over a hill, it's silly to shoot them willy-nilly.

If we were to teach fire control orders, ie, how to shoot at the enemy, by definition we would also teach how to not shoot at civilians. There is one heck of a grey line between teaching military tactics, which was not my job, and teaching implementation of the Law of War, which was my job. When Rwigamba and I met not long after that conversation with Nyamvumba, Rwigamba threw me a surprise.

"I think we can start the Law of Armed Conflict training now, Andrew".

I had initially envisaged training along similar lines as in Yugoslavia, where we would train the senior officers in classroom-type scenarios and then the senior officers would train their junior people. Rwigamba had other ideas.

"We want you to teach all of our non-commissioned officers (sub-unit commanders) the basics of the Law of Armed Conflict and Fire Control Orders. It will need to be practical training because our guys don't do classrooms well". He was talking about many thousands of soldiers.

Be careful of what you wish for, so the saying goes. The ICRC wanted to train the Rwandans in the law, and now a Rwandan was asking me to train all of them. The Red Cross had the mandate to teach the law, but not military tactics. It was a very fine line to say that you needed to teach soldiers how to shoot straight in order for them to avoid shooting civilians, as opposed to teaching them to shoot straight in order to shoot soldiers. I wasn't sure that we could cross that line so thought of ways to avoid the problem.

Before Gulf War One, General Norman Schwarzkopf said, "When given a task you think is too big, ask for so many resources to do it that the boss will change his mind and not ask you."

I put a proposition to Rwigamba so large that I thought he might reconsider and take us back to the train-the-trainer model.

"Well to do that, you would need to let me know all your basic tactics and manoeuvre groups, give me a platoon of special force soldiers we can train up as a demonstration platoon, and then give us access to all your training grounds so we can find the best training terrain."

This was like asking for the entire operating methodology of their army to be given to me, a foreigner. But I forgot lesson two from Schwarzkopf. George Bush Senior actually gave him all the stuff he asked for.

"Okay, we can do that," said Rwigamba. "When do we start?"

To achieve the objective, support from the Armed and Security Forces section of ICRC headquarters would be needed. We would need to source additional staff members to undertake this training. It would be more than a full-time job, and there was my standard dissemination work to do as well.

First call would be to Yves Daccord, and then to Jean-Jacques Garcond, Head of the Armed and Security Forces section. We needed the correct level for the additional trainer. The person would need to be ex-military, focused on infantry minor tactics and neither too senior nor too junior. My feeling was mid-level, training major, anything more senior would be too highbrow. Ideally, it would be good to get someone from the region – from central or East Africa.

"One question, sir," I asked Rwigamba, "What is your basic manoeuvre group?"

"Similar to your army," he said. "A section of ten men made up of one scout, gun group of three, rifle group of three, section commander and second in command, and the signaller to carry the radio, sat phone, generator and laptop."

I had no idea if he was joking or not about the last bit. After all, an Australian army section is made up in a similar way, but back in 1998 our manoeuvre groups didn't carry laptops, so what was an African army doing with them? "Why the laptops?" I asked.

"Because we pass our command orders by Hotmail."

That was a surprise, but a very clever one. Back in 1998 email was new and back then the use and security of a Hotmail password would have been sufficient for operational security. It was novel, clever and again reminded me about Dominique's comment about "smart" and how wrong he was.

Like Gowing's comments about the media, the Rwandans understood information control. That having been said, Rwigamba was exaggerating slightly as not every section had a laptop, but the significant commanders did.

Now the search was on to find a suitable person to help do the training. ICRC headquarters originally found a retired colonel from the Swiss Air Force to be a trainer. This was a bad choice. What was needed in Rwanda was a person who would have credibility in front of a fighting African army. A retired colonel from the Swiss Air Force wouldn't cut it in my view, the rank of colonel was too senior, the air force was the wrong branch of the services, and to be frank the Swiss military hasn't fought for generations.

The Right Fit?

Hans Hatting, a colleague in Nairobi, told me of a Kenyan training major who had just retired after a few decades in the Kenyan Army, including time assisting ICRC training in that country.

"Perfect, let's get him".

Unfortunately, some in headquarters took significant time to adjust to the idea of a Kenyan major being a better fit than a Swiss colonel. Some in the Kigali office took even longer. Kilele 'Ben' wa Kivunzyo was eventually approved for a deployment to Rwanda after nearly three months of negotiations about why black was better than white, regional better than European and major better than colonel.

Usually, when an expatriate staff member is deployed to an ICRC mission, particularly in a difficult country, for security reasons the staff member is sent to share a house with other expatriates. My residence had three others, Pascal: an Administration Delegate; Crystelle, a Detention Delegate; and Kathryn, a Health Delegate. All three were Swiss. You can imagine my surprise when Pascal, a mission administrator, told me Kilele was to be put in a small hotel in Kigali at the request of Pascal's boss, Marcel, the head administrator. This had to be a mistake. Expatriates were put in houses. Downtown hotels in Kigali circa 1998 were neither appealing or secure, particularly the small flea-infested one that Kilele was put in.

"Why isn't Kilele in an expatriate house?" I asked Marcel later.

"Because he is not an expatriate," said Marcel.

"He's from Kenya. We are in Rwanda. That makes him expatriate."

"But he is black," said Marcel. No guilt. No sense of how wrong that was.

I insisted that he be put in an expatriate house and eventually Marcel relented and said that if Kilele were to live in an expatriate house then he would have to live in mine. I agreed. Kilele moved in and then Pascal moved out. This story was reported to headquarters and written up in my end of mission report, but was filed in the same file as, "That is just Dominique".

Kilele eventually found housing in an appropriate house. He was a great guy, conscientious with the light-hearted laid-back African style that works well with Australians. Always ready to laugh and with a comfortable attitude to life, Kilele and I became friends, and worked well together. Kilele spent a lot of his time fathering me and calming some of my frustrations with the organisation. The racism pissed him off, but Kilele had dealt with it a lot longer than me. He had been suffering racial vilification all his life. He was more sanguine than me.

Reinforcing my views that our actions were closely monitored, Andrew Rwigamba thanked me for defending Kilele. How he knew, I can only guess. But if it was through electronic monitoring, then one cannot underestimate the impact that the racism had had on entire ICRC operations. I wrote in my end of mission report in early 1999: "The key word concerning relations with the military is 'Sensitivity'. The RPA is very weary of international influence and perceptions of international arrogance towards the country. They are also exceptionally sensitive about the events of 1994. Therefore any actions or activities concerning the RPA must be made from an appearance of humility and understanding, whilst representing the ICRC in accordance with the Fundamental Principles."

Humility and understanding did not sit well with Europeans with racial tendencies. I went on:

"Between 1990 and 1994 Lieutenant-colonel Kalimba was an operational Battalion commander, despite his medical training. He says that in 1990 a delegate demanded access to areas under his control. He says that her approach and demands (rather than requests) caused him to issue a standing order banning the ICRC from access to any area under his control. This standing order lasted until 1998 when Lieutenant-colonel Rusagara intervened to organise a meeting to discuss the first-aid training program."

It was very frustrating for me to realise that the majority of our block-ages were on style rather than substance – and often these came down to racism. Again, in my end of mission report in 1999 I wrote regarding internal racism: "Internally the treatment by certain members of the delegation of Kilele (Ben) wa Kivunzyo when he joined the delegation to assist with the Armed Forces program was inexcusable.

"At first he was given no house, car or computer as he was, in the words of the responsible administrator 'not a real delegate". When he was eventu-ally 'permitted' to live in an ICRC residence one of the delegates changed house in protest."

Another delegate pulled me aside and accused Kilele of having an 'affair' with a delegate (a rumour I have no reason to believe). When I responded asking what the big deal was, as many delegates 'sleep around', she re-sponded, "But Andrew, it's different for him, he is African".

Another more shocking example involves the drafting of the document, "An ICRC delegate and Rwandan culture", written by all of the dissemina-tion field officers. When the first draft was being circulated one delegate be-gan to correct the document. I asked this delegate if they knew more about Rwandan culture than 15 Rwandans and the delegate replied, "Yes, they are wrong here, here and here". The same delegate also resisted the idea of the field officers briefing the delegates on culture as, in this delegate's opinion:

"We would not want the field officers to think that they are teaching us something."

Internal problems would be one thing, but more concerning were poten-tial external problems that could impact on operations and lives. I wrote in my end of mission report: "Externally to the delegation such attitudes provide huge dissemination problems as interlocutors rebel against the feel-ings of racism (at worst) or paternalism (at best) that such delegates exude."

Above all, when examples such as this were brought to the attention of the Head of Delegation his reaction was one of inaction.

It is in the above context that I am not surprised when I read that both Human Rights Watch and African Rights are considering reports on racism within the international aid community.

Incidents like this really got to me and on occasions I would come home, sit on my bed and cry out of sheer frustration. What got to me was not the violence or poverty of the country, but the bureaucratic inertia that seemed to slow things down to an unnecessarily cautious level – and this cost lives.

The Invasion of Congo

Kilele and I had worked with Patrick Nyamvumba and Andrew Rwigamba to create a structure for the training we would do. Rather than just train in the Law of Armed Conflict in classroom-based isolation, we thought we would take four scenarios, and train the Rwandans on all tactical issues (with that component taught by Rwandan instructors), and incorporate Law of War factors, such as the treatment of prisoners of war, into their standard training scenario. This way the subliminal message would pass that law points are just as legitimate as how to shoot a rifle. We would focus on four incidents: an offensive operation, a defensive operation, a checkpoint operation, and a cordon and search. Each scenario needs a particular type of terrain.

Rwanda is a stunningly beautiful country of green hills, tropical forest, red soil, banana trees and lots of eucalyptus. I felt at home with the nature. Lake Kivu in the west is breathtakingly gorgeous and Rwanda remains one of the few habitats of the wild mountain gorillas. We came across a beautiful valley.

"You know, Andrew," said Kilele with a beaming smile and taking a huge breath of the clear African air. "This valley is like heaven. I can imagine perfection in this valley. Just me, my wife and one million cows!"

What a pleasure it is to be with a good friend, doing some useful work in beautiful terrain.

After the training grounds were identified, we got to work. True to their word, the RPA gave us a demonstration platoon, and access to training areas, and we started enjoying our training, creating competitive spirit between Kilele's group and mine over whose group would receive higher marks. Training was often held in extremely high spirits.

On one occasion we were to undertake some training on the edge of the Akagera National Park with the full access we were promised. What we didn't realise, but since has become public, is that the North Koreans, Chinese and Americans were all providing secret training support to the Rwandans in different parts of the country, each without the other countries knowing – another example of the Rwandans demonstrating diplomatic tact. When we were taken to our training area we found ourselves right next to the North Koreans' rocket training. The Koreans were extremely surprised to see a white guy, and thought their secret was blown. The Rwandans explained that we were trustworthy as we received this information in a confidential context, and the ICRC's confidentiality can be trusted. This shows how much we had developed a sense of trust.

When the North Korean presence later became public, Rick Skow noted over a beer in the Officers' Mess how surprised he was that the North Koreans were in Rwanda.

"Not at all," I said, "I knew a month ago when I saw them at Akagera."

"Well why didn't you tell me?" Rick asked.

"Because you are the US Military Attaché, and I am the ICRC," was my reply.

By late June 1998 our training was progressing well and clearly we had gained the trust of the RPA. We had developed good friendships with people like Andrew Rwigamba and Patrick Nyamvumba. Dominique Dufour didn't quite believe what we were doing, but we had lots of support from Yves in Geneva. There is no doubt in my mind that we were achieving results, and indeed Rick Skow let me know that CIA estimates of civilian casualties in conflict had dropped from 800 a week when we started the training to 400 a week a couple of months later. I am convinced that the training was contributing to that decrease in casualties. The delays in the training – first in getting Kilele in place, and secondly in pushing through the institutional blockages cost lives. Kilele was delayed three months. That's 12 weeks. Four hundred lives saved per week times 12 weeks. Four thousand-eight hundred lives. Sleep well, Marcel.

Patrick Nyamvumba had gone missing. We could not get meetings with him and we didn't know where he was. Andrew Rwigamba assured us he was fine, but it made me wonder what was happening. Rwigamba piqued my interest more when he asked us to accelerate the training so that it would be finished by August 1, without giving any reason why. What was also curious was that each soldier who passed through our training was deployed to the west of the country, near the border with the Democratic Republic of the Congo (DRC).

I'd also been swimming in the small kidney-shaped pool at the Army Officers' club on the outskirts of Kigali one weekend. Access there was also a sign of trust. One weekend Kagame arrived with Yoweri Museveni, the President of Uganda, Rwanda's northern neighbour. Kagame used to be head of Museveni's intelligence services when he was living in Uganda before the 1990 RPF invasion of Rwanda. Uganda also shared a western border with the DRC. There had been no public announcement of a state visit. This was secret and got me thinking.

The next week, in a pause in the Law of Armed Conflict training, Kilele and I noticed a group of soldiers practising an "advance to contact". An advance to contact is the main infantry manoeuvre to attack an enemy. In my time in the army we had practised platoon advance to contact (about 30 men) and a company advance (about 100 men). Kilele had done a couple of battalion operations in his day (about 600–1000 men), so naturally the soldier in each of us came out and we just started counting to see how big this group was. As men started to advance I turned to Kilele and said, "Looks like a battalion." As the men kept coming, he said, "Brigade". The men kept coming; it was beyond a battalion and a brigade. We knew something big was on the horizon. No army practises brigade plus advance to contact without a reason.

We called up my colleague in Uganda to ask what was happening there. He told us troops were moving to the south-west. We knew Rwandans were moving north-west. We knew that Museveni had been in Rwanda, Colonel Patrick Nyamvumba, the Head of Operations, had become so busy we never saw him, and we had the critical deadline of August 1 by which to finish training.

"They are going to invade Congo," said Kilele, "soon after August 1."

We sought advice from Dominique, the Head of Delegation, but he didn't believe us. So what to do? What do you do when you have advance notice of one country invading another when confidentiality requires silence, and your chief doesn't believe you? In the end we passed the message to Yves so preparations could begin at HQ. No statement was made though as this would breach confidentiality and put at severe risk not only the relationships in Rwanda, but in every other country. Trust is key. It cannot be visibly broken or all operations become at risk. This is one heck of a moral dilemma.

I went to Kibuye and Gisenyi in the west of Rwanda in the last week of July and first week of August 1998. On August 2, I was woken by artillery and witnessed another advance to contact. I heard the gunfire and the results. The war that began that day was to last more than a decade and involve at least eight African nations, with ramifications and unrest continuing today. The war is now recognised as the most deadly in Africa's history, and the most murderous in the world since World War II. Estimates indicate that there were between 5 and 20 million deaths, although true casualty figures will never be known, given the country has no way of accurately counting its population.

I witnessed the first of those deaths, heard the first of the shells, and felt the first of the blasts. Standing on the border that night was, in African terms, the equivalent of standing on the Polish border as the Germans invaded in 1939.

African and Expat Life

Africans have a fabulous sense of humour. For a country affected by such misery, the children seemed to be happy. There were four boys who lived in the slum area across the road from my house in Kigali. Each afternoon they would wait for me to return just to wave, salute and laugh with me when I came home. Sometimes we would play football together in the street. To play a game the boys first had to make something that resembled a football from whatever scraps of cloth and rubber they could find.

In Rwanda one would often give gifts where in normal circumstances one would not. I am a committed anti-smoker. One of my Swiss colleagues lit her cigarette as we came out of a meeting. A small child ran up and asked for a cigarette. He was about the size of an Australian 10-year-old, so given the malnutrition of the kid I guessed his age at 15.

"*C'est très mal pour ta santé*" (It is very bad for your health) I said.

"*Monsieur, regardez moi*" (Sir, look at me) was his response. I looked him up and down. He was malnourished, had scabies and would be extremely unlikely to live long enough to get cancer. We gave him the cigarette.

There was a group of beggar children that waited at one of only three sets of traffic lights in the country. I passed them most days. They always tapped on the window.

"*Monsieur, donnez-moi quelques chose*" (Sir, give me something).

While we would rarely give money, we would often give a comic book or similar. One time a box with 100 or so Chinese-made imitation ICRCbranded Swiss Army knives arrived at the Delegation. Apparently someone in headquarters had figured out that they were cheaper than the genuine Swiss item, but their quality was so poor we could not give them as gifts to our interlocutors. Shipping was too expensive to return them so we were told to throw them away. I had a box of them in the back of my car when I stopped at the traffic light and had a swarm of kids asking for "something".

Normally giving out knives in a violent country to beggar boys would not be a good idea. In Rwanda they all had knives, machetes and various sorts of weapons anyway. Ignoring the changing green light I made sure each kid received a cheap imitation ICRC pocket knife. The next day at the same traffic light there wasn't a kid to be seen. Just before the light changed a small kid ran from behind some bushes, knocked on my window. He smiled and said, *"Monsieur, merci beaucoup pour la couteau"* (Sir, thank you very much for the knife) and then handed me a Rwandan twenty franc coin to say thanks. Twenty francs is worth about one third of one Australian cent. It is not much money at all, but that one beggar kid was so pleased with his gift, he had to give something back. For me that return gift said so much about humanity and for years I carried the coin with me and eventually had it framed.

The behaviour of many expatriates in war-like circumstances is strange. In general, people choose to cope with daily threats to life in one of two ways: retreat into themselves (my preferred option), or seek physical comfort from others. When you add this to night-time curfews, it means that if you went to an expatriate party you had to arrive before dark and leave before dark, or stay all night. Expatriate parties tended to last all night and often became sexually active, as well described in the book *Emergency Sex and Other Desperate Measures*.

An ICRC nurse once told me the HIV infection rates among aid workers in the early 1990s, before HIV training became compulsory, approached 25 per cent. This figure might at first seem shocking. But when you consider that the HIV infection rates among prostitutes in many areas of Africa exceeds 99 per cent, and given the physically uninhibited environment in which aid workers often operate, it would only take one male visiting a prostitute in Africa for HIV to enter the expatriate community. Florida 2000 was a well-known nightclub in Nairobi, Kenya. One of my Swiss colleagues would boast that he would sleep with a different prostitute every night he was there and, "never wear a condom". When I asked him if he was concerned about HIV his reply, somewhat astonishingly was, "No, because I am Swiss." To this day I don't know if he was foolhardy, naïve, or so deranged he actually believed his Swiss passport would prevent HIV infection.

One female colleague had slept with six partners in her first three months. Kathryn, my nurse house-mate, explained the HIV statistics to her. The question for her was not if she had slept with an infected person. Statistically she had. The question was had the disease transferred. Now that is a wake-up call.

Threats to Aid Workers

On March 31, 1999, near the end of my time in Rwanda, two Australians working for Care Australia in the former Yugoslavia, Steve Pratt and Peter Wallace, together with their local translator, Branko Jellin, were arrested by Serbian authorities while trying to cross the border into Croatia. They were charged with spying.

On April 1 the Pratt and Wallace story was all over CNN.

I headed off for a regular afternoon visit to the Rwandan Army Officers' Mess. I approached the gates expecting the guard to salute and open them. The car drew nearer, the window lowered, the car slowed yet the gates stayed firmly shut. I stopped at the guard house, bemused and then frightened as the guard simply put his AK-47 to my head. This was one of three times in my life that I feared death. "Steve Pratt and Peter Wallace are former Australian military NGO spies. You are former Australian military and an NGO worker. You have 30 seconds to convince me you are not a spy."

In circumstances such as these there are two ways to respond. Beg and grovel, or bluster. Both mechanisms are dangerous, but one has dignity.

"Fuck-off and get Colonel Nyamvumba", I said.

Bluster worked. The Colonel let me in, and the guard was never to know just how scared I was.

Australians were ready to think of Steve Pratt as a hero "wrongfully detained" by the 'evil Serbs'. However, an investigation in 2000 by journalist Graham Davis of the Australian SBS network suggested something more balanced. His report revealed an arrangement between CARE Canada and the government of Canada, to recruit a team of people, including former military personnel, to help 'monitor' events in Kosovo during the Yugoslav civil war. Perhaps the Serbian government was right to be concerned as actions shown in Davis' report would have been a breach of Yugoslav law, and indeed would have been a breach of similar law in Australia. The Serbs may very well have been justified.

The actions of an aid worker in one part of the world can immediately threaten the lives of another aid worker's half a world away. This is why we could not breach confidentiality about Congo. We would never understand the impact of our decision if we had done so. Aid workers can only be effective if they have access to conflict zones. If we have no access then we can't deliver aid. This means that we need to win the trust and confidence of some dodgy people. Confidentiality in what we see and do is critical. If a commander on the ground thinks that you are a risk of allowing secret information to flow, you will either be removed from the area and prevented from delivering vital aid, or killed. That's why confidentiality is so important. It is, literally, a matter of life and death.

Frustration and a Bad Decision

About halfway through my time in Rwanda, in early 1999, a sense of frustration began to build. The frustration was not due to the conflict, the sadness, poverty, or the difficulty of living in Rwanda, but from bureaucracy. The ICRC is the best and most effective organisation in the field of humanitarian assistance. However, I make the subjective judgement that the ICRC is about 20 per cent efficient. If one concentrates on the 80 per cent that it could do, but doesn't, it can get enormously frustrating. But if one concentrates on the 20 per cent that nobody else does then the work can be quite uplifting. I was deeply frustrated in Rwanda by the approach that the ICRC was taking with both the local government and the community. The neo-colonialist approach was unnecessarily hindering the effectiveness of the ICRC work program. The inherent racism, demonstrated by the treatment of people like Kilele, was having a broader impact on operations. I felt this strongly and was losing sight of the 20 per cent and instead concentrated on the 80. This adversely affected my decision-making.

The ICRC can and does have an impact on people and fundamentally improves their lives. There is no doubt in my mind, that even with its flaws, the world is a better place with the ICRC in it. It does some incredible work, it could do it better, but the things it does well no one else could do.

At any rate, my decision-making process was diminishing and I had decided to leave the ICRC after my mission had finished. Robert Ray and Duncan Kerr, two Australian politicians, had said they would help me gain pre-selection for public office and I was going to follow that path. It was the start of some bad decisions for me.

A couple of weeks before I was due to leave Rwanda, Rick Skow and I were having a couple of beers in the Mess. We were looking at the UN-AMIR (United Nations Assistance Mission for Rwanda) maps of Rwanda and noted three small words *source du Nil* (source of the River Nile). Following its discovery in 1863 by John Speke, the source of the Nile used to be considered Ripon Falls outside Kampala in Uganda at the exit point of Lake Victoria. Recently, geographers have noted the lake has feeder rivers of considerable size. The Akagera River, which flows into Lake Victoria near the Tanzanian town of Bukoba, is the longest feeder and flows from Nyungwe Forest in Rwanda, giving the Nile a length of 6758 km. So what do two alpha males with a couple of beers under their belt decide to do when they realise that the Source of the Nile is really near them in the Nyungwe Forest in Rwanda?

The ICRC has six golden rules. You may never travel to an area declared off-limits for security reasons; never travel before sunrise, or after sunset; never travel in someone else's vehicle; never go anywhere without telling the Delegation; and above all, never, absolutely never, carry a weapon. If you break any of them you are dismissed and removed from the country.

People often ask ICRC Delegates if they are armed. A Rwandan army captain once asked during one of our Law of Armed Conflict training programs. He clearly didn't believe we were not armed, nor did the room full of officers. "Do you have a side arm?" I asked. He did. "Make your weapon safe and pass it over." He did so.

"If you knew I had this pistol, would I be a threat to you?"

"Yes," he said, "and I would use a rifle against you."

"And if I had a rifle?" I asked.

"I'd use a tank." he said.

"And if I had a tank, you would use an army. The thing is, we could never carry enough weapons to effectively protect ourselves. Our only protection is to prove to you that we are not a threat to you and that therefore you should not use this pistol, let alone a rifle or tank against us." His military mind understood immediately and he believed we carried no weapons. He thought we were crazy and said so, but he believed us. The truth is, the logic doesn't always work and too many of our colleagues die, but non-armament is the ICRC's best protection.

The problem with visiting the Source of the Nile is that Nyungwe Forest in 1999 was incredibly dangerous and many thought Interahamwe were based there. Skow and I wanted to go. I was bitter, stressed and had poor decision-making. So a couple of days later, without telling anyone (rule one), we left before sunrise (rule two), to go with Rick in his armoured vehicle (rule three) to the Nyungwe Forest which was off-limits (rule four), returning well after sunset (rule five) and given the nature of where we were going we were armed and didn't have other military personnel with us (rule six).

We managed to drive down a small track to within 4 km of where the map had the source marked. As an infantry guy, the compass and map were my responsibility as we set about navigating 4 km through potentially hostile central-African virgin jungle. After a few hours we finally hit the small stream trickling about 50 m south of our objective. We followed it up to a peat bog, checked the map, and looked at each other with big grins. We were standing in a bog that was the source of the River Nile.

Naturally, that sort of thing doesn't stay secret. As Benjamin Franklin once said, "three people can keep a secret only if two of them are dead". When headquarters found out I was told in no uncertain terms that if I hadn't already decided to leave the Red Cross, I would have been removed and would not be welcome back. In retrospect I am torn with a number of conflicting emotions. I am bitter, but not at the ICRC. They did the right thing. The rules are there for a reason and I broke them all. *Mea culpa*.

A Brighter Future for Rwanda

On my last day in Rwanda I went to visit Kagame to say goodbye. "Tell me, sir," I said, "what do you really want to do with Rwanda?"

"I want reconciliation between the Tutsis and the Hutus," he said.

"Cut the crap, it's my last day, you don't need to give me the diplomatic answer. What do you really want to do?"

"Andrew, I am Tutsi, my children are Tutsi. If I do not get reconciliation there will be a fourth genocide and my children will die." He sold me. Kagame is a rare breed: one of a few leaders of a developing country that genuinely wants to bring his people out of poverty. And he has motivation to do just that for the future of his and his children's children.

In 1994, immediately after the genocide, Rwanda was unambiguously the worst country in the world. Today, Rwanda is a relative island of stability, with improving trade, corruption shrinking, quality of life improving and employment and investment growing. Rwanda has also become an extremely interesting example of independent thinking and reliance on private-sector solutions. Because the country mistrusts the UN and NGOs, it has developed a methodology to encourage business rather than aid, looking to trade as its way to wealth, and it appears to be working. Today, Rwanda is an incredible country. It remains beautiful, it is safe and it makes a powerful case study in changing the way the world looks to addressing poverty.

Like Yugoslavia before it, and Pakistan after it, a little bit of me will always be Rwandan. And for any Rwandan who may read this, when I see you, make yourself known. Let's have a drink and finish with agashyingu-racumu. Andrew Rwigamba's last lesson to me was its true meaning, more than the literal translation. If you become a true friend of a Rwandan, they may only then explain its true meaning.

In late 1999 I left Rwanda and the ICRC with the promise of support to run for parliament, so long as I gained pre-selection. After Rwanda and Yugoslavia it seemed to me that Aid was a tiny plaster on a bleeding wound. Would it not be better to stop the bleeding in the first place? Could that be done through politics? I was still young enough to take a risk and try for public office and use it to assert an influence on bleeding wounds. If the attempt failed, then a return to Aid was possible. It initially felt good to be back home in Melbourne – but it was surprisingly difficult to re-adjust after being in Yugoslavia and Rwanda.

"Welcome back to the real world", my stepmother Caroline said to me when I first arrived back in Australia.

"This is not the real world, this is fantasyland. I've been in the real world", I said. Australia is a wealthy country, and the majority of Australians can live their entire lives free from hunger, threats to their lives, or abuses of their basic human rights, and yet many Australians still find something to complain about, such as public transport, infrastructure or the political parties. Australia takes its lifestyle for granted. In 1999 no more than half a dozen countries in the world could claim a better quality of life than Australia. Melbourne first gained the title of 'World's Most Liveable City' in 1990 and has never left the top 10 since, winning again in 1999, 2011 and 2012.

Strangely, in 1999 I found it much harder to adjust to coming home than going away in the first place. Before going to war or conflict zones one has time to mentally prepare for the things that will be seen, the tragedy witnessed, and the sheer futility of war, but no one tells you that once you see these horrors, you are changed. It's a gift to no longer take everyday peace for granted. The challenge, however, is how to adjust when confronted with frivolous wealth.

4.

Time in Timor: Are Small NGOs Different?

From an early age the issues in East Timor and its independence were important to me. My best friend in primary school, Evan Shackleton, was the son of murdered Australian journalist Greg Shackleton, killed in East Timor in 1975. When the international community, with a little help from the Asian Financial Crisis, persuaded the Indonesians to allow a referendum, it was natural that I might want to play a small part in whatever possible way. On August 30, 1999 the people of Timor were due to vote in a 'free consultation' (or referendum) for their independence from Indonesia.

On August 23, a C130 Hercules aircraft made its way to Dili, the capital of East Timor with me in the back. I had joined the Australia East Timor Volunteer Project (AETVP) with no idea of their background or knowledge of whether they were particularly professional. I just wanted to do my bit to help.

Meanwhile, in Dili, a woman cast her eye down the list of incoming volunteers. Her eye stopped at my name and she thought – him, we'll get him. When I disembarked in Dili that same woman was holding a sign with my name on it.

"Andrew MacLeod?"

"That's me."

Off I went. The woman introduced herself to me as Janelle Saffin. It later emerged that Janelle, an Upper House Labour Party member of the New South Wales Parliament, had come to East Timor with the International Commission of Jurists, together with Supreme Court Judge and former Liberal Member of Parliament, John Dowd. Janelle had thought that AETVP wasn't effective. She had come across my name somehow and decided that it would be better if we were together. Janelle deliberately arrived at Dili airport before the AETVP, wrote my name on the card, picked me up and took me away before I even realised that I shouldn't have been with her. She is now a Federal Member of Parliament and we joke to this day that we first met when she 'kidnapped' me. So there I was in the wrong car with the wrong people.

Janelle Saffin is an incredible person. She left home in rural Australia at the age of 14, worked in an abattoir until the age of 18, eventually achieving a law degree. Later in her life, she would sneak across the border into Burma from Thailand to give pro-democracy training to Aung San Suu Kyi and her people, acted as a main conduit for the Free East Timor Movement in Australia, and to this day is a leading advocate of freedom for Western Sahara. While doing all this she remains an active and strong supporter and fighter for her constituents. Janelle is magnificent. People underestimate her at their peril!

Janelle, John and I were to monitor the referendum around the Ulmera polling station. The chief of the village was also the chief of the Indonesian-controlled militia so we anticipated difficulty. Corvahlos, the village chief, was no supporter of independence. His brother had been killed in the lead up to the poll, so he was by no means sympathetic. No one knew whether the polling day would end in violence and we had to be prepared for all eventualities.

We played a local role to keep things calm for polling day as international monitors. While the militias did occasionally ride around on their motorcycles, wielding machetes and threatening with the AK-47s, the day remained largely calm, as it did throughout Timor until the arrival of the *60 Minutes* TV crew led by Richard Carleton. After their arrival all hell broke loose. In Ermera district, where *60 Minutes* had been filming, a UNMET (United Nations Mission in East Timor) staff member was murdered after the close of the polling booths. That was an absolute tragedy in a day that was relatively calm.

On referendum day, Richard Carleton, against all advice provided by the United Nations and the International Journalists Federation, asked people how they intended to vote or how they actually did vote, right under the noses of the watching militia. These actions were provocative to the militia, and directly endangered people's lives. It is my view that if it hadn't been for the actions of the *60 Minutes* crew, no one would have lost their life that day. Richard Carleton was expelled from East Timor not long after that because of "visa irregularities". When he left he didn't have time to take his luggage with him, which included a number of cases of wine and cheese that he had brought. These were later enjoyed by a number of journalists.

Some years later, in 2006, Richard Carleton was visiting Pakistan covering the earthquake relief. We shared a helicopter ride with the Australian Defence Force to their hospital compound in Danni, in Pakistan-controlled Kashmir. When we got off the helicopter, I smiled at Richard and thanked him.

"What for?" he asked.

"I never had the chance to thank you for your wine and cheese in East Timor," I cheekily replied.

Other than the Richard Carleton incident, polling day in East Timor was very special, and in many ways, a quite magical day. When we arrived half an hour before the opening of polls, long queues had gathered as the population lined up to have their say about the future of their country for the first time in their lives. Nearly 2000 people at our polling station in Ulmera marked the ballot paper.

As the population was largely illiterate, people would mark their ballot by pushing a nail through their chosen box. For me, there have been few moments more pleasurable than to stand in a polling station and watch the smile on an old man's face as he placed a marked ballot paper into the box. After depositing his ballot he walked back to the front door, looked at the crowd outside, smiled and raised his arms in victory. He was crying tears of happiness for the opportunity he had for the first time in his life to vote for the future of his country. On the bottom of one of the 'all clear sheets' used to certify that the vote in that ballot station was free and fair, is my signature. I had done my little bit.

Janelle, John and I knew something was up when our vehicle didn't arrive to collect us. We had one Indonesian soldier assigned to protect us and no vehicle. As night started to close in, we sat on a bench beneath a flickering light bulb as the militias began to circle in the shadows. Janelle convinced a passing Indonesian army truck to take her to Dili so she could sort out transport for John and I. I photographed Janelle as she hopped on the truck, hoping that the photo would not be needed later in a missing persons enquiry. The photo of Janelle and a couple of armed Indonesian soldiers still sits on a noticeboard in Janelle's Parliament House office.

After polling day the violence took off. People may recall the images on their TV screens of militias out of control, of Indonesian soldiers putting on wigs and dressing as civilians and then perpetrating horrific acts of violence. Janelle and John had to leave Timor early but Janelle instructed me not to leave East Timor until all of our team, and selected pro-independence leaders, were successfully evacuated.

At one point a ship chartered by the International Committee for the Red Cross had arrived in Dili harbour. As the small world theory would have it, the head of logistics for the ICRC in East Timor was Robert Mackay, with whom I had worked in Rwanda. It would be a severe breach of ICRC neutrality to put people on board an ICRC merchant vessel. Robert let me know that, while the ICRC had chartered the vessel to come into East Timor, it was a free agent and not an ICRC vessel when it left the country. I managed to smuggle a number of people on board and into the engine room. We managed to get others out overland to West Timor in cars. The militia caught wind of our actions and at one stage shot towards the port. AK-47 rounds fire at supersonic speed so when they pass close overhead one doesn't hear a whistling sound, but a small crack like a sonic boom.

My mobile phone rang as I was huddling behind a block and the bullets 'twack-twacked' just above me. The Australian phone company Telstra had parked a satellite above Timor to ensure communications during the referendum. The phone was the only form of communication I had. When it rang, I answered.

"Hi Andy, it's Dad", said the voice from Melbourne. "We see the violence on TV. Are you OK?" I chose not to tell my father what was really happening at that point.

"Sure Dad, I'm fine." Twack. "I'm kind of busy just now though." Twack-

twack. "I'll call you back later." Not being able to call back for around 48 hours reminded me that when one enters difficult circumstances it puts tremendous pressure on those back home.

The militias were actively hunting pro-independence leaders and supporters. One of the pro-independence leaders that Janelle asked me to help flee the violence was Abel Guterres. Abel was due to take the penultimate flight out of Dili. He was, understandably, nervous and fearful of his fate should the militia capture him. I escorted Abel to the airport, and used my accreditation to join him in the waiting lounge after security. We had been operating on the assumption that as the Indonesian police continued to control the airport then once Abel was inside the waiting lounge he would be safe. We were wrong.

An armed group of militia entered the waiting lounge to take Abel away. As the militia approached I placed myself between Abel and his assailants. Abel stayed behind me, spoke only English and showed his Australian passport. Many pro-independence leaders had lived many years in Australia and had dual nationality. As the militia approached with Abel behind me, I sought to bluff saying "you take this man and you have just started the war between Indonesia and Australia".

A Mexican stand-off ensued. The militia were too scared to take Abel, but also couldn't leave without him. Media in the waiting room unpacked their cameras as they gained the whiff of an event. The room went silent and the atmosphere chilled. I was tapped on the shoulder by someone who whispered into my ear "I am from the Chilean consulate, hold these people off, I will get help." I never saw this man's face but he ran to get help. Within a few minutes both security and Australian diplomatic representatives arrived and forced the militia to leave. Abel boarded the plane and escaped. He was saved by both passport and the mystery man who tapped my shoulder.

My actions brought me to the attention of the infamous Aitarak Militia, led by Eurico Guterres (no relation to Abel). When the Aitarak militia presented a list of Australians that they were hunting to the diplomatic corps, my name appeared on the list. The militias wanted me out of the way. Gone, or dead. John McCarthy, the then Australian Ambassador to Indonesia, persuaded me to leave on the last flight out of Dili. As the militias were hunting me, and all of Janelle's team had been evacuated, I kept my promise to her and sought to leave. Once at the airport, I found that the Aitarak Militia leader, Eurico Guterres was on the same flight from Dili to Jakarta via Denpasar. I asked my translator Helio, "He doesn't know what we look like does he?"

"No, but he wants us dead," said Helio.

So, surrounded by protection provided by the Australian embassy, and sure that Eurico knew our names, but not what we looked like, we approached the notorious militia leader and cheekily asked for a photo. To this day it appeals to my sense of humour that I have a photograph of me and Helio at Dili airport with a man who wanted us dead, but who had no idea what we looked like.

East Timor Again

In early 2001, again under the auspices of the International Commission for Jurists, I was sent a second time to East Timor, this time to help prepare the country for the parliamentary elections. After the successful independence referendum in 1999, Timor was to go through a period of transitional authority with sovereignty vested in the United Nations while the structures of the new country were created. Political parties and the political process had to be created from scratch. Xanana Gusmao was the leader, but the United Nations had sovereignty.

My role was to train party activists in election-monitoring techniques so they could monitor their own elections free of international involvement if they so chose. I was pleased to be in East Timor, this time free of Indonesian control. We prepared around 100 people to monitor ballot boxes, ensure that there was no fraud in elections, and have faith in the election process that would soon be theirs. Many admired the work of Xanana Gusmao who was soon to be the country's first president. I asked my translator, Innes Almeida, if it was possible to meet the president. She said she would pass my message on. The next day, while training a class of election volunteers, the whole room stood and went silent. I turned to see the man who would be the first free president of East Timor.

"Andrew," Gusmao said, "you are here to help my country. You do not need to come to me, I will come to you." This was typical of the humility of Xanana Gusmao

2002 saw my third trip to Timor, this time to attend the official handover ceremonies and to welcome East Timor's first day as a fully independent nation. I went with John Thwaites, the Victorian Deputy Premier, as one of his team of advisers. When Bill Clinton arrived we all wanted to talk with him.

"I would love to get my photo with the President," said John. So after a quick chat with the former President I took John's photo and then John took mine.

"You are a cheeky bugger, Andrew," said John mischievously, "you are the only ministerial adviser in the world that gets the Minister to take the adviser's photo!"

We attended the official dinner and at midnight we had the honour of being at the official ceremony at which Xanana Gusmao gave his first speech as the first free President of East Timor. When he came off stage as President just after midnight, Xanana shook hands and thanked the United Nations Secretary General, the President of Indonesia, the Prime Minister of Australia, President Clinton and then caught my eye. He came over, remembering me from the training the year before and gave me a hug.

The next morning the sun rose to East Timor's first full free day. As well as the rest of the Victorian team, we also had with us Shirley Shackleton, the widow of Greg (murdered in a town called Balibo by Indonesian troops during the 1975 invasion of East Timor) and mother of my best friend in primary school, Evan. The death of Greg in 1975 started me on the journey that ended here in Timor. The Balibo house where Greg was killed is now a community facility for the people of Timor, funded by the people of Victoria. It's a good project.

Shirley and I took a car and drove the few hours' to Balibo. There, for the first time, Shirley was able to see the place where her husband had been murdered 27 years before. We sat on the stoop outside the house, turned on my mobile phone and called Evan in Perth. The three of us had a long chat. It may have taken 27 years but finally, the good guys won.

In 2010 a large earthquake hit Chile. I received an email from a friend Duncan Harris who, knowing my work in post-earthquake Pakistan [see later chapter], asked me to assist in Chile. In my reply I recounted the story of the day in Dili. I wrote that I had never seen the face of the Chilean diplomat who helped me, nor did I know his name. But owing a debt of gratitude I was happy to help. The Chilean Consul General was copied into the email.

Diego (the Consul) replied.

"I know the story. That was me."

Abel had just been made Timor's Ambassador to Australia, and John McCarthy had just retired from Australia's diplomatic service and returned to Melbourne. I organised for the four of us, Diego, Abel, John and I to have dinner. One night in 2010, 11 years after the event, four men of three nationalities who shared one experience in Dili, East Timor, were reunited over steak and very good red wine in Melbourne, Australia. It was a wonderful night of storytelling.

It makes you think. In Australia we have compulsory voting. Sometimes you hear people complaining and asking for voting to become non-compulsory. Just over 78 per cent of Timorese voted for independence. Two of my treasured possessions now are a nail that was used in the voting and a marked ballot paper that the UN let me keep after the counting was complete. They have huge significance for me because I have seen people die trying to win their right to vote. For me, voting is not a right, it is an obligation.

5.

My Own Election Campaign

After my first trip to Timor in 1999 the Labor Party chose me as their candidate for the electorate of McEwen, Victoria, at the 2001 federal election in Australia. McEwen, was one of the close constituencies, having changed hands each time – bar one – that government changed. It was a seat we needed to win.

Through 1999 and 2000 the polling was looking good for Labor to win the election and replace John Howard, the Liberal Party Prime Minster, with Kim Beazley, the Labor Party leader.

Then came 2001 and the Tampa. In 2001, increasing numbers of people attempted to travel to Australia by boat in order to seek asylum as refugees. While Australia had been previously generous to asylum seekers, concern started to rise within the electorate about the border protection for Australia. Previously refugee and asylum issues had been dealt with in a bi-partisan way, with only those on the extreme right seeking to make a political issue. The Howard government moved to the right.

Many asylum seekers arrived off Christmas Island, an Australian territory in the Indian Ocean, 2000 km off the northwest coast of Australia and 500 km south of Jakarta, Indonesia. Hundreds of people arrived on tightly packed, unseaworthy vessels, and many paid large amounts of money to people smugglers for their passage to Australia. At dawn on August 24,

2001, a 20-metre wooden fishing boat, the *Palapa 1*, with 438 mainly Hazara unauthorised arrivals became stranded in international waters about 140 km north of Christmas Island. On August 26, Rescue Coordination Centre (RCC) Australia, which had been aware of the vessel's distress requested all ships in the area to respond. Of the ships that acknowledged the request, the MV *Tampa*, a Norwegian freighter was closest to the site and proceeded towards the distressed boat.

The Howard Government in Australia refused permission for the Norwegian freighter to enter Australian waters, even though under international law the vessel had the right to do so. When the *Tampa* entered Australian water, the Prime Minister ordered the ship be boarded by Australian Special Forces. Bruce Oswald, my colleague from Yugoslavia days, was the Legal Officer on board the Australian navy vessel carrying the Special Forces. His response was to immediately resign his post in protest – that is how wrong the action of Prime Minister Howard was.

Within a few days the government introduced the Border Protection Bill into the House of Representatives, saying it will confirm Australian sovereignty to 'determine who will enter and reside in Australia'. The government introduced the so-called 'Pacific Solution', whereby the asylum seekers were taken to Nauru rather than to Australia where their refugee status was considered.

Boats of asylum seekers, like that intercepted by the *Tampa*, contain both genuine and disingenuous asylum seekers. That said, if one sees a car accident on a lonely country road in which one person is obviously hurt, and one is obviously OK, most people would stop and help because one person is hurt, rather than continue on because one is OK. Likewise a boatload of asylum seekers should be treated as if the passengers are genuine, as some are, not treated as 'illegal' because of a few. Later processing can sort out the real from the phoney. But we should start with the Australian sense of 'fair go'.

We must remind ourselves of the conditions from which genuine refugees flee. We must also re-examine the number of refugees that we consider to be our 'fair share' of the 22 or so million people currently considered as refugees or in their terminology 'people of interest' to the United Nations High Commission for Refugees (UNHCR).

To the first question: what are the conditions from which genuine refugees flee?

I have witnessed refugees through work in five conflicts on three continents. I remember Maria. What had she seen? What could have happened to her? Why would we turn our backs on people like her just because they arrive here by boat? Why would we lock her up on a remote island in the Pacific? I think the Australian political discourse in and since 2001 has demonised these people and in the process has devalued Australia. Not only was Australia wrong to turn its back and detain children, it is wrong to think that Australia has even come close to doing its fair share

In the lead up to the 2001 election the polling for the governing Liberal Party did not look good. However, following *Tampa*, the Liberal polling improved. By early September the boost in Liberal polling began to fade. Just as the mood started to turn again, the clock clicked from September 10, to September 11, 2001. Evening Melbourne time, Tuesday September 11 (morning New York time), I was attending a party fundraiser with Labor Leader Kim Beazley, and Labor Victorian Premier Steve Bracks. Anthony Leong was taking the photograph of the three of us to be used in later campaign literature. We were all fans of the US TV program *The West Wing*, airing that Tuesday night. We were all joking that we were missing the best politics of that night – the TV program not the fundraiser.

At that moment Kim's security team leaned in and told him that a plane just hit the World Trade Center. The election was lost at that moment.

Following the terrorist attacks of September 11, 2001, Australia, like many countries, was fearful of terrorist attacks and vulnerable to manipulation of hatred of all things 'Muslim'. It became worse for the Labor Party with what became known as the 'Child Overboard Affair'.

In the early afternoon of October 6, 2001, a southbound wooden-hulled "Suspected Illegal Entry Vessel" designated SIEV 4, carrying 223 asylum seekers and believed to be operated by people smugglers and carrying largely Islamic asylum seekers from Iraq and Afghanistan, was intercepted by the Australian Navy vessel HMAS *Adelaide* 190 km north of Christmas Island and then sunk. The next day, Immigration Minister Philip Ruddock announced that passengers of SIEV 4 had threatened to throw children overboard in an effort to force the Australian vessel to 'rescue' them and take them to Australia. This claim was later repeated by other senior government ministers including Defence Minister Peter Reith and Prime Minister John

Howard. Howard's polling went up, and the election for him was won and for me was lost.

A later Australian Senate Select Committee found that no children had been at risk of being thrown overboard and that the government had known this prior to the election. The government was criticised for misleading the public and cynically "(exploiting) voters' fears of a wave of illegal immigrants by demonising asylum-seekers".

Ask yourself this: Is a western political leader, Australian or otherwise, who deliberately creates a falsehood around asylum seekers in order to garner votes, any different from a Serbian political leader deliberately creating a falsehood around Albanians throwing stones in order to garner votes?

Where is the moral distinction? If you remove for a moment the actions of Milosevic in the 1990 wars, and look only at 1989, ask yourself this: How different are today's politicians who chose to stoke fear and hatred?

The Australian sense of national generosity that was lost in 2001 was never recovered. I recommitted myself to work for UNHCR. If my country wouldn't help those in need, I certainly wanted to.

6.

Moving to the UN: Aid in Disaster

I came to the United Nations expecting *The West Wing*, and what I got was *Yes Minister*. Who would have thought that by the time I left the UN, I would hold the view that military dictatorships, may, in the right circumstances, do more good for the people than the aid world does?

The British do comedy very well. In the 1970s and 1980s the sitcom *Yes Minister* and its successor *Yes, Prime Minister* followed a bumbling fictional politician named Jim Hacker. Hacker strived to make a difference but was often blocked by his main civil servant Humphrey Appleby. Humphrey always had an ingenious way of sending issues to sub-committees, investigations, commission or some such way of talking about things but never actually doing them. The interaction between Humphrey and Hacker was often hilarious and one wondered how true it all was.

The US drama *The West Wing* was a program set in a fictional White House under President Jed Bartlett. Bartlett's character was a super smart Nobel Prize winner surrounded by brilliant staff perpetually busy getting things done. *The West Wing* and *Yes Minister* were diametric opposites.

By the early 2000s I had left Australia and found a job in the United Nations in the tried and true way: by jumping on a plane, flying to New York and knocking on the doors of people I knew and asking for a job.

Forty-three doors later, no luck. Next I flew to Geneva and did the same. Twenty-seven doors later, I found myself about to enter the UN system with great hopes of being surrounded by 'West Wingesque' smart people and heroic leaders scurrying around trying to save the world.

In early 2003 my first steps echoed down the corridors of Palais des Nations, the United Nations European home. My visions of young, bright people hustling and bustling from office to office, filling corridors full of enthusiasm, idealistic hope of a brighter world, and passionately driving towards the dream of bringing the world out of poverty, filled my mind. How wrong I was.

The corridors of Palais des Nations were strangely quiet, with little energy, and few people scurrying anywhere other than the cafeteria. Still idealistic and naïve, I began a three-month contract working with the Small Arms and Demobilisation Unit (SADU) of the Bureau for Crisis Prevention and Recovery (BCPR), itself a component of the United Nations Development Program (UNDP). I began my lesson in acronyms and quickly learned my employer was SADU in BCPR in UNDP. In Geneva no one speaks in full names.

In 2001 the international community came together and created the Program of Action on the Elimination of the Illicit Trade in Small Arms. The program was initiated in July 2001 to keep a check on the ever-growing illicit trade on Small Arms and Light Weapons (SALW) and to help countries, combat this pernicious problem. Nation States were due to meet for their first two yearly reporting requirements under the Program of Action in 2003 and it was my job to come up with a plan to assist 20 Nation States to properly analyse and report on the progress they had made against the commitment in the international agreement. This was a relatively small contract, but it was my foot in the door and provided an education in the peculiar internal workings of the United Nations.

After a couple of months in that role a job was advertised for an 'Early Warning Specialist' for the United Nations High Commission for Refugees. I applied and finally found myself where I wanted to be: UNHCR. One of the things I liked most about working for UNHCR was the multinational aspect of working life. When the Emergency and Security Service of UNHCR got together, it always amazed me that in a room of 40 people we had 35 or so different nationalities represented. It was a real meeting place and mixing pot for nationalities and cultures. I loved UNHCR, but not the whole system.

There are dozens of 'funds', 'programs', 'specialised agencies' and other sub-organisations within the UN system. There is also the UN Secretariat itself. The problem is that there exists no coherent command and control structure that brings these agencies together. They largely act independently of each other. Hence there exists an Interagency Standing Committee (IASC) designed to help coordinate the actions of United Nations agencies and the plethora of NGOs and organisations that exist in the humanitarian space. Part of my role in Early Warning and Contingency Planning for UNHCR was to sit on the IASC subcommittee for Early Warning and Contingency Planning.

I met both Carlo Scaramella who worked for the World Food Program (WFP) and Everett Ressler who worked for the United Nations Children's Fund (UNICEF). These two people were deeply committed to trying to do the best they could for people in need and were often creating systems of early warning that would actually work. They were rare risk-taking innovators within the system.

They, like me, knew the unfortunate truth that few of the world's major conflicts were either unpredictable or unpredicted. Regardless of the strength of an early-warning system, no response will come if there is no political will. In the case of conflict, victims needed the political will of member states to stop violence. This political will is so rarely in evidence.

We developed a very strong relationship with Shell International, based in London. Shell, like many of the resource giants, has an incredibly detailed early warning and contingency planning process to look at vulnerable assets around the world, in particular in West Africa. I met with Shell once every three months or so to compare notes and analysis. The information Shell shared made UNHCR and the IASC subcommittee better informed on potential escalations of violence, particularly in West Africa. This was a good but unexpected partnership. Shell would usually be perceived by those on the left as a 'big evil resource company'. Given the right circumstances the private sector was not always the bad boy that many paint it to be. Here was Shell freely sharing information, intellectual property and analysis for no other reason than they thought it was the right thing to do.

In both Yugoslavia and Rwanda I had seen it was possible to build good collateral partnerships between professional military officers and the humanitarian world. I was also beginning to discover that there were some people in the private sector, even in large multinational resource companies, who were willing to share corporate information for no other reason than the greater good of humanity. It certainly wasn't for publicity, as we kept this exchange very quiet.

Perhaps the public perceptions of corporates as 'always evil' and the aid world as 'always good', may not be right. Some in the private sector and military surprised me, while many in the aid world disappointed me. Some of the 'good guys' were not so good, and some of the 'bad guys' were not so bad.

The Psychological Impact of Being an Aid Worker

UNHCR has a Workshop for Emergency Managers (WEM), the purpose of which is to prepare people for emergency deployment. Many of those running the WEM course had been through a number of emergency operations and were dealing with the psychological after-effects in a variety of ways. During the WEM we had individual and collective psychological briefing sessions. The collective session was phenomenal.

The facilitator for the session had been a Scandinavian peace-keeper in Bosnia who, upon returning home, discovered a lack of psychological and psychiatric services available for people like him. His solution was to become a specialist counsellor for peace-keepers and aid workers. The facilitator went around the room, asking each of us why we had chosen to be aid workers. When it was her turn, one of the more senior and experienced emergency workers said "it is not that we want to kill ourselves, but sometimes I think we wish to put ourselves in a circumstance where someone will do it for us".

The room went silent because this statement resonated with a differing degree of truth for each of us. It took me back to the end of my mission to Rwanda working for the ICRC. My own decision-making process had so degraded that I took the risk of visiting the Source of the Nile in very dangerous circumstances. Was I then thinking something similar? Was the logistician who worked with me in Rwanda and boasted about sleeping with so many prostitutes and never wearing a condom secretly thinking the same thing?

When asking emergency aid workers about their motivation, some will say it's a search for adventure, coupled with a genuine desire to help. Others are running from something back home or running from something inside them. For me it was a bit of both: The thirst for the world and running, trying to make up for the untimely death of my mother. This collective session in Norway really hammered home the feeling of collective understanding. We all shared a common bond as we knew what others felt. We knew that for some parts of our lives, fellow aid workers understood what we thought and in many ways would replace family.

Reform: Could 'Clusters' Make Aid Effective?

One would think that if the United Nations and humanitarian systems functioned well, collaboration would be a normal way of life. One would think that a specific office like the Office for the Coordination of Humanitarian Affairs (OCHA), set up just to coordinate humanitarian action would not be needed. One would hope that the sense of a common goal would have people collaborating naturally. You would think that this would be particularly true of the UN family which includes organisations such as the World Food Program, World Health Organisation, UNICEF and the myriad other organisations. Unfortunately, the truth does not live up to this hope.

If you thought the common goal should be to alleviate global suffering, you would be right. Unfortunately, the goal of many organisations seems to be the longevity of the organisation itself. Given that many developmental and humanitarian organisations are fighting over the same limited donor funds, from governments such as the United Kingdom, United States, Australia, Scandinavia and others, one quickly learns that the financial incentive is towards competition rather than collaboration. That is why, strangely, there is the need for the OCHA.

In 2005 my job changed from UNHCR to being the Asia Pacific desk officer for OCHA based in Geneva. Having come from two other UN agencies (UNDP and UNHCR), and having worked for a non UN organisation, ICRC, I was asked to take part in an inter-agency review process looking to reform how UN agencies and humanitarian NGOs, such as Save the Children, MSF and World Vision, operated in times of emergency.

The 2004 Southeast Asian tsunami operation combined with the discoordinated and dysfunctional response to the genocide in the Darfur region of Western Sudan emphasised the need for a review. The international community had been slow to respond, acted in an uncoordinated manner and saw duplication of services in some areas, lack of service delivery in others, and a lack of a coherent narrative towards the political leaders, resulting in a weak response to a huge crisis that continues today.

The poor responses to those events showed the truth that the humanitarian world did not work well and urgent reform was needed. The process of review became known as the 'Humanitarian Response Review' (HRR).

Through the northern summer of 2005, the wide-ranging consultation process came up with the recommendation that humanitarian response be divided into nine sectors or 'clusters': Health, Food and Nutrition, Water and Sanitation, Logistics, Camp Management, Emergency Shelter, Emergency Telecommunications, Legal Protection of vulnerable groups and Early Recovery. The clusters were created to overcome flaws identified by the HRR that "humanitarian response was simply not good enough, and that the disparate organisations were unable to collaborate".

The failure of the humanitarian system is a betrayal of those who hope for a better world and put their faith in the 'system'. It is a betrayal of those who work in the system, striving for change and hoping to make a difference. It is a betrayal of the funders, the taxpayers and those who donate to charity in the hope that the organisations will do the most good possible. But above all, the failure is a betrayal of the people who need it most: those victims of conflict, disaster and poverty. The betrayal existed because many assumed the humanitarian response worked within a well-functioning system, staffed by well-educated, well-trained and well-meaning people supported by a collaborative framework of professional organisations who worked hand-in-hand with each other. HRR had finally told the world and the humanitarian system that the assumption was not true. There were deep flaws in the humanitarian system which were only just beginning to be made public.

True flaws existed in the system, and the need to help the most vulnerable should not be less important than bureaucratic concerns. The challenge would be to fix the flaws once identified. Would the system accept that which Benjamin Franklin once said: "Our critics are our friends for they tell us where to improve"? Through the identification of this problem, the HRR finally acknowledged that one of the problems was poor quality senior management. Further criticisms were aimed at recruitment policies, training, and the reliance on voluntary staff.

Criticisms began to raise the awareness that humanitarian response mechanisms are too important to rely upon 'well-meaning amateurs'. Since humanitarian operations have an impact on people's lives, they make decisions about who lives and who dies, quite literally, by the way they conduct the delivery of food, water, supplies or other essential items. Frankly, if one staffs humanitarian operations with 'well-meaning amateurs', one will see amateur responses. Amateurism, no matter how well meaning, kills people. By contrast, the HRR recognised the need for 'well-meaning professionals' which implies a more professional pay scale, training mechanism and more importantly, a professional recruiting mechanism in which people are hired and fired according to ability, not just nationality or gender.

If personnel was one issue, the underlying structural faults of the system were another. Humanitarian organisations simply didn't work well together, didn't prepare together and had a complete lack of unified humanitarian response to all major emergencies. The victims of conflict, natural disaster or manmade disasters needed better response from the humanitarian organisations than that which had, up until now, been provided.

When catastrophe strikes, the people of the world look to the United Nations for help. But how does a massive bureaucracy charged with peace-keeping, arms control, political dialogue between states and myriad of other tasks, realign itself for rapid onset emergencies? How do the hundreds of NGOs and dozens of UN agencies work with host governments facing a huge crisis? It's vital to stress that the United Nations is not one single monolithic organisation with key focused goals. It has six principal organs: the General Assembly; the Security Council; the Economic and Social Council; the Secretariat; the International Court of Justice; and the United Nations Trusteeship Council (which is no longer active).

In addition to the principal organs, there are more than three dozen funds (such as UNICEF the United Nations Children's Fund), high commissions (such as the United Nations High Commission for Refugees, or the United Nations High Commissioner for Human Rights), specialised agencies (such as the World Health Organisation or the International Labour Organisation), 'programs' (such as UNDP – the United Nations Development Program), many offices and departments (such as the Department of Peace-keeping Operations and the Office for the Coordination of Humanitarian Affairs) and lots of research institutes (such as the United Nations Institute for Disarmament Affairs). Each of these funds, offices, programs and commissions has their own rules, reporting requirements, mandates and methods of raising money.

The United Nations Secretary General is in charge of the Secretariat of the United Nations, but not the agencies, organisations, funds or other components of the system that report back to Member States in very different and confusing ways. While the Secretary General has persuasive authority over organisations such as the World Health Organisation or the World Food Program, the Secretary General has no actual authority. The second thing to understand about the UN is that it is confusing, disjointed and nowhere near as effective or as efficient as it could be precisely because this is how the Member States wish it to be. The UN is, after all, nothing more or less than the manifestation of compromises worked out between the 197 or more Member Nation States.

The third thing to understand is that when people ask for 'the United Nations to do something', whatever the 'something' is must be agreed by the majority of the Member States, or at the very least the Permanent Five members of the Security Council, Britain, France, the United States, China and Russia. As we saw with Rwanda, if one of the Permanent Five decides to block any remedial action, then the entire system becomes hamstrung. In the case of Rwanda it was the French threat to use their veto power in the Security Council to stop any action. Russia in 2012 blocked actions in Syria. China, US and even Britain have at times asserted their veto in their single national interest and consequently prevented the entire system from functioning.

It is too easy to blame 'the United Nations' when there is no effective response to the Rwandan and Darfur genocides or other mass atrocities, or because 'a coherent single United Nations organisation' simply doesn't exist. The UN is the manifestation of the collective will of Member States. Member States are to blame for inaction – including Australia. The truth is that for each and every one of the recent political or military conflicts, political decision-makers knew in advance, through early warning mechanisms of each new conflict. There are no surprises. Inaction doesn't come through lack of knowledge but through lack of will. Decisions are taken either to intervene, or not to intervene. Sometimes the act of omission can have horrible results. In Rwanda and Darfur we also saw that the act of omission and inaction can be equally as devastating.

7.

Pakistan and the Earthquake:
The Army to the Rescue

"Life's challenges are not supposed to paralyse you; they're supposed to help you discover who you are." – Bernice Johnson Reagon

Pakistan has a split weekend. Friday afternoons are for prayers and non-working time. Saturday is a normal working day and a school day. Sunday is a day of rest. "Situation normal" was the right phrase to describe October 8, 2005. On that early morning the school bells had rung. Children crowded into rural classrooms in mountaintop hamlets. Impoverished towns and villages kicked into daily life.

The earthquake hit at 8.30 am, just as the day was beginning. It measured 7.6 on the Richter Scale and hit close to the major city of Muzaffarabad and was shallow in depth. The quake shook the earth for approximately one minute, destroying 500,000 homes and damaging 200,000 others. In that one minute 2,394 km of road, 5,348 education facilities, 307 health facilities, 3,994 water supply systems and 715 government buildings were destroyed. Three and a half million people were made homeless; 30,000 square km of land was affected. Nearly half those killed were school children. A total of 75,000 people gone, twice as many again severely injured.

The political realities were important in Pakistan. The earthquake had an impact on an area stretching from Indian-controlled Kashmir, through Pakistani-controlled Kashmir, through the North-West Frontier Province (NWFP) and Federally Administered Tribal Areas (FATA) of Pakistan and into Afghanistan. Although the vast majority of the people killed and affected were in Pakistan's NWFP and Pakistan-controlled Kashmir, more than 1,000 people were killed in India and a smaller number in Afghanistan.

It is very difficult for people in the West to understand the enormous difficulty that Pakistan has in asserting influence on the tribal areas between Afghanistan and Pakistan. It is no surprise that after the War in Afghanistan following the American invasion in 2001 the tribal areas became the home of the fleeing Taliban and, before his move to Abbottabad, Osama bin Laden. Under traditional customs of hospitality the obligation fell upon local villages to protect both the Taliban and bin Laden.

Next to FATA, when travelling east, is the NWFP, renamed as Khyber Pakhtunkhwa though still referred to as NWFP, with its capital in Peshawar. Peshawar is the gateway to the Hindu Kush on the road to Afghanistan. It is a traditional market town with a long history and is recognised as one of the oldest living cities in Asia. It is a city with many romantic associations of frontier exploration. The smugglers' bazaar that sits on the outskirts of town sells almost everything you can imagine that can be bought, from weapons to drugs and even people.

The world's three mighty mountain ranges, the Hindu Kush, the Karakoram Range and the Himalayas all converge at one point in NWFP, where the mighty Indus River flows to separate the ranges. Original parts of the ancient Silk Road can be seen carved into the side of cliffs not far from the point where Alexander the Great reached the Indus River and decided to go home. What an amazing place it is.

Heading east from FATA through NWFP one reaches Pakistan-controlled Kashmir. The Partition of India following British colonial rule brought into being the two independent states of India and Pakistan. The Hindu rulers of Kashmir chose to side with India even though the majority of the population were Muslim and perhaps would have preferred to have joined with Islamic Pakistan. This divide has led to a number of conflicts between

Pakistan and India over Kashmir, with roughly one third of the territory now administered by Pakistan and two-thirds administered by India. The cease-fire line last saw active fighting in 1999, and remains tense.

Perhaps second only to the Israel-Palestine dispute, the Kashmir conflict is one of the rallying cries for Islam. This is where the disaster hit.

The Geology of an Earthquake

Taken together, FATA, NWFP and Kashmir redefine the word "scale". Thirteen of the world's 30 tallest peaks are in Pakistan. Five of the 11 mountains reaching 8,000 metres are in Pakistan. K2, the world's second largest mountain looms on the border between China and Pakistan. The longest glaciers in the world outside of the Antarctic sit in this area of Pakistan.

It has often been said that those who love natural beauty and awesome silence should meet in these mountains and witness the wonders of the world in serene silence. It is a magical and awesome place. It is the place where you come to understand the meaning of the phrase 'young mountains'. In geological terms the three mountain ranges are caused by the on-going subjunction of India under Asia. The subcontinent split from ancient Gondwana during the Cretaceous period some 90 million years ago, and then drifted north before colliding with the Eurasian Plate about 50–55 million years ago. This massive collision gave birth to the Himalayan range and the Tibetan plateau.

During a particularly difficult time in early negotiations with the Pakistanis, I joked that the earthquake was all 'India's fault'. This gross over-simplification intended as a joke brought the desired laugh at a very tense time. Geologically speaking, the joke is true. The Indian subcontinent, by continuing to push north-eastward and under the Asian continental plate at 5 cm per year, is the cause of the region's considerable tectonic activity. This results in many earthquakes and an on-going pushing up of the mountain ranges, making the entire terrain unstable. Regular massive landslides and geological movements give the impression that this part of the world is still being born. The magnificent geography, unstable history and the political turmoil meant that when the earthquake hit, the word 'devastating' could only be used as an understatement.

When natural disasters hit, the world usually measures the scale by the number of people who died. By that measure the Pakistan earthquake was at the top end of the scale. This is a flawed measure, however. Humanitarian workers know the cold truth. The number of dead people is not as important as the number of people who survive. To put it bluntly, dead people don't need help; the living do. The people who need help are the survivors and the injured. In planning a response to a major natural disaster, one must measure the impact and size of the event by the number of those who have been seriously injured and survived, and then take into account circumstances in which the survivors find themselves.

The 2004 Southeast Asian tsunami killed, on revised figures, 198,000 people and injured approximately 120,000. Those who survived the tsunami lived in mild climatic conditions. Survivors would find themselves relatively close to unaffected areas, certainly within a day's walking distance. In comparison, the Pakistan earthquake killed about 75,000 people, injured approximately 1.4 million more and left 3.5 million homeless in highly hazardous terrain and brutal climatic conditions. Those affected would be significant distances and many days' walk from help. If you believe the headlines of newspapers, then the 2004 Southeast Asian tsunami had a bigger humanitarian impact than the Pakistan earthquake because more people were killed. The truth is the impact and challenge of the 2005 Kashmir earthquake was monumentally larger than that of the 2004 tsunami.

In terms of scale, a larger territory was affected by the quake than that affected by the Asian tsunami. The terrain, rather than flat and coastal, was mountainous and rugged. The weather, rather than temperate and tropical, was Himalayan, threatening and lethal. The freezing winter temperatures were less than two months away. Predictions of massive second waves of death caused by infection, starvation and cold were realistic and frightening. Disease could be expected, calamity was thought to be a certainty.

As a general rule of thumb, a poorly executed response to a natural disaster would see a second wave of deaths from secondary infection, hunger or exposure equivalent to that of the disaster itself. For Pakistan that would mean an additional 75,000 would die if the response was managed poorly. The reduction in the second wave of deaths from a potential 75,000 to as small as possible, would be the challenge. The problems faced were large, and the constraints on the planners were significant. By any reading, the impact of a natural disaster on the Pakistan scale was going to test any government, let alone a developing country government in particularly difficult circumstances. Faced with a massive catastrophe without precedent in modern times, the Pakistan government had to react, with or without help. Expectations were bleak and the task was immense.

For six months the government led an operation that was to see the world's largest helicopter engagement ever. More cargo was carried by air than in the Berlin airlift following the separation of East and West Berlin which marked the start of the Cold War. More than 70,000 Pakistani soldiers bravely carried huge amounts of aid up some of the world's highest mountains. After six months, the government of Pakistan with the support of the Pakistani people, international agencies, organisations and foreign volunteers, was able to declare relief operations over and could measure themselves against the threat of 75,000 potential secondary deaths. How did Pakistan stack up?

Not only was the second wave of deaths avoided, the death toll of 511 was a lower-than-normal death rate for winter in the same area. Deaths from the cold were fewer, no one starved to death, no disease breakout occurred. The quality of life indicators for the population had actually increased after the earthquake. Just under one million tents were distributed, nearly 400,000 emergency shelters were built, water supplies were rebuilt, and the closed areas of Kashmir were opened to foreign assistance. In less than six months the Pakistan government, with the help of the international community, was able to say, "Job well done, now let's look to rebuild." After 18 months of reconstruction, new schools and hospitals had been built, fundamental land reform had been achieved, and girls' enrolments in schools had increased 50 per cent. By any measure, the quality of life for the survivors had improved during the relief effort and had been significantly enhanced in the reconstruction.

In a BBC special *Children on the Frontline*, which looked at the way children responded to natural disasters and war, a father from Kashmir was interviewed about the earthquake. When the interviewer asked him, "What did you think about the earthquake?" one would perhaps have expected an answer that suggested the event had brought devastation.

"Thank God for the earthquake. My daughter can now get the education my wife never had," he said.

The earthquake relief and reconstruction had done more than keep people alive and rebuild their towns and lives. It had, to use the catch-phrase, 'Built Back Better'. Pakistan had achieved some remarkable social change as part of the relief effort. This was astonishing. The story of how this all happened is a story of trust with incredible partnerships, ending in friendship, family and love.

How Pakistan Responded

In Pakistan local search and rescue operations started immediately. In any natural disaster a general rule of thumb is that 70 per cent of an emergency response is made by local people on the ground, 20 per cent by national governments, and 10 per cent with the assistance of the international community. Pakistan was no different. The vast majority of rescues conducted in the first six to eight hours of an emergency are by people pulling friends, colleagues, sons, daughters, fathers and mothers from underneath the rubble of their own homes, well before any international response could possibly mobilise.

People sometimes forget timelines too. When they see the first reports on international news, people often ask, "Where is the international assistance?" not realising that it takes time to assemble a team from all over the world and deliver them to the affected region, even in the very best scenario. It takes time to pack the necessary supplies and equipment. Twenty-four hours would be a rapid deployment and anything up to seven days would still be quick.

Given that the earthquake struck and had effect in both Pakistan-controlled and Indian-controlled Kashmir, including across the Line of Control (still an internationally monitored ceasefire line between two nuclear powers) it was natural that both the Indian and Pakistani military were mobilised. Many people also ask, why use the military at all? What is the military's "value addition" to a humanitarian situation? Don't armies just fight wars? An emergency of this size cannot be dealt with by existing infrastructure and systems alone. With so many government structures and key personnel potentially wiped out, a rapid replacement of capacity is needed. This is why in any natural disaster of this size, a stable government turns to its military for immediate response. No one else can do it.

The military has assets, mobility, means, organisation, and the wherewithal and can provide national, district and local coordination infrastructure for NGOs, civil society and international support. Most importantly, they can work in far-flung areas, and hard-to-reach and perhaps 'insecure' regions. The military, particularly if well trained, has knowledge, and the ability to think and adapt.

But then if the military is so good, why use NGOs or other agencies at all? While the military may have some expertise in fighting wars, peacekeeping operations and control in civil strife, they don't have knowledge or expertise specific to humanitarian operations. Nor do they have the understanding of the political paradigm that exists in the middle of a humanitarian operation. The military specifically lacks advance practice and training in critical standards, such as the SPHERE Standards (international humanitarian standards), which are the minimum standards for humanitarian delivery and cover such practical issues as how many litres of water per day a person needs, how to set up an Internally Displaced Persons (IDP) camp, how to ensure food distribution equitably, and a whole plethora of other indicators and standards.

Death, cold, starvation and thirst are enemies in humanitarian operations, not an opposing military force. When operating in the humanitarian environment, the military needs to change its mind-set. Does the army collect sex-disaggregated data and understand its importance in planning, monitoring and 'mid-course corrections' based on gender and age? Does the military know how to set up an IDP returns process and ensure that aid deliveries in a relief operation don't cause a long-term 'dependency syndrome'? Most military personnel would have received no training in any of the above concepts, let alone know how to implement them. Yet the military has an enormous capacity to provide logistical support. Nevertheless, without the help of humanitarian experts, it cannot use its logistical and manpower strengths to their best advantage. It must be willing to learn and adapt.

Knowledge and experience in humanitarian and natural disaster response exists within NGOs, both national and international. It must be tapped into so that the maximum benefit is gained from the military's logistical skill. Their respective skill sets and intrinsic capabilities must combine to produce optimal results. Additionally, particularly in a large disaster, international organisations can help to mobilise more resources, give understanding of the political dimension and provide a coordination network.

While humanitarian organisations and the military may not be natural bedfellows, they both must learn to adapt and coordinate with each other in disaster settings. Civil-military co-operation is critical in natural disaster settings, even more so than post-conflict settings. I mentioned in earlier chapters that in the mid-1990s the world of civil-military coordination was new. By the mid-2000s progress had been made.

Although it took some days in the affected region to re-establish full command and control mechanisms to replace senior, middle level and junior level commanders who died in the earthquake, the Pakistan army was able to respond in varying degrees, depending on the strength and ability of remaining personnel in each location.

Initially though, these responses were localised and ad hoc, based on the skill of the officers on the ground. Military forces were activated for search and rescue for civilians and soldiers alike, to assess damage, and secure the frontier, which had been brutally fought over in previous years. In those first few hours and days, as communication links were out of order, as command structures had been decimated and key personnel wiped out, order had to be restored, law enforced, and most importantly, thousands upon thousands of medical emergencies had to be dealt with. These early interventions were coordinated and commanded by well-trained professional officers who were among the survivors in the affected region. Pakistan did well with the strong response of local people acting independently, while centrally information started to come in and coordination began.

Geneva Mobilises

In November 2004, I had bought a small chalet on 2,000 square metres of land at the foot of the Jura bordering Geneva, but just inside France. Fifteen minutes' drive from Geneva airport and 22 minutes' drive from the UN base in Geneva, this house was perfectly located for me.

In mid-2005 I had started some significant renovations, which took most of my weekends. By October 2005 the house was close to uninhabitable. The previous weekend saw my old kitchen hit the dust heap in preparation for a new one, on the weekend of October 8, 2005. It was my turn to be the

United Nations duty officer that weekend, but nothing ever happens on a weekend, does it? It was 5.30 am, October 8, 2005, Geneva time, when my phone rang to give me the first hint of the unfolding tragedy.

Just over 100 were said to be dead and one building had collapsed in Islamabad, Pakistan's capital. By 7.30 am reports started to filter in about the impact – a few hundred people had died. No panic yet. Experienced operators know that you need to completely ignore initial death toll reports for they are extremely unreliable. To determine the size of a natural disaster and the likelihood of international response, one needs to examine, in the case of an earthquake, the size of the earthquake, its depth and proximity to population centres. Everything in my background had prepared me for what would happen next. My time in the military, legal training, my 1990s aid work with the Red Cross in Rwanda and Yugoslavia, my political stints around 2000 and the time in UN Headquarters from 2003–05 would all contribute.

This earthquake was big, shallow and close. It would need help from the outside, but only if the Pakistanis were to ask for it. An international assistance team cannot be deployed without the support of an affected government. We needed the UN to get ready. At 7.45 am I headed off to UN headquarters in Geneva to discuss the response to Pakistan, assuming it wouldn't escalate and I would be back working on my house before long.

I never slept a night in that house again.

In the early stage of a natural disaster, especially one on a massive scale, accurate information is always scarce and yet assumptions and actions need to be made. By 8 am I found myself with Arjun Katoch in the office of Gerhard Putman-Cramer.

Gerhard ran the Emergency Services Branch of the United Nations Office for the Coordination of Humanitarian Affairs (OCHA). He was always well groomed and meticulously dressed, and was very senior. Some people assumed that Gerhard was pompous, or that he would be completely disinterested in any field operation that might get mud on his shoes. This couldn't be further from the truth. Gerhard loved the days when he could go to field operations and get deeply involved. While some would argue that he was too senior to be allowed, Gerhard believed that you did need to have senior operatives on every mission. There is no doubt that his deployment was made easier, given that it was a weekend, by the absence from headquarters of people who may have sought to block his departure.

Arjun worked for Gerhard and was responsible for the Field Support Section which, among other things, ran the deployment of United Nations Disaster Assessment and Coordination (UNDAC) teams. Arjun was a man of good humour, and as a retired colonel from the Indian Army, had always hankered to see the Pakistan side of Kashmir.

In the normal course of events, if the earthquake hit on a working day, people would be buzzing around the office trying to look busy in fear that they would get in trouble for not looking busy, regardless of whether they had something to do or not. This is real *Yes Minister* stuff. But being earlier than 9 am on a Saturday, most people in the United Nations system in Geneva were still at home, blissfully unaware of what was taking place in Pakistan. This was to work in our favour! Rather than wasting time running from meeting to meeting, informing people of something they didn't really need to know, but feared not knowing, Gerhard, Arjun and I were able to make decisions without dealing with unnecessary bureaucracy. The only people involved in the early planning were those we wanted to be involved. No baggage. Consequently some people would later query some of the decisions we made because the bureaucrats had not been 'informed'.

UNDAC teams cannot deploy without an official invitation from the host government. There are a number of practical reasons for this, the first of which is that the host government issues the visas. If the government doesn't want support, there is no point sending a supporting team.

As soon as Arjun heard of the earthquake he contacted Air Marshal Toor. Toor was Director General of Civil Defence in Pakistan, based in Islamabad, who was well aware of UNDAC. This early contact played a critical role in the early hours, acting as the interface between the United Nations system and the office of President Musharraf, who was also an army chief. Toor passed information to us about the size of the natural disaster and also persuaded General Musharraf that he should formally request support from an UNDAC team.

In many ways dealing with military dictatorships can be easier than dealing with civilian governments in times of emergency. A good military commander understands that it is much easier to return unneeded resources than to mobilise them late. The best response to a crisis is to mobilise a team without waiting to be fully sure you need them and cancel the resources later if they aren't needed. The alternative of waiting for certainty of need, hesitating and delaying, can cost lives.

We were quickly given very strong indications from Toor that a formal request from Musharraf would come sometime during the afternoon. This was a good start to the response, and we needed to put an UNDAC team on standby.

The way an UNDAC team normally deploys is as follows: there is a roster of pre-existing trained personnel, some of whom are UN staff members and some of whom are staff of donor governments and agencies. When it seems likely that an UNDAC team will be needed, an alert SMS and email is sent to the entire roster asking who is available and where they are located. Members of Arjun's team would then go through the replies and determine the best make up of an UNDAC deployment, based on language skills, previous experience and location. That is the normal process, and Arjun swung it into action, but with one difference. Arjun, Gerhard and I were standing in Gerhard's office as we were discussing potential team deployment.

"I would like to go," said Gerhard.

With a twinkle in his eye, Arjun responded, "Me too."

It was an interesting exchange with an underlying dynamic. Many have argued that Arjun shouldn't have been deployed to an earthquake in Pakistan-controlled Kashmir given his history in the Indian armed forces. Even though United Nations staff members travelling on a United Nations passport have technically "no nationality", diplomatic niceties would normally dictate a little bit more discretion in choosing the nationality of a team member.

However, it was becoming more and more clear that Pakistan was going to be a major natural disaster in which the best people would need to be deployed even if there was a risk in their deployment. If the earthquake had hit during working hours, on a working day, there would have been many other people crowded into Gerhard's office. Many would have had a view on Arjun's nationality and the appropriateness of his potential deployment. But it was a Saturday, Arjun would know part of the terrain and culture, but would also be a welcome senior interlocutor for incoming search and rescue teams. There were only three of us in the room, and we all got on well – an essential prerequisite for an emergency response team.

"Me too," I said.

Although I wasn't qualified to go on an UNDAC team as I hadn't been UNDAC trained, my role was the Asia Pacific Desk Officer so it could be my responsibility to write the initial situation reports for the earthquake. A silent deal was done. All three of us had confidence in the other in playing a significant and effective role in an UNDAC team. My role would be to write the situation reports and coordinate the initial communication back with Geneva headquarters, and I would be labelled the "desk officer in place" and thereby get around the "no UNDAC training" hurdle. Boy, did this change, big time, once we hit the ground.

When other senior officials discovered the make-up of the UNDAC team there were attempts to stop the deployment of both Arjun and I, with Gerhard having to go all the way to the United Nations Emergency Relief Coordinator Jan Egeland to stop the blockers. These late attempts really made us glad that the earthquake had hit on a Saturday. For most of the day we prepared, freed from the unnecessary hindrance of intervening bureaucrats.

Other members of the UNDAC team were notified of mobilisation from Britain and other parts of Switzerland so they could join our team in Geneva for an initial deployment of seven. By 10 am we started our mental and physical preparations for a deployment. Jesper Lund, one of Arjun's staff, began to put together the emergency response kits, which included communications, laptops, tents and clothing necessary for us to be a fully self-sustaining unit upon deployment. He activated a pre-existing standby agreement with the government of Switzerland for an air ambulance to be converted for immediate transport. The Learjet was reconfigured and sent to Geneva in readiness for flying us to Pakistan.

I rushed home to pack.

The Unfolding Story

While billions of dollars were donated to support the tsunami victims, funds given for Pakistan earthquake relief would turn out to be slow and scarce. In addition, the international relief community was part way through a process of self-examination following poor coordination and massive duplication of effort seen after past operations. The Humanitarian Response Review discussed above finalised its recommendations in September and were due to be discussed and agreed at the meeting on December 12, 2005. In between the September recommendations and the December meeting was the October earthquake. It was limbo-land for international disaster response. No one knew which system to use: the old discredited one or the new yet to be endorsed one?

So this was the challenge: A massive natural disaster, a military dictatorship, questionable security, international terrorism, and a flawed humanitarian system part way through a reform process that no one fully understood and with no systems yet in place and no one willing to fund the response. How would you like to be caught in the middle of that?

At Pakistan Army General Headquarters (GHQ) in Rawalpindi, just outside Islamabad, senior commanders became more and more aware of the size and scope of the disaster as information flowed in from village after village. The Joint Chiefs convened meetings to coordinate data collection and response, mobilise forces and analyse the continuous flow of new information. It soon became clear that this crisis was too big for any country to handle alone. Hence the reason they were open to a deployment of an UNDAC team.

While some have criticised the Pakistan army for its 'slow' response in the first few hours, the forces were coordinated and largely functional within three or so days – this compares very favourably to other natural disasters in other parts of the world. It compares much better than other armed forces, particularly after Hurricane Katrina in the United States, and in the 2004 tsunami-affected countries. On that first day the initial response by civilians, local military commanders, and communities banding together, saved many lives well before any international support could possibly be mobilised. Criticism of Pakistan in the early days is not warranted.

Three key factors helped to produce an unusually fast UNDAC mobilisation. Firstly, Pakistani officials such as Air Marshal Toor had been trained in the UNDAC system. Secondly, a pre-existing standby agreement with the government of Switzerland was activated to provide a special aircraft for our team. Thirdly, a potential UNDAC team was identified from pre-existing rosters, and members were put on four hours' notice to move. Personal and institutional preparations began.

By the middle of that Saturday afternoon the President of Pakistan officially requested the United Nations to mobilise support, including the UNDAC team. Our standby became real. The British-based members took a connecting flight from London to Geneva. By 10.30 pm we all gathered at the private craft section of Geneva airport to pack our emergency gear aboard the Swiss plane.

I had forgotten to lock the front door of my house. The last thing I did in the country was to telephone a friend whom I asked to go around and lock-up. Just before 11 pm we taxied to the end of the runway, and took off, headed towards south Asia.

"Good evening," said the pilot over the intercom. "Our flight time will either be eight or 12 hours. We will either be landing in Islamabad or Dubai depending on whether we get over-flight permission for Afghanistan. I'll let you know." It was the first and only time I've got on an aeroplane without being sure where we were actually going to land!

We tried to get some sleep during the flight, but we also had some very big questions. Would we be welcome in Kashmir or was this merely a diplomatic exercise? How would terrorist groups respond to foreign people on their soil? Would the Pakistan military be cooperative or uncooperative? How were we going to work with a military dictatorship, and who in the government would we be dealing with? Would the international community be providing financial support? For Gerhard there was an additional question. Eight hours without a cigarette: "Will I be able to smoke on landing?"

UNDAC Arrives

We arrived around 8 am, barely 24 hours after the earthquake. Gerhard rested in the arrivals hall of Islamabad airport, cigarette in hand, comfortably sitting, puffing gently directly under a no smoking sign while our goods were cleared by customs. Only one other foreign team, the Turkish Red Crescent Society's search and rescue team, reached the affected zone as fast.

We were given 72-hour visas, presumably because those who were in power thought the problem would be resolved within three days. Such under-estimations are not uncommon in natural disaster responses.

The first thing we needed to figure out was who we would be dealing with in the government of Pakistan. The Department of Economic Affairs in conjunction with the Ministry of Foreign Affairs had been historically the focal point for dealing with foreign organisations and NGOs, but we knew the power was with the army.

In Rawalpindi the joint chiefs of military staff met again at the general headquarters of the Pakistan army. They, like everybody else, had a lack of information and a growing sense that the disaster was larger than was first expected. Some of the generals even began to feel that the disaster was bigger than they could handle. A sense of hopelessness is extremely frustrating for a military commander, particularly one that is used to being in complete command. Some senior army staff had a temptation to continue with their own plans without building a partnership with the United Nations or foreign NGOs. For them, it made more sense to leave the international collaboration to the civilian and bureaucratic arms of the government.

Pakistani Civil Defence officials, specifically those trained by UNDAC, met the arriving team and organised internal transport to the key affected region. The pre-existing United Nations country team organised office space and coordination meetings with UN agencies and key international development focused NGOs present in Pakistan prior to the earthquake.

This was one of those times to note the difference between 'humanitarian aid' and 'development aid'. Prior to the earthquake there had existed a UN Country Team in Pakistan. Largely made up of development-focused staff looking at macro-economic reform, agriculture enhancement and anti -corruption measures, the development-focused staff work under a paradigm of slow incremental change following rules and procedures.

Humanitarian emergency staff don't do slow and don't do incremental. The culture clash between the different personality types is always hard to manage, and in a sense the first meetings between 'development' staff and 'emergency humanitarian' staff exist to lay the ground rules: you do development in other parts of the country, we do the emergency. Some people understood the difference, others didn't and still insisted on controlling their patch, even if they were unsuited to it.

International agencies, NGOs and governments were busily despatching emergency response teams from all corners of the globe. The question now was how all of these incoming teams would be coordinated and plugged into a mechanism for collaboration. The UNDAC team's rapid arrival, with Pakistani government and UN in-country support, allowed for the rapid creation of three vital elements. First, the immediate establishment of an onsite coordination centre in Muzaffarabad, headed up by Rob Holden. Muzaffarabad was devastated. Most of the buildings were destroyed, telecommunications were lost, and there was no electricity, running water or food. Within this environment Rob had to set up a mechanism for coordination of all the incoming search and rescue teams from a tent. He and the team in Muzaffarabad did a magnificent job.

Second, a welcome centre for international humanitarian assistance and volunteers was established at Islamabad airport. This is a critical element in the first stages of a natural disaster as it is the "traffic cop" that directs incoming teams to the place where they are most needed. Third, a functioning coordination office was established in Islamabad. The role of the Islamabad office was to make the top-level connections with government, embassy, and military partners as well as informing the "information beast of headquarters in Geneva". Initially my role was to act as the information coordination point between Islamabad and Geneva, but my role was to change radically and quickly.

The UNDAC team's other initial tasks were also critical. Principal among these was the role of information focal point for incoming international search and rescue teams, donors and NGOs, through the online Virtual OSOCC (on site coordination centre). The online Virtual OSOCC is a very powerful tool managed by OCHA. When search and rescue groups from various countries make their decision to deploy to a new emergency, they register on the virtual OSOCC, indicating their departure and likely arrival times. They include the make-up of their teams and list their arrival needs.

International search and rescue teams are used to working closely with each other in different disasters around the world. Nearly 20 years prior to the Pakistan earthquake the need for better coordination of international search and rescue teams had been identified. The International Search and Rescue Advisory Group (INSARAG) was established in 1991 following initiatives of international search and rescue teams that responded to the 1988 Armenia earthquake. The United Nations was chosen as the INSARAG secretariat to facilitate international participation and coordination. The Field Coordination Support Section (Arjun's team), located within OCHA, Geneva's Emergency Services Branch (Gerhard's Group), functioned as the INSARAG secretariat.

While teams are en route, the OCHA team at the airport scans through the arrival times and begins to organise groups to work together based on their language and capacity matches. Teams with search dogs are matched with teams without, and initial areas to search are allocated to those teams. By the time a search and rescue team arrives in a country the 12 hours or so travel time has been well used to set the search and rescue priorities and allocate teams to task immediately.

One of the first tasks of at least one of the UNDAC team is to find the timber and oxyacetylene gas. Search and rescue teams are incredibly courageous people who dig their way into the rubble of buildings to rescue people who may have survived in air pockets. An enormous amount of wood is needed to prop up the unsafe concrete rubble to minimise the likelihood that a rescuer could become trapped should the rubble move during an aftershock or from the instability of the collapsed pile. Strong timber beams are needed but are very heavy to transport and are best sourced on arrival.

In an urban environment many of the concrete structures are reinforced with steel reinforcing bars making the removal of concrete difficult unless it is cut with oxyacetylene torches. It is highly dangerous to carry oxyacetylene gas by air, so this needs to be sourced locally.

We were acutely aware that it was all very well to set up coordination structures in Islamabad, but the epicentre was just outside Muzaffarabad. Arjun dispatched Rob Holden to set up the OSOCC in the devastated town. Arjun was supposed to go to set up the OSOCC in Muzaffarabad but the Pakistanis refused him permission to leave the Islamabad area because he had been in the Indian Army 15 years previously and turned him back from the Chaklala military airfield in Islamabad.

One cannot underestimate the hardship and challenge that Rob had to face. He had to enter a devastated city, surrounded by death, cold nights, no electricity, with only the food provisions he brought with him. Working out of a tent, he had to establish a safe operating environment for the incoming search and rescue teams, including identifying areas for sleeping and eating while also determining the list of priority buildings to search. Without people like Rob and his colleagues in the OSOCC on the ground, initial search and rescue would have continued to be haphazard, but with Rob's work many people's lives were saved.

While all this was going on, I wrote the first situation report for headquarters. In the early days of a large emergency such as this, it is the UN-DAC situation reports that are a primary source of information for many agents, including key donors and other organisations that may be considering deploying emergency teams.

Pakistan saw the novel experiment of the 'reverse situation report', whereby the headquarters, at the request of the field operation, would provide the field with a daily update of important issues for the field, much like the field situation report provides daily information for the headquarters. This novel idea only lasted four issues before the headquarters stopped this support service citing 'too heavy a workload' to headquarters, while still requesting a situation report from the field. One headquarters' official went as far as to say, "Remember, Andrew, you are there to support headquarters, not the headquarters to support the field operation." I couldn't have disagreed more.

Cluster Management Begins

We decided that the situation report should be written using a simple format based on the Humanitarian Response Review cluster recommendations. In essence, this 'cluster approach' divided up humanitarian response into a number of sectors including but not limited to health, food, water and sanitation, camp management, shelter, etc. An agency takes responsibility for that sector (WHO for Health, the Red Cross for some shelter scenarios, the World Food Program for food, for example) and aims to coordinate and have visibility over that sector.

Through the cluster system, the humanitarian actors can be asked to ensure that there is no duplication of action, and no unknown and unmet gaps – or at least try to. In making this simple decision we had effectively said that we would not coordinate the response in the same way as past humanitarian responses. Without saying as much, we recognised that the international system had been heavily criticised in Humanitarian Response Review process, and that we were going to implement the new mechanism. Given that it is very difficult to implement a new system that had not yet been agreed, approved, or trained for, this was a risk. But what were we to do? Implement a former system that we knew was discredited, or take the risk with a new one?

Flash-funding Appeal

As the initial coordination structures began to take shape we turned our minds to money. Emergency operation does not run for free and a mechanism is needed to inform the international donor community of the level of funding that is likely to be needed. The flash-funding appeal is the process by which a rough estimation of the overall emergency response costing is sent to the international donor community to begin to get national budgets ready. We decided that we would try to avoid the delay in funding by preparing a flash appeal and returning it to headquarters within 72 hours. This would be the fastest flash appeal ever.

This target was not as simple as it seems. Although it was a 'rough and ready' document, a whole series of assumptions needed to be made. Principal among these assumptions is a guess about how large the affected population was. The size of the affected population is the main variable in the cost of major operations. This is calculated more by educated guesswork than by factual analysis of data, because that simply doesn't exist that early in the crisis.

Secondly, to put together a flash appeal based on the HRR cluster process we needed to bring each of the agencies already on the ground into a central location, explain the process and what we were going to implement, all without the agencies having authorisation from headquarters. To complicate the matter further, the United Nations Resident Coordinator, nominally the most senior person in the country, was not present. Jan Vandemoortele had recently been appointed as Resident Coordinator and was in New York being briefed at the time the earthquake hit. He was en route to Pakistan while we were beginning to put together the initial funding appeal.

We had decided that the flash appeal would be based on the clusters identified by the HRR process, with one additional cluster of 'emergency education' that had been rejected in the HRR process. Emergency education is a critical element in a natural disaster response. It involves sourcing emergency tents, books, pens and all similar items needed to re-establish children's schooling as fast as possible. While there is an important aspect of continuing children's education, the largest immediate impact is to put children in care for at least eight hours a day so that parents can begin to rebuild the family life as fast as possible. The psycho-social impact on children is also critical as rebuilding begins to return a 'sense of normality' to fragile and delicate young minds. It is always strange to me how in the developing world this is often understood better than in the developed world.

We invited all NGOs, international organisations, donors and interested parties that were represented in Islamabad to a meeting at the World Food Program's Islamabad office where a draft guideline for a flash appeal, a short description of the 'cluster process' and cluster leads appointed based on the HRR recommendations were distributed. An aftershock later measuring 6 on the Richter Scale hit Islamabad and a room full of emergency workers sat as the huge oak meeting table bounced and the chandelier swung wildly. Everyone looked to the walls, hoping that they wouldn't crack.

With little guidance, no terms of reference and no background to draw upon, these lead agencies were asked to rapidly pull together draft projects for consolidation into the flash appeal. In order to have a common planning figure I put the question to the room: "How many people do you think have been affected by this earthquake?" Numbers ranged from 2.5 to 4 million people with a collective agreement to settle on a planning figure of 3.5 million people affected, and 500,000 houses destroyed. In the after-action analysis we were able to show that our initial estimations were almost spot on, proving that if you get enough experienced people in the room and asked them to give an educated guess, the collective result will more often than not be very close to accurate.

The important thing to know about a flash appeal is that it is intended to raise money to cover the first three to six months of emergency operation. When putting together project requests, agencies need to take into account that if the request is funded, then those funds must be expended within a three- to six-month period. The flash appeal must be taken seriously by the international donor community and there is a huge risk that if agencies overestimate costs it will blow the credibility of the whole process.

Within 24 hours of the decision to draft the appeal, initial proposals had been formulated for emergency response projects totalling US$2.6 billion. This was an outrageously high amount of money and would have smashed all records of the previous flash appeals. Clearly some had not understood the process evidenced by the distinct difference between the proposals brought by people who had a development background, and people who had an emergency background.

People with emergency backgrounds are acutely aware that money will be tight. They tend to only ask for essential items. People with a development background may be tempted to take a perceived opportunity to grab funding for their pre-existing underfunded development programs. If we submitted an overly ambitious and deeply flawed flash appeal it would lose credibility and we might receive almost no funding. The appeal had to be credible.

One of the programs put forward by the Food and Agricultural Organisation (FAO), a developmental organisation, was US$50 million for planting crops and restocking herds. This was never going to be implemented in the following six months as a country entered a Himalayan winter. Even if the money was obtained, it simply couldn't be spent within the defined limited period, and the donors would know this. While the restocking was not a good emergency response program, it would be a good early recovery program to implement later in the cycle. In removing the request from the flash appeal, a formal complaint was made from the FAO office in Islamabad to headquarters back in Europe, creating an enormous amount of unnecessary work by people who simply didn't understand the system.

Equally, the UNDP office put in a submission for US$1.2 billion for their early recovery programs and activities, even though there was simply no possibility that US$1.2 billion could be spent within the timeframe.

I looked at that budget line item and said to the UNDP country director (who is second in command of UNDP behind the resident coordinator) that he needed to cut the request. He said with a bit of work he might be able to drop the program down to $1.1 or maybe even $1 billion.

"You don't seem to understand, let's drop the zero, halve the amount and halve it again." I was not very popular. We took his request and turned it into a much more credible US$30 million.

Jan Vandemoortele, the resident coordinator arrived at that moment and walked into the room as we were having this discussion. This was the first time I had met Jan. He was wearing a light beige woollen vest, corduroy pants and sandals with socks. If one were to judge a book by its cover one would have very little cause for happiness. Sandals with socks? In Pakistan? Give me a break. Fortunately, he was an exceptional leader for the time.

When you first meet Jan you gain the impression that he is a quiet, humble man. The more you learn of him, you realise that within this quiet exterior is a man of extreme courage and character. He was a rare personality in the United Nations. If more people were like him it would be a much more effective organisation. He asked what was going on. When I told him, he backed my judgement.

Jan was and is a man entirely without ego. He was also very conscious that he was selected prior to the earthquake based on his macroeconomic knowledge and the assumption that the UN's presence in Pakistan was to assist with on-going macroeconomic reform. Jan had never experienced an emergency and had no knowledge about how to handle one. A person less secure in his own skin might have tried to bluff or bluster. Jan on the other hand, watched, observed and supported the UNDAC team and began to assert control only as his knowledge and understanding grew to a point where he would add value to a discussion. In the two and a half years we worked together, I grew to respect Jan enormously as a mentor, a boss and as a fundamentally decent human being.

By the end of the first flash appeal coordination meeting we had a realistic target of US$311 million. The severe reduction came as the emergency workers in the room asserted their influence over the development workers. It was a win for logic over optimism. The development workers did have one card to play when a number of them complained to their headquarters. For political and diplomatic reasons the flash appeal was revised upwards by the OCHA office in Geneva to $521 million. A number of pet projects were included to placate other agency headquarters, including FAO's restocking program. Six months later, at the end of the relief effort, the total actually spent during the six-month flash appeal period was $330 million. None of FAO's money had been spent so the funds did not flow through to the agency and they were not able to claim their 'administration fee'. While I may have been proved tight, FAO still didn't like me.

This first flash appeal coordination meeting was more than just about funding, it was a critical step in resetting the mental state of many of the United Nations and NGO workers already in Pakistan. They had to move from the mind-set of development to the mind-set of emergency. The rules of the game had to be changed.

There is a special lexicon of language within the United Nations and

NGO world. Before arriving into this world I had always assumed that 'humanitarian work' and 'development work' were the same thing, one being a subset of another. This is not the case. 'Humanitarian' refers to an immediate emergency assistance post-conflict or post-disaster. 'Development' refers to on-going programmatic interventions in developing countries as part of on-going efforts to bring those countries out of poverty.

Why is this important? The personality types of people in humanitarian work differs greatly from those of people in development work. By its nature 'humanitarian' work demands that people respond quickly to incredible demands, tight timelines and have a sense of urgency brought on by rapid onset disasters and conflict. Development work, on the other hand, requires people who manage slow incremental change. Given that 'humanitarian' and 'development' work can be done in the same country, these workers often clash around questions of speed, results and effectiveness. The process of the flash-funding appeal highlighted this difference.

With the flash-funding appeal completed our attention turned to a larger question: How will the international community coordinate and interface their relief operations with government structures, institutions and the military? Jan Vandemoortele quickly established his leadership, relying heavily on UNDAC advice, particularly that of Gerhard and Arjun. Together, they had divided the senior tasks among themselves, with Gerhard taking responsibility for high-level government and diplomatic liaison, while Arjun concentrated on setting up the mechanics of the UNDAC team and initial coordination structures.

To Cluster or Not to Cluster?

Jan accepted that the cluster recommendations of HRR would be implemented for this natural disaster response. A new and experimental approach would be used. Clusters which were created, first for the situation report, then the flash appeal, now made a permanent mark on the relief operation. They were formalised, leaders appointed and coordination structures and mechanisms put in place. Experimenting with a new approach for a large emergency did have its drawbacks because no-one knew the rules of the new system. We were inventing it as we went along.

One great strength of the cluster approach became apparent long after the event. Because no-one knew how it worked, no one knew how to stop it. This took away the great strength that some of those in the bureaucracy of the United Nations who seek to avoid doing "nothing wrong" by doing "nothing" had. This was the great defeat for the *Yes Minster* types. Those who normally know how to manipulate the rules to stop innovative action, new thinking or accountability found themselves out in the cold. Because no-one new the rules of the new system. We were inventing it as we went and as perverse as it sounds, this was a great advantage.

Two key institutions developed. Firstly, the UN country team convened regularly to discuss UN administrative issues that were critical in solving problems such as customs clearances and visas for emergency workers.

Secondly, the cluster heads forum brought together all cluster coordinators. With the backing of Gerhard and Arjun, I empowered the cluster leads to be the ultimate decision-making organisation at the initial stage of the relief effort.

Key cluster coordinators represented emergency shelter, camp management, health, food, logistics, water and sanitation, emergency education, legal protection and early recovery. Most of those responsible withstood significant pressure from their agencies and chose to work in the context of the overall needs of the operation, not just the needs of their own organisations. Many were criticised by their headquarters for not putting their agency's priorities first. It may sound ridiculous, but many within the United Nations' system had still not got the point of the Humanitarian Response Review: we were supposed to act as a team.

By now the reader may be wondering if this was becoming over complex? Have we moved too far away from the disaster and too far into the minutiae of the bureaucracy? The frustrating answer is that in the UN the bureaucracy is the point. This is the greatest frustration of the emergency response worker. You have to know how to navigate the interpersonal petty bureaucracy.

By the end of the first week the Pakistan's Department of Economic Affairs had persuaded the military to meet us. The Pakistan High Command, meeting in Rawalpindi, came to that conclusion as well. One of the problems the Pakistani military had to wrestle with was the question of coordination of international aid organisations in a militarily sensitive area such as Kashmir. So how does a military operational commander seek and gain visibility and control over an entire operational area, if a key interlocutor in that operational area has skills and knowledge needed, is undertaking activities, but is reluctant to share information and will not be controlled? The military had to find a way through all of this.

With lobbying from the Department of Economic Affairs, the UN offices and through expert diplomacy from United States officials, particularly Ambassador Ryan Crocker, USAID focal point Bill Berger and military liaisons Sandy Davidson and David Keefe, we were summoned to attend the Operations Room at General Headquarters Rawalpindi on the following day. This was good news.

By this time we had also established a Civil Military Coordination Cell under Chuck Royce. Chuck managed to build links and confidence with the NATO military commanders, particularly US and UK officers. This gave additional credibility and strength to the attempts to win over the Pakistanis and played a critical role in convincing senior generals to take United Nations seriously. As the relief effort unfolded, civil military coordination officers were deployed to each of the field coordination hubs. They all played a critical role in building strong personal contacts with key army officers on the ground.

The bad news was that almost no money was coming in through the flash appeal. No donor agency or government seemed to be interested in what was happening in Pakistan. Many people speculated as to why this was so. Some thought there was international donor fatigue created by the huge outpouring of funds to the Southeast Asian tsunami a little less than a year before. Stories of inefficiency and ineffectiveness in the tsunami operation were starting to be reported in major international newspapers and some thought this was having an impact on funding available to Pakistan.

Additionally, there is a concept called 'proximity'. People take more interest and donate more money to things that are proximate to them. In the case of the Southeast Asian tsunami the perception of proximity was created as many in western countries could imagine themselves on a holiday resort beach and being struck by a wave. The fact that many foreign tourists died in the tsunami added to this impression. People simply couldn't imagine what it was like to be in a remote village in Kashmir and so many in the West found it difficult to empathise with the people of Pakistan. Images of fundamentalist Islamic terrorism certainly didn't help.

The most empathetic of countries would be the closest – but the list of neighbouring countries is a roll call of difficulty. India: currently at war with Pakistan. Afghanistan: itself a basket case. Iran: on the opposite side of the Sunni/Shia divide. China (yes, Pakistan does border China) would provide bilateral aid (that is not through the UN system, but directly government to government). The fastest responding country was Turkey.

While the cluster coordinators hoped that we would get money, we had to devise an alternative. The early ideas of a contingency plan based on no funding started to form in our minds. If we didn't get funding we would need to pull out most of the UN staff and leave a small number of experts to advise the government of Pakistan. It was critically important to develop a strong relationship with the military in case our role would shrink to humanitarian advisers to a military operation. This first meeting with the military would be critical to develop strong relations in case we did get funding, and develop even stronger relations in case we did not.

The most senior UN official and global head of OCHA, Jan Egeland visited Pakistan at about this time. His gathering of knowledge added weight to the importance of coordination and strength to his calls internationally for additional funding. He appointed Gerhard as Deputy Humanitarian Coordinator and in so doing strengthened Gerhard's capacity to get things done. Egeland is a good and sensitive man. On the return helicopter flight from Muzaffarabad we crammed a number of injured people in to take them to hospitals in Islamabad. With great sadness one small child died with us en route. Egeland continued to work tirelessly to get whatever support he could for us in field operations. We knew we had an ally in him in headquarters. His visit also helped in building relations with the Pakistani military.

Gerhard knew of my military background and knew that there was no way Arjun, being Indian, would be allowed inside the Pakistan army headquarters. Given that Gerhard had made the decision that I was to stay in Pakistan, and had created the title 'Chief of Operations' for me to gain credibility with the military, he asked me to lead the negotiating group.

These are moments when, given my background, I wonder how I arrived in my current situation. Having been a young officer cadet and commissioned officer in the Australian Army a decade and a half earlier and after being in Pakistan a little over a week to make situation reports, I now found myself inside the super-secret operations room of the Pakistan military. How the heck did I get here? With me were half a dozen or so other UN officials representing the World Food Program, the World Health Organisation, UNICEF and UN High Commissioner for Refugees, all of whom had roles as cluster coordinators. Critical among these people was Philippe Martou, the focal point of the United Nations Humanitarian Air Service (UNHAS), the providers of UN helicopters.

On the Pakistan side, the delegation was led by Major-General Mohamed Yousaf, the Director-General of Military Operations. For the first 20 minutes of the meeting we were comparing notes on how big we thought the disaster was. Even then we were still operating on incomplete information and were underestimating the scale of the problem. Then Yousaf did the bravest thing I've ever seen an army general in any country, in any time, do. He put his head in his hands and said, "Honestly, we do not know what to do".

In most countries an army general would never admit to a foreigner that he didn't know how to handle a problem in his own country. Such lack of admission and realisation of a lack of capacity to respond to a natural disaster was a contributing factor to the poor response of the United States to Hurricane Katrina.

It takes an enormous amount of strength, confidence, self-awareness and selflessness to realise the needs of your people are greater than the pride of your organisation. One cannot underestimate the strength and courage of Major-General Mohamed Yousaf.

I looked across at him and said, "Sir, honestly, neither do we." I asked Philippe to outline the type of resources we could bring to assist. With a UN helicopter airlift supplementing that of the Pakistan army, and with the assistance of UK and US military forces from Afghanistan, perhaps there was a light at the end of the tunnel?

While Philippe was outlining how and what sort of rotary wing airframes the United Nations could bring to bear, I wrote a small note to General Yousaf. "Sir, this is the biggest challenge of your life, but together we will win." I passed the note across the table. When he read the note he smiled. He walked over to my side of the table, put his arm over my shoulder and said, "We can work together." Yousaf asked us to give the army 48 hours to consider the framework that we would put in place.

General Nadeem: Didn't Want His Arse Kissed Either

We were called back within 24 hours. This time the meeting was led by Major-General Nadeem Ahmad, the Vice Chief of General Staff. This was to be the first meeting with a man who I later came to know as one of the most 'rolled gold' human beings I have ever met. He is a man with few character flaws, a prodigious sense of service and was incorruptible. He is a brilliant, empathetic man who is like a big brother to me. This bond would take time to develop. There are few, if any, people I have as much respect for as this man.

General Nadeem proceeded to tell us that he would instruct the NGOs on what and where they would work and he respectfully welcomed our assistance. I knew two things. Firstly, never contradict a senior army officer in public. Secondly, there was no way NGOs would take orders from the Pakistan army.

"Sir, can we have a word alone for a moment?" I asked.

We went into a side room. I told General Nadeem the story of Brigadier Rowe, Commander Ninth Brigade and how he hated when people tried to kiss his arse. Nadeem laughed his agreement.

"So let me tell you when I think you are wrong," I said.

Nadeem appreciated that. Mind you, he was right more often than me. We developed a level of trust and friendship between us such that he expected me to disagree when I thought he was wrong. It was my job in his mind to do so. It is a rare asset for a general to have people speak their minds. Nadeem wanted facts, honest interpretation and strong opinion. While we were still in the side office, Nadeem asked me to share my thoughts. It is my view that one of the greatest dangers is if a decision-maker makes a decision based on a wrong assumption. The Pakistan army had assumed that the international aid world was a homogeneous and well coordinated group that could be treated as a single interface. This was wrong. If the Pakistan army were to plan on a flawed basis, they would only be disappointed and disillusioned with the assistance that could come. In my mind it was very clear that Nadeem needed an accurate perception of the partnerships that he could, and could not, rely upon. I had to take a punt and be blunt.

"The first thing you need to understand, sir, is there is no such thing as the United Nations. There are a whole bunch of organisations with the letters U and N in front of their name, a fascination with the colour blue and an organisational structure that means they are more likely to compete than collaborate.

"Secondly, the NGOs will guard their independence and will leave the country before they take a tasking order from you.

"Thirdly, NGOs are often thought to be a homogeneous group that can be handled in one category. This is wrong. NGOs are a huge range of different organisations, from 'one-man' operations to multinational professional organisations. It is simply not possible to assume they are all one group of similar organisations that can be handled in a similar way.

"In your role, you need to understand the fourth thing: if you want to get things done you need to be more diplomat than soldier."

Nadeem became a very good diplomat. We went back into the main meeting. Nadeem instructed the chief of the army air wing to co-operate with Philippe in seeing what air assets could be brought into the country. He also asked me to attend the Federal Relief Commission (FRC) meeting the next day to get a preview of the Public Needs Assessment that the government of Pakistan was going to make known to the international community.

The FRC was set up by the government of Pakistan after the earthquake to make up for the fact that there was no pre-existing National Disaster Management Authority. The FRC, headed by Major-General Farooq Ahmed Khan, had two wings, a civilian wing to deal with the civilian bureaucracy and the military wing to task the military assets in the relief operation. General Nadeem, as Vice Chief of General Staff, was in charge of the military wing. The next day, in a heavily guarded Prime Minister's Secretariat in Islamabad, I attended the first of my many FRC meetings.

The Prime Minister's Secretariat is a tremendously handsome building and looked somewhat like a hotel in its architecture. It was constructed when Islamabad was created. Islamabad, like Canberra, Washington, DC and Brasilia, is a purpose-built capital city created after the Partition. The Greek architect of Islamabad, Konstantinos Doxiadis, is said to have taken part of his inspiration from Canberra.

I used to joke with the Pakistanis that Doxiadis had designed a capital with self-contained suburbs with their own shopping centres, just like Canberra. He had designed wide streets in a city seen as "bat-shit boring", also just like Canberra. This usually brought a chuckle to Pakistanis who had an expression that Islamabad was 16 km from Pakistan as that is how far it takes to drive to Rawalpindi. Islamabad is not a Pakistan city in the cultural sense. It is not chaotic. It is organised and clean. Living in Islamabad, one does not experience the 'real' Pakistan. In terms of lifestyle, Islamabad is a very easy city to get around and there is a great mix of architecture.

At the meeting of the FRC General Farooq outlined the structure of both the civilian and military wings of the organisation he was to command. As we were walking from the FRC meeting room back to Nadeem's temporary office in the Prime Minister's Secretariat he asked me for my view of the structure.

"I don't know, sir, it seems a bit complicated."

"What would you do?"

I explained that we were implementing the experimental cluster approach and drew a diagram of it on a piece of paper. Nadeem asked if it were possible to implement something similar in the FRC. Together we thought they could. "If you did that, we would be running the experiment together. It certainly wouldn't be imposed from outside." Nadeem liked the concept of the clusters and the concept that it would be a joint experiment conducted by both Pakistan and the international community together. The next day at the public announcement of the FRC structure and Pakistan National Action Plan, we saw that Nadeem and Farooq had indeed implemented a synergistic structure.

A Humanitarian/Military Alliance

Relations between humanitarian workers and the military now had a clear, identifiable, and agreed structure. The military's medical corps could liaise with the health cluster, the logistics corps with the logistics cluster and so on. As time went on the critical personal relationships between the cluster coordinator and the Pakistani civil or military counterpart became key. Also, Jan had by then been appointed Humanitarian Coordinator and with me as Chief of Operations/Cluster Coordinator, we were able to strengthen personal relations with the Federal Relief Commissioner through General Farooq and the FRC's Head of Military Wing, General Nadeem.

The cluster approach, implemented by both the FRC and the UN, was the one critical element that made all the countless government bodies, including the armed forces, work together with agencies and NGOs. Before then, partitions between ministries, military, civilians and internationals were seemingly impenetrable. Although it should not be the case, often the effectiveness of collaboration will depend on how strong the personal relations are between the key players. The strong interpersonal relations allowed for the creation of another key group – the Strategic Oversight Group. It also allowed us to set up similar coordinating structures in each of the field operations that we had called 'humanitarian hubs'. In any emergency, the first two weeks are haphazard at best – and Pakistan was no exception. By the end of the second week, multiple international search and rescue teams were on the ground, augmented by the Pakistan military, with good direction by local military commanders and the UNDAC OSOCC in Muzaffarabad.

Despite the growing structures, logistical problems were a mounting nightmare. Many mountainsides had collapsed, meaning that roads had slid away and simply ceased to exist. Helicopters were vital. The Pakistan military stock of helicopters was insufficient to deal with the massive needs, even augmented by US military support. The UN had been able to initiate a handful of helicopters, but even as funds began to trickle in, poor and slow donor response meant that few could be leased. Early estimates assumed a need for more than 100 helicopters – which would make this the largest helicopter aid airlift in history.

While local military, international and spontaneous national groups were doing all they could for emergency medical evacuation, aid deliveries and rescue, what was still missing in those early days was a strong central direction. Given that no functioning National Disaster Management Authority existed, and given that the military was set up to deal with conflict not aid, the urgent need for the newly created Federal Relief Commission grew. In the meantime the army continued its role.

Two organisations not used to co-operating are an active military and a sceptical humanitarian world – especially in sensitive zones. Prior to the earthquake in Pakistan only a handful of foreigners were allowed by Pakistani authorities to access Pakistan-controlled Kashmir. The Line of Control was sensitive, with major exchanges of artillery between India and Pakistan a fairly frequent occurrence. Most major governments, including

Britain, USA and Australia – the national homes to many aid workers – had travel advisories recommending against travel to Kashmir. The North West Frontier Province of Pakistan, which shared the force of the earthquake with Kashmir in almost equal measure, was known as conservative, and was thought by some to be a potential hiding place for Osama bin Laden.

It was only in 2011 that we realised how accurate that suspicion was. The compound in which Osama bin Laden was killed is 500 metres from the accommodation tents used at the UN helicopter hub in Abbottabad. Travel advisories also recommended against foreign travel in this zone. In such difficult areas the military can be understandably hesitant to open up controlled areas to a host of poorly regulated and loosely aligned foreigners as part of a large and disparate group known as 'aid workers'.

Aid workers, for their part, often have deep institutional mistrust of the military. In many countries 'army' does not mean 'professional organised force'; rather it might describe a 12-year-old boy, drugged and carrying a Kalashnikov. Although this is clearly not the case in Pakistan, institutionally many organisations find it impossible to work closer than at arm's length with the military. Added to this, the requirements of earmarked funding, mandates, and principles of neutrality and independence, mean that many institutions, and many individual aid workers, have never worked, or ever want to work, with the military. What had become clear was that the huge area of the earthquake required the establishment of several field co-ordination hubs. We ended up creating four of these in Manshera, Battagram, Bagh and Muzaffarabad. In each we would need to replicate the cluster system and in each we would need to foster the creation of the interpersonal relations between the international community and the military. While in Islamabad we concentrated on the coordination at the high level with the government, the really hard and dirty work was being done by our colleagues in the forward field hubs.

Early on, Nadeem and I took a Pakistan army helicopter and flew to each of the field coordinating hubs and held meetings jointly with the NGOs, UN agencies and local military commanders. Nadeem was a pilot and I was to spend many flights on-board helicopters with him during the two and a half years I was in the country. This relationship was unusual. Some look back today and are tempted to think that the strong relationships and inter-operability between international NGOs and the Pakistan military was 'normal'. In those early field meetings, military commanders were suspicious of the foreign aid workers, and likewise the foreign aid workers of the military. Many aid workers had deployed from emergency settings in Darfur or other conflict environments where close collaboration with the military can be dangerous. It was initially a very difficult task to convince the humanitarians and the military that these two worlds could make good collaborating partners. Nadeem and I set about creating a framework for a collaboration. He had the authority simply to instruct the army officers that they had to attend the humanitarian hub cluster meetings and had to participate in full honesty and transparency. In the first meeting in Muzaffarabad he said, "If I get a piece of information from an NGO and conflicting information from the military, I will believe the NGO, so you'd better collaborate with them." When a statement like that comes from the Vice Chief of General Staff in an army like Pakistan's, it's not a suggestion, it's a command.

I couldn't match the strength of Nadeem for many reasons. As Chief of Operations for OCHA I had, at best, persuasive authority and no command authority. I said that the United Nations endorsed the program and requested the NGOs to do the same. It was weak and limp in comparison to Nadeem, but it was all I had. What began to develop throughout each of the field operating hubs was a series of partnerships between the health cluster coordinator locally and the local military commander in charge of health. Same for the logistics, food, water and all of the other clusters. By the end of the operation many people would look back upon friendships made between foreign NGOs and Pakistan military officers that would last for life, but the relationships were built over time and based on trust that had to be earned.

After about two weeks we had some structures in place that could do some real work. It had been more than a week since the flash appeal had been launched and not enough funds were coming in. UNHCR had expended almost all its emergency reserves, as had WHO, UNICEF, IFRC and other major organisations. Crunch time was coming so a small group of selected people in addition to cluster coordinators met in the basement of the World Food Programme (WFP) office in Islamabad to discuss a couple of ideas.

WFP is the cluster lead for logistics as they have an enormous capacity to move food around the world. The WFP head of emergency operations had come from Rome, bringing with him ideas, wine and prosciutto ham! These were a fine addition to a planning meeting. We did what most people did in a crisis. We gathered at the WFP office, drank wine, ordered pizza and then discussed each cluster area, one by one.

Priorities were re-examined and advice generated. With no money coming in, this informal group put more detail on the contingency plan that would have seen the almost complete withdrawal of the UN from operational work, restricting itself to technical advice only. We also considered asking the Pakistan authorities to fund the vital UN helicopters out of bilateral funds provided by the government of Saudi Arabia. Without more funds or an alternative source of revenue we were only days away from grounding, let alone expanding, the helicopter fleet.

At this meeting the OCHA 80/20 strategy was semi-formalised – agreed in Islamabad and not at headquarters in Geneva. In general terms, it was thought that the Pakistan military would probably deliver 80 per cent of relief goods, and the humanitarian world maybe 20 per cent. These figures were not scientific; they were a rough guess based on the huge resources the Pakistan army was putting into the earthquake relief. At the high point nearly 70,000 soldiers were involved. In many cases it was hard to differentiate who delivered what. If goods were carried on UN helicopter to Muzaffarabad and then carried up the hill by the Pakistan military, who delivered it? Answer – both did. That was the strength of the program.

But if we were to and improve the knowledge and skill base of the Pakistan army to deliver the 80 per cent in the most effective way, then they had to be willing to learn a whole new lexicon of language based on humanitarian operations – not military operations. If weapons' calibres, rates of fire and muzzle velocity are unknown concepts to the humanitarians, 'earmarked funding', 'feeding supplements' and 'sphere standards' are unknown to the military. As we neared the end of the substantive part of our meeting the phrase 'humanitarianising the military planning process' became part of our vocabulary.

In the early days, without the benefit of assured, available funding, other decisions also had to be taken. In conjunction with the UN's Emergency Relief Coordinator, an aggressive media strategy to raise awareness of the funding situation including a countdown of days left for helicopter funding, then less than seven, was made public, as was a call for tents, tents and more tents.

I did a live interview on BBC World Service that night, saying:

"The humanitarian community here is underfunded by hundreds of millions of dollars. To be frank, I just don't think the world gets it. We have one of the best organised relief operations here and we are just not getting the funding. If the second wave of deaths hits, it is the major donors that are going to have to look at themselves in the mirrors – and ask, why?

"There are more than 15,000 villages and towns in the affected region and many of them are going to be cut off from around about 1 December because of the decreasing snow line."

At this point in the interview I became quite emotional.

"We – we have such a short time to be able to give assistance to the most vulnerable. This is not the time for people to be penny-pinching."

The emotion in the interview summed up the feelings of many within the operation. We had done a really good job in setting up a coordinating framework and structure, and a great collaborative partnership with the Pakistan military that would actually work. More importantly, we had set field operational hubs so that the strategic decisions made in Islamabad could be implemented through effective collaboration and co-operation mechanisms in each of the field hubs. Before long, this mechanism would enable the main focus of the operations to shift to the field operations where the needs were, from Islamabad, and allow the capital to evolve into a supporting function that would ensure the on-going strategic operational framework. It was after that interview that perhaps coincidentally money started to come – but only just in time. We were literally only a matter of hours from grounding the entire United Nations helicopter fleet.

The UNDAC team expanded after the initial two weeks, establishing four 'humanitarian hubs' in Muzaffarabad, Bagh, Battagram and Mansehra – each with a civil/military liaison officer provided by OCHA in Geneva. The objective here was to increase and facilitate interaction between the military and the civilian world at the field level.

At the Islamabad level the UN designated an experienced civil/military liaison officer to facilitate contacts with the Pakistani military, and the newly established Federal Relief Commission. In essence the 'dirty laundry' of the aid community was shared in order for the military to understand where the strengths, weaknesses and boundaries of the relationships would lie.

Another key partnership developed. As helicopters became more important, and numbers became available, air coordination became critical. Eventually more than 100 helicopters filled tight valleys, making air-traffic control and flight tasking difficult.

Three key actors, the Pakistan Army Air Wing, the UN Humanitarian Air Service, and the US Navy combined to formulate the air relief operation. Each of the air assets was combined into a common pool, tasked by its particular capacity, the cargo it carried and where it needed to go.

It is only when we look back, with the current discussions of difficult inter-operability between United States and Pakistani military forces in mind, that we can fully understand the power of the collaboration that was achieved in the Air Operations Cell. Indeed, near the end of the operation, the United States for only the second time in its military history, gave up control over its assets. They did so due to the faith and confidence the US had in the operation of the AOC.

What started off on paper as two unlikely allies, the humanitarians and the military, developed the potential to become a strong, united team – with two strong provisos: The disparity of funding and some personal mistrust between individual military and humanitarian personnel. The second of these worked out over time, with a lot of effort by the Pakistani leadership to 'sell' the humanitarians to the military, and by UNDAC and OCHA to likewise 'sell' the military to the humanitarians. While bonds were strengthening centrally, military and humanitarian actors worked increasingly well at the field operational level. The cluster coordination mechanism put in place at Islamabad was replicated in the field hubs, with all parties seeking to work through the natural distrust that military had with humanitarians, and vice versa, until strong relationships were built.

Gerhard made the decision that he and Arjun would leave after the first three weeks (after the initial search and rescue had been completed and co-ordination structures established for the relief operation) but that I would remain until at least the end of the year.

Operation Winter Race

Three weeks after the earthquake the initial search and rescue phase was winding down. Hope of finding new survivors decreased. The coordination mechanisms were beginning to work. A National Action Plan was launched by the FRC but an enormous problem loomed: there were 3.5 million people without shelter and only 30–40 days before the Himalayan winter was due to strike. High-altitude villagers were beginning to migrate down the valleys and it was important to stop them or huge camps would coalesce around destroyed urban centres. With little flat land to spare, camps would have huge population densities, disease would spread and thousands could die.

If on the other hand people stayed in their villages, they would have no home, no food and no chance of survival. Thousands could die. When the relief operation began most tents were not designed with extra protection and flaps for the cold. For most people, the words 'winter' and 'camping' don't normally go together. Almost every available winterised tent was sent to Pakistan, but there weren't enough. Half a million tents minimum would be needed; less than 40,000 were thought to have existed in the world. The Chinese who make the best, increased production of winterised tents and donated 50,000 to Pakistan, but that still left hundreds of thousands of families, more than 2 million people, potentially without adequate shelter. Although people could survive in the lower altitudes with a standard tent, those at high levels were in deep peril. A dozen ideas were offered as a solution to the high-altitude homeless problem. One was 'Paniflex', a Pakistani product used for advertising billboards. This product is a heavy-duty plastic that advertising is fused onto, and discarded once the advertisement has run. It could not be re-used as advertising, but it could be used as an emergency tent covering. In the early days of the relief effort one would fly over the earthquake-affected region and be confronted by advertising for anything from soap to motorcycles. Paniflex would put but a small dent in the problem. We had a major crisis.

The OCHA office in Islamabad was staffed by a couple of UN employees like me, and had been augmented by a large number of volunteer interns from universities in Islamabad, as well as staff that we were hiring locally with the assistance of UNDP. A brilliant young girl named Ammarah Mubarak had been allocated to assist me from the start. She came to simply call me 'Chief'. I smile when I hear in my own mind the cry of 'Chiiiiieeeeffff' echoing through the hallways. Ammarah brought one of the young male interns to me who said, "You are not using our brains."

I replied to him, "Of course we aren't."

The reason we didn't use interns in that way is because they had another critical, albeit menial task. When arriving in an unusual country like Pakistan interns are very useful for letting us know the basic stuff. Where do you buy paper? Where do you buy pens? Where do you get telephones connected? Where do you buy food? Which restaurants can you trust to eat at? Which ones wouldn't you trust? There are a lot of normal day to day things that one needs to find out about a country when one first arrives. In an emergency, we simply didn't have the time to find this information out for ourselves. Interns are good for that.

This young man was insistent. He wanted me to put him to work on something significant.

"Okay, if you want to use your brain, here is a dilemma. We have 3.5 million people homeless. We are running out of money. These people are disbursed through difficult geographic terrain, have had their homes destroyed and are running out of food. We are considering a plan of forced evacuations from high altitude to low-altitude displaced persons camps, but if we run out of money and cannot run helicopters how would we do that?"

Much to my surprise he returned the next day to say that he thought he had a solution. He told me of a former Navy Seal (US special forces) from the United States who made his own way to Kashmir and was showing villagers how to construct 'one warm room' from the rubble of destroyed houses. The earthquake did not vaporise building supplies, it merely collapsed them. The idea of instructing and encouraging people to build an emergency shelter to last them through the winter was an idea with some merit. If this worked we had a much cheaper option of delivering food to the people, not people to the food.

This young intern said that he could get this Navy Seal to come in for a meeting. In the intern walked with the former professional surfer, B-grade movie star and former trainee for the Navy Seals. Matthew George made an appearance with two small models of A-framed designs that he thought could be used to build shelters throughout the earthquake-affected region from the rubble of homes. After he had presented his models and descriptions of emergency one warm room concepts, Matt Hollingworth and Philippe oversaw a pilot trial with one helicopter sent into a village to do a rapid assessment of the housing material needs, then a second called forward with equipment and personnel. The second helicopter would offload material and demonstrate the building of one A-frame house that could house a family and be architecturally more stable in the area prone to aftershocks.

After these initial experiments we thought that this would be a small-scale project, with 5,000 to 10,000 shelters being built before winter descended. After looking at the idea, Nadeem instructed the Pakistan army to test the concept with the army engineers and the Pakistan Architects Association, with the construction of a test A-frame design at Chakothi.

Chakothi is a town nestled right up against the Line of Control and Nadeem had been based there in his early days as a Brigadier. When we flew to Chakothi to examine the first A-frame design constructed, Nadeem also took me to the primary school that had been destroyed during the earthquake. Nadeem had personally sponsored that school since the days of his posting there as a Brigadier. We stood on the collapsed walls and looked out over blood-stained school books, still littered through the rubble. Nadeem and I shared a sombre moment and it reminded us why we had to work hard and fast; so no more children would die.

We looked at the A-frame designs and Nadeem smiled and said, "This will work."

For this idea to work we needed helicopters from the Pakistan army, US and UK military as well as the United Nations. A plan we were to call 'Winter Race' began to take shape. Nadeem allocated 12 engineering battalions to the task of dispersing throughout the earthquake-affected region, instructing villagers on how to build A-framed emergency shelters. The entire focus of the relief effort then shifted to the production and distribution of corrugated iron sheets, which soon became the most valuable item in our relief arsenal. So important were the corrugated iron sheets to the relief effort that General Musharraf himself authorised the importation of CGI sheeting from India, so long as the 'Made in India' stamps had been removed.

Pakistani steel mills churned out hundreds of thousands of roofing sheets, thousands more were imported. The 12 engineer battalions, 300 Pakistani volunteers and hundreds of international teams were assigned to this monumental task. Instead of 10,000 shelters, nearly 400,000 emergency housing units were built in the immediate relief period. The result was startling. The feared flood of displaced people coming down the valley stopped, indeed some people left displaced persons camps and went home up the hills. The consequential massive overcrowding didn't happen, no disease outbreaks occurred, and there wasn't a second wave of deaths. Operation Winter Race worked because problems were worked on together – ideas and concepts, not just information, were shared. The whole concept demonstrates how much can be achieved by coordination.

By this time the Strategic Oversight Group (SOG) had been put in place within the Federal Relief Commission that oversaw all operations. The core four-person team of the SOG were the Federal Relief Commissioner, Major General Farooq Ahmed Khan, the Humanitarian Coordinator, Jan Vande-moortele, General Nadeem and myself. Subject matter experts were called to SOG meetings to advise on whichever relevant issues we were discussing at any given point. The SOG, important though it was, was downplayed. It didn't appear in situation reports and many people didn't know of its exist-ence. It was thought that many players, both military and civilian, would have been uncomfortable if it was known how closely the strategies were linked.

By the time November came to an end the overall operation was taking shape. The FRC was up and running, the UN cluster system was up and running both in the field hubs and in Islamabad, the SOG was functioning, but things were not easy. The operation may have been 'working' but it was only working because people, Pakistani civilians, military and internation-als were all working long and arduous hours, and for those in the field, they were doing so in very tough conditions. While the 'big picture' was looking good, the details were not always so. Communication flows needed fixing, terms of reference needed writing, administrative details needed tightening, and, as always, the 'information beast' of UN headquarters needed feeding.

Communication flows and information gathering and analysis were two aspects of the operation that never ran well: neither for the government nor for the internationals. Baseline data simply didn't exist. A compre-hensive village list did not exist. Rapid information assessment and co-ordinated analysis were often not possible. For UN agencies that had to submit extensive data to various headquarters, silence was a difficult message. Headquarter units naturally need detailed information in order to prop-erly advise donors on emergency requirements, yet detailed information gathering is a difficult and time-consuming task – hence field operatives have to constantly balance their time between delivering aid and gathering information required to get the resources for that aid. There is an on-going tension created between the headquarters' units, whose need for information often seems to be greater, balanced with the field desire to make assumptions and move on to get things done.

As it turned out, the key assumptions that were made in the first flash appeal meeting in the first 48 hours were good and stayed relevant right through the relief stage: 3.5 million people affected, around half a million houses and 30,000 square km. Two months after the earthquake the relief operation was on track. Aid was being delivered, and a feeling of optimism was starting to creep in. The biggest fear became complacency.

The media also played a very important role in the operation both locally and internationally. We quickly brought the international media inside our tent. We were acutely aware as the relief operation unfolded that there would be pockets of people that we had missed because we simply didn't know where they were. In a search for 'bad news stories' the media often found missed populations before we did. We told the media that they played a vital role in the information flow and very soon they understood that when they found a population that had been under-delivered in aid, that by telling us we could rectify the problem, so it was best to tell us rather than criticise us.

Many aspects of the Pakistan earthquake response were experimental. In seeking to bridge the military world and the NGO world, a new model was tried based on the cluster approach. Nadeem and I eventually called the model 'Non-interfering Coordination'. We formalised the theory in a number of published documents after the event, but could summarise it as follows:

The military should share an open and honest assessment of needs between the military and the NGO and humanitarian world, including the United Nations. The military should allow humanitarian actors to choose what operations they will undertake, rather than dictate activities. The military should ask NGOs to inform central commanders of the choices made. Central commanders can then identify unmet gaps in humanitarian delivery, which can then be filled with the Army and other government agencies. This sounds simple, and in theory it is, but in practice consolidating that information, and tracking and monitoring the promised 'delivery' is extremely hard and challenging both for the military and for NGOs – both have to fight institutional reflexes that prevent them from sharing with each other. On the positive side though, this mechanism means that independence of NGOs can be respected, while their activities can be coordinated with the back-filling efforts of the military forces.

Collating, consolidating and sharing information within the humanitarian community is difficult in itself, even when removed from a need to coordinate with the military. In Pakistan the military adapted to the cluster system. Indeed, for the military 'clustered' thinking is the norm. The military already had a logistics corps, a medical corps, and the like, so intellectually understood clustered coordination. Ironically, the military found it easier to adapt to the new cluster mechanism than did the humanitarian world. By marrying up the military 'clusters' with the humanitarian 'clusters', a mechanism for identifying and filling gaps was created. In essence, the clusters would form the backbone of 'non-interfering coordination" by being the hubs through which information was shared.

As Pakistan had no designated National Disaster Agency at the time of the earthquake, the ad hoc structure created to deal with the aftermath (the Federal Relief Commission) decided to structure itself using the cluster approach as well. What resulted was a rare if not unique series of key personal contacts between the national and international coordinators, and between civil and military actors in the clusters. It was these personal contacts within the cluster framework that allowed for the ironing out of some 'perspective problems'.

The Pakistan military often focused on 'what has been done?' while the humanitarian world brought with it a perspective on 'what is left to be done?" While the difference in perspectives could cause problems, the ability to talk through issues and raise concerns within the context of cluster meetings allowed for solutions to be found. Once senior commanders understood the logic of cluster coordination and passed command orders down the chain, mid-level officers simply accepted the mechanism as the 'way things would be done' as that is what they were ordered to do.

Within the world of the multiplicity of humanitarian organisations things were more difficult. As the cluster system was tried for the first time in Pakistan no pre-existing terms of reference, guidance notes or pool of experience existed. Additionally, as the cluster system was rolled out earlier than planned because of the unexpected nature of the earthquake, many NGOs had not received 'guidance' let alone 'orders' to implement the system.

The clusters thereby became not only the method of internal humanitarian coordination, but by virtue of a military presence in the cluster meetings, the system also became the heart of the civil-military coordination structure.

Beyond Relief: Recovery

The Pakistan government decided to close the Federal Relief Commission by late March 2006, and introduce another new body known as the Earthquake Reconstruction and Rehabilitation Authority (ERRA), late in 2005. The question was how would we move the entire operation from a 'relief' focus to a 'recovery' focus, and how would we move the bureaucratic responsibility without losing the service delivery efficiency?

At the end of relief operations, a lull often occurs before the recovery and reconstruction phase begins. Aid workers leave an emergency zone, contacts and momentum are lost, and the humanitarian impetus to coordinate is replaced by dysfunctional planning.

As early as late November 2005 Nadeem and I were confident that we had the structures in place to successfully undertake the relief operations. We needed to look beyond the relief effort towards the post-relief phase.

By December Nadeem and I shared our concerns that the Earthquake Reconstruction and Rehabilitation Authority didn't seem to be making adequate headway in preparing the ground for recovery on the domestic side, nor did the OCHA/UNDP seem to be doing the same on the international side, to maintain the best of the system that had worked so well.

We were particularly concerned because by the end of 2005 Nadeem was due to return full-time to the military, be promoted to Lieutenant-General and become one of Pakistan's key corps commanders. Under the rule of Musharraf Pakistan was effectively controlled by the 'Corps Commanders Conference' so to become a Corps Commander was to become part of the most important group of people in Pakistan. This was an enormous compliment to Nadeem.

On my side, I was due to return to Geneva at the end of 2005. The strong relationship that had developed with Nadeem was seen as a threat rather than an asset to many within the United Nations system. Despite Jan's protestations, OCHA had made it clear that my contract would not be extended by the end of the year. From late November I had moved out of the OCHA office and had been effectively taken on secondment into Nadeem's office and acted as a bridge between him and Jan. This close relationship to two key people made others uncomfortable.

This was a shame as the concept of transitioning from relief to recovery was very new. What do you do when the emergency finishes, but normality has not yet been restored? How do you plan that transition from relief to recovery? How do you transition from the emergency personnel leading back to development personnel leading? This had never been done effectively before.

In one cluster-coordination meeting in December, Tim Pitt, who had been running the OCHA in Islamabad after I moved into Nadeem's office, went so far as to say, "Andrew, there is no such thing as a transition and when the relief period ends the clusters will end because OCHA has a copyright on the clusters." Such a view remains ridiculous. If the coordination framework could work well in a relief period, it could work equally as well in the reconstruction and recovery period and act as a bridge in the transition between the two. It was a strange position for me to be in as it was almost as if the stronger my relationship became with the Pakistanis, the weaker my relationship became with those in authority in the United Nations. The one exception to this was always Jan who at every time gave me full support, backing and encouragement.

Regardless of where our career paths were going to take us after December 2005, for Nadeem and I it seemed pointless to do all the good work in the relief effort and not get the transition to recovery right. If we did what was done in previous natural disasters in most countries in the world then a lot of the good work of the relief would be undone in the period between relief and recovery.

The Pakistan government had already planned to close the FRC under General Farooq in early 2006 and have ERRA, commanded by another general, Lieutenant-General Zubair, takeover. The government had not yet planned the transition. We went to see Zubair, who as a Lieutenant-General was the senior officer. Over a series of dinners Nadeem and I came to the conclusion that Zubair did not get the point of a transition and there was a serious risk that things could go awry.

After the last of our dinners with Zubair Nadeem asked, "Andrew, have you ever had Kashmiri tea?" I hadn't. We got into Nadeem's staff car and drove down the backstreets of Rawalpindi until we found a little street-side vendor selling Kashmiri tea. You have to picture this. Pakistan can be a dangerous country and at times the military can be a target for Al Qaeda or other terrorist organisations. Nadeem was in full military uniform and we were in a military staff car with only a driver who also acted as bodyguard.

We pulled up to Nadeem's favourite Kashmiri tea vendor, ordered two cups of the pink, milky, sweet tea and sat by the side of the road to drink it. There could have been nothing more unusual in the backstreets of Rawalpindi than a general in full uniform and a foreign aid worker sitting in a gutter drinking Kashmiri tea from foam cups. While we enjoyed each other's company, we were so pissed off and disillusioned about poor recovery planning that we paid no attention at all to our security.

"I am going to have to tell Musharraf," said Nadeem.

I received a call from Nadeem the next Sunday afternoon. "Andrew, I'm coming to see you" he said. By that time I had a temporary office in the Prime Minister's Secretariat and an office in the United Nations building and would choose which office to go to each day, based on whether most of my work was with the Pakistani or international community. That Sunday I was in the United Nations building.

"Sir, you're the general, I will come to you."

Something was up. He insisted on visiting my office. Pakistan was a military state so it was highly unusual for an army general in uniform to turn up on a Sunday afternoon in the United Nations office. Nadeem and I sat and chewed the fat.

Nadeem told me how he raised the issue of transition with Musharraf and expressed his view that Zubair was not up to the job. Nadeem started to talk to me about the options of leaving the army to take up the role to coordinate ERRA or to stay in the army and take the role of Corps Commander. He took me through all the options including the impact on his pension and his entitlements on retirement at different levels. In the end Nadeem made a deal with Musharraf. He would stay in the army, would be promoted to three-star General, serve two years in ERRA and then become a Corps Commander.

"So, Andrew," he said, "you cannot leave. If I am going to stay in this operation, so are you."

"But sir, the money runs out for my position at the end of December."

Nadeem called up the British High Commissioner and asked for one more year's funding for my position. He called the American ambassador and asked for the same. He got an affirmative from both.

"I have got the money, now you are staying two more years," he said with a smile. There was still one problem. We might have had the money, but I had no contract.

Nadeem and Jan met to discuss this problem. Jan agreed that he would transition my contract from one overseen by OCHA to one overseen by UNDP. He also promoted me to a specially created position in his office as Senior Relief to Recovery Transition Advisor. This was a position that had not been created in the UN before. After making it very clear to UNDP headquarters that the government of Pakistan (read Lieutenant-General Nadeem) had an expectation that role should be filled by only me, reluctantly the human resources system agreed. I now had a two-year contract to remain in Pakistan to help with the transition from relief to recovery, but we'd pissed off an enormous number of people in both OCHA and UNDP because we had circumvented almost every rule and regulation that there was. Planning for post-relief continued with Nadeem in ERRA and me seconded into his office and remaining as the relief to recovery transition advisor to Jan.

Given that the relief effort in Pakistan was experimental in its development of the 'cluster approach', the transition from relief to reconstruction would also be 'experimental'. While no detailed guidance existed on how one transforms relief clusters to the post-relief phase, the Inter-Agency Standing Committee had sent guidance in early December on the modification of relief clusters to early recovery clusters. Clusters such as 'camp management' would be phased out, whereas new clusters such as 'livelihoods' and 'housing' would be phased in.

Following detailed discussions with different organisations, a decision was taken in mid-January to remove the cluster coordination system for the early recovery phase. This decision to close the clusters was premature. The degree of cohesion and coordination within the international community would be diminished and the interface between local authorities and international actors would become less clear. By the end of March we formally closed the Federal Relief Commission and moved the residual relief staff into a new Transitional Relief Cell (TRC) as a component of ERRA. While the main component of ERRA began the process of massive reconstruction and rehabilitation with a budget estimated to be around US$6 billion, the TRC ensured that people didn't fall through the cracks, and made sure that transitional arrangements remained in place to look after people needing residual relief until their livelihoods could be restored. By April it had become clear that the closing of the clusters had been a mistake, so Nadeem and I reinstated them.

A General, A Jock and a Feminist

Over the next two years through to the middle of 2008 some incredible achievements were made under Nadeem's leadership. The enrolment of girls in schools had increased by 50 per cent; significant land reform was achieved; schools and hospitals were built; and the quality of life for people in Kashmir had significantly improved. I particularly like the story of how girls' enrolments in schools were increased.

I don't like it when feminism blinds us to problems that are open to both genders. While feminists will speak of 'women only households' they rarely consider the problems confronted by 'male only households'.

The United Nations has within it many gender advisers that come to post-conflict or post-disaster settings with a feminist lens. To the gender advisers the reason girls were not going to school was because of the repression of females by Islam. In early 2006 the Canadian Embassy had suggested the secondment of a gender adviser into Nadeem's office in ERRA. Nadeem and I met Christine Oullette, a French-Canadian. Christine introduced us to the concept of 'age and gender disaggregated data'. That means that when making a base analysis, there is a need to breakdown information according to both genders, and according to age differentiation. For example, it isn't good enough to say '3.5 million are homeless'. We needed to know what the gender and age breakdown was, since different ages and genders have vastly different needs.

Christine made a passionate case that to plan an operation, we need to analyse the difference in problems faced by males and females and not favour any particular group. Data should be analysed for the root cause of the problem. Christine was the first gender adviser I had ever heard who didn't push a 'feminist' view exclusively. Gender issues apply, by definition, to both genders.

Christine was warm and affable, and smart enough to know that to bring gender-related issues dressed up in the lens of feminism would really piss off an army general and an Australian bloke. She framed the issue as a question of analysing data and understanding real problems. Through this approach we discussed the problem of girls' attendance at schools and realised that girls were not absent because of repression in Islam; they were absent from school because they spent between four and eight hours a day collecting water.

"So let us build taps," said Nadeem. And so, a new policy was implemented that in order to gain compensation to rebuild a home the homeowner needed to install a tap in the house. Girls would then be free to go to school.

Land reform was a major issue in Pakistan since much of the country still operated under a feudal landlord and tenant system. The government of Pakistan had made the decision to give compensation for each destroyed house. But who would receive the compensation – the landlord who owned the house or the tenant who was now homeless? The landlord had no obligation to provide housing for tenants when the house was destroyed. A tenant had no rights, and certainly no rights that would be considered normal in the more advanced economies.

In Pakistan the question of land reform was highly controversial and fraught with danger as it fundamentally challenged the remnants of the feudal system. Nadeem's reforms would challenge entrenched power structures by giving the compensation to the tenant to build a house. If the landlord saw the new house and decided to take the house and remove the tenant, then the landlord would have to pay the tenant the equivalent of the compensation. In effect, the landlord still owned the land, but the tenant now had rights over the house.

Did the Relief and Recovery Work?

While there were difficulties in implementing a new system in the midst of a major emergency, the cluster approach in Pakistan produced results that speak for themselves: One million tents, six million blankets, 400,000 emergency shelters delivered or built through a coordinated and consolidated effort. Military and humanitarian logistic capacities were combined and cargo grouped collectively and allocated according to need, not by the agency that was dispatching it. In total, 350,000 Internally Displaced People (IDPs) were housed over winter, with 95 per cent returning to their homes in the first year after the relief, thanks to a unique combination of humanitarian and military management. All medical measures showed an improvement in the rate of cold-related infections compared to standard years. All schools and hospitals were able to remain functional; first in an emergency setting, and then in a transitional setting. It was the largest single relief effort ever.

Statistics such as these, and a recognition of the joint role of the military and the NGOs in the clusters led to Jan Vandemoortele, the United Nations Humanitarian Coordinator in Pakistan, dubbing the operation "[The] most successful civil and military co-operation ever." The early deployment of the UNDAC team was an essential element. Jan Vandemoortele, while addressing a donor meeting on the Pakistan earthquake in Geneva a few months after the earthquake, was asked by a donor representative what the UNDAC team did for them. Jan said that, 'The UNDAC team brought order out of chaos through their calm professionalism and made us feel that we could deal with this emergency when we were overwhelmed by the event.' This was high praise from a man who doesn't give high praise lightly.

The establishment of the cluster approach as the key coordinating mechanism was controversial. In the end, the clusters provided a mechanism for information and idea exchange between civil and military actors alike. A sharing of a common understanding of 'who is doing what and where' allowed for gaps to be identified. The level of information sharing seen in the Pakistan earthquake was rare if not unique. I don't believe that the senior officers of the Pakistan army fully understood how special the earthquake operation was until major floods hit Pakistan some time later, and the relief effort was less successful. It was only after the event that many of those involved realised that in 2005 we had a close-to-unrepeatable series of events including a new coordination mechanism that no one knew how to stop, and open-minded military, and critically, a whole series of key personal relationships that just happened to work. In short, it worked like no other operation either before or since.

Together, we also tackled the challenge of 'transition' from relief to recovery. The transition is handled very poorly in most natural disaster operations including the major bushfires in Victoria in 2008. There is generally a lull after relief but before reconstruction. We avoided this in Pakistan. The recovery also worked. The creation of the Transitional Relief Cell within ERRA was an essential element in maintaining continuity of service to those who needed it.

In my two and a half years in Pakistan I grew to like Nadeem and respected him immensely. He didn't see the challenge of the earthquake as merely to keep people alive, he saw the challenge as one to improve the quality of life of people and in that he succeeded. Nadeem and others in Pakistan forced me to question the preconceptions one has of countries such as Pakistan when information comes only from the international media.

Pakistan also relieved me of a self-imposed burden. I had developed in my mind an obligation to 'use my skills for the betterment of other people'. In Pakistan I felt that I had made a difference. It allowed me to start my life free from that weight.

During the time we were implementing the recovery phase of the earthquake operation in Pakistan, the United Nations went through a global process to examine potential reform of the normal developmental activities of the United Nations. In many ways this process would supplement the Humanitarian Response Review process that had created the cluster approach for emergency relief operations. It turned out to be 'just another reform'.

The United Nations Secretary General had appointed a High Level Panel to explore how the UN system could work more coherently and effectively across the world in the areas of development, humanitarian assistance and the environment. The panel was led by the Prime Minister of Pakistan and the Prime Minister of Mozambique.

Between May 24 and May 26, 2006 the High Level Panel took evidence in Islamabad from members of the diplomatic community, NGO community, government of Pakistan and members of the United Nations system. Usually these organisations would all give evidence separately. Nadeem had another idea. He had said to me that the cluster approach had worked so well that he didn't quite understand why the United Nations was going through the whole process of asking itself how it could perform better. In Nadeem's mind the earthquake relief operation in Pakistan was a very good example of how the UN could develop system-wide coherence.

Ryan Crocker, the United States Ambassador to Pakistan, agreed. So did I, so we decided to give evidence together. I believe this was the only time a UN official, a serving army general, and a very senior ambassador all representing different viewpoints and from different countries, gave combined evidence to a UN panel. Our point was simple. To get system-wide coherence, the United Nations needed to recognise that there is no such thing as the United Nations. There is a bunch of 'discoordinated agencies'. What was desperately needed was some degree of authority and command. As outlined in the previous chapters, the UN Secretary General has no command and control capacity over the different agencies of the United Nations. Likewise, the United Nations Resident Coordinator in the country has persuasive authority and no command and control over agencies in any given country. Our evidence was quite simple. If you want system-wide coherence then someone needs to be in charge.

One of the great strengths of the earthquake relief operation was that the Pakistan army was able to give someone in charge. When the High Level Panel delivered its report it initially came up with the idea of creating a 'One United Nations', however, once the bureaucrats in headquarters grabbed hold of these recommendations the catchphrase changed from 'One United Nations' to 'Delivering As One' because people didn't want the perception created that there was only one organisation. For me, the moment that the catchphrase was changed any substantive reform would face the same future as all previous attempts at reform: failure.

Aid in Development

Like me, one of the junior ministers in the Pakistani government was also a swimmer, so we trained together on some days. At the end of a lap one morning I asked him why he was involved in politics.

"I'm here to protect my family's land interest," he said. It shocked me that there was no pretence at good governance, nor government for the greater good of the Pakistani people. His involvement in politics was about the wealth of his family, pure and simple.

Take that matter-of-fact statement and recognise it as a realisation that in most post-feudal or post-tribal societies those in government are merely the former feudal overlords or former tribal leaders dressed up in a cloak of democracy. The mistake that we make in the West is that we look at our governments and assume they are trying to do the right thing for the people. If the government doesn't do what is in the best interests of the people that government will get voted out at the next election. We transpose this presumption on to governments in the developing world and fail to recognise that more often than not the interests of the people and their government may not coincide.

In 2005, more than 100 nations came together in an attempt to improve the effectiveness of foreign aid. The meeting resulted in the Paris Declaration, which was aimed at reducing a feeling of 'neo-colonialism' from donor countries. The declaration stated that aid should be given on the host government's agenda not the donor government's agenda because donor governments' agendas were often perceived as controlling and restrictive – almost colonial.

The Paris Declaration went much further than previous agreements of a similar type. At its heart was the commitment to help governments of developing countries formulate and implement their own national development plans, according to their own national priorities, using, wherever possible, their own planning and implementation systems. The problem with this declaration is in the presumption that the governments' 'own national priorities' match those of the people of that country.

Reflections on Pakistan: A Different View of Muslims

I am often asked what it was like to spend two and a half years in Pakistan. In the West many people have a perception of Pakistan based on television news, but all that one sees is the negative part of Pakistani culture – terrorism, political dysfunction and cheating at cricket. While there is some truth in each of these, they represent only a small part of what is Pakistan.

In Pakistan it is the culture more than the law that determines how people live. The divergences of culture can be a trap for locals, not just foreigners.

The history and geography of Pakistan makes the country a melting pot of small Christian communities, a number of Islamic communities and even a small animist community said to be left over from the days of Alexander the Great. Even within Islam, the culture can diverge radically in a short geographic distance.

A woman may walk the streets of Islamabad wearing jeans and a T-shirt, hair flowing freely, eat McDonald's and live a life similar to that in many major capitals around the world. A mere 100 km to the north as the crow flies, the small town of Bana represents a more conservative life. When I first went to Bana if a woman saw me walking down the street, she would turn her back, squat down, cover her head and wait for me to pass. The culture of that area deemed that she may allow no man's eyes other than those of her husband and family to see her.

When the earthquake operation began we needed to hire local drivers. Given the nature of United Nations work, drivers were often a long way from home. We started to receive reports of drivers being beaten by local villagers. At first we thought these attacks were aimed at the United Nations and foreigners. It was only after we did a thorough examination that we found something far more unusual and parochial.

In some parts of Pakistan the most important seat in a car is the rear seat and should be reserved for men. In other parts of Pakistan a woman may not sit too close to a non-family member male driver, so she should not sit in the front seat. We found that on occasions male drivers who came from the parts of Pakistan where the back seat is reserved for men had female passengers in the front seat in accordance with their own local culture, but were driving through villages where the cultural requirement was the reverse. In extreme circumstances the drivers were taken from the car and beaten.

The second thing to learn about Pakistan is that the vast majority of the population are extremely tolerant of other religions. I had no expectation of a good Christmas in 2005, having gone to bed on Christmas Eve huddled around a single gas fire in a tent in the earthquake-destroyed town of Muzaffarabad. Snow was falling; people were still buried under rubble. I thought that Christmas Day would be a day like any other during the emergency operation.

I woke and was surprised to find that people, who did not believe that Jesus Christ was the son of God, and who had lost everything in an earthquake a few weeks before, managed overnight to put up big signs in every village saying: "Christian Brothers thank you for being with us on your special day. Let us be your family." Outside our tents on Christmas morning lines of villagers and townspeople who had lost almost everything brought us cake, fruit, and whatever small gifts they could make. They expressed their humanity by understanding that we were thousands of kilometres from home in order to help them. In return, their hospitality was unforgettable.

For Muslims, Jesus Christ is the second most important prophet in Islam, behind Mohammed. If one were to over-generalise, the followers of Judaism regard the Old Testament as a holy book. The Christians regard both the Old and New Testaments as holy books. Muslims regard the Old and New Testaments and the Qur'an as holy books. In my experience the Muslims understand that their religion worships the same God – the God of Abraham.

For the everyday Pakistani, to be a person of faith, Jew, Christian or Muslim, is acceptable. To be a non-believer was bewildering. I spent many hours in conversation with many people trying to explain why I was a 'non-believer' with the normal reaction being "if only you were a Christian we would understand".

Far from being a country full of dogmatic terrorists, I found most Pakistanis to be a lot more open, tolerant and understanding of others' political or religious views than in Australia, the United States or Great Britain.

The third thing to learn about Pakistan is for the moderate Muslim it is the radical terrorist who is destroying the religion and good name of Islam, not the United States or the West. The average Pakistani does see that Western countries, inadvertently or not, assist the radicals in their recruitment of young and illiterate rural classes, simply by being the West or the 'enemy' that the radicals use in motivation.

What we see in Pakistan is the real frontline in the War on Terror. In my view it is a battle between moderate and radical Islam for the winning of the hearts and minds of poorly educated rural Muslims. Drone attacks, invasions into other countries, and fundamental misunderstandings by radical southern United States preachers burning the Qur'an in ignorance of that holy book which supports the same God as their holy book, only serve to inflame and power the extremists.

In late 2006 General Nadeem sent me to Peshawar and Muzaffarabad to check with the two Provincial Relief Commissioners (Kashmir and NWFP) that they had made adequate plans for the upcoming second winter following the earthquake for those still homeless. I had been working with Nadeem for more than a year and most Pakistanis in the earthquake operation no longer viewed me as a 'foreigner'. Rather, they saw me as part of the government team and as a representative of Nadeem not the United Nations. In this context it was not unusual for me to go to a provincial official and ask for them to report to me.

There were satisfactory contingency plans in place in Kashmir but the same could not be said for North-West Frontier Province. I went to visit the Provincial Relief Commissioner for that region in his office in Peshawar. There is no doubt that Peshawar is a much more conservative, and in some ways fundamentalist area than Muzaffarabad. In addition, the Provincial Relief Commissioner was an Islamic cleric. When asked why he had no adequate contingency plan the Provincial Relief Commissioner fundamentally changed the way I look at the issue of religious extremism. "You need to understand something, Andrew," he said. "God sent the earthquake because the people were bad and he punished them. If the people have been good this year, this winter will be fine. If they have been bad, God will punish them again, and who am I to get in the way of the will of God?"

I went straight back to Islamabad, somewhat bewildered, and said to Nadeem, "Sir, it's like he believes that God sent the earthquake."

"He does," Nadeem said.

"No sir, I mean it is like he believes that God pushed a button and the earthquake happened."

Nadeem smiled and said, "Andrew, he does."

I must have looked really confused because I found the notion that God 'caused' the earthquake a bit of an anathema.

"I want you to think about it this way," said Nadeem. "He believes God sent the earthquake because he read that in a book. You believe that tectonic plates caused the earthquake because you read that in a book. Whose book is right?" Only then did I realise that the main battle is that between moderate Islam and radical Islam. By its nature it is easier to motivate people around radicalism than it is around moderation.

The Provincial Relief Commissioner was a very conservative man. He was not in any way offended or threatening to me, given that I wasn't a Muslim, or even a believer in Christianity. When I told him that I 'did not believe', his reaction was a genuine feeling of sorrow and sympathy that I wouldn't go to heaven. His principle emotion was one of regret that I wouldn't join him in eternity.

It is bizarre that a person can hold strong religious beliefs and accept that another has the right to hold different beliefs, even if those beliefs ran counter to theirs. Friendship and hospitality is indeed a trump card. I am not sure people of other nations display that tolerance. Motivating people to be 'moderate' and tolerant is the challenge of our and future generations. It is a challenge that exists in each country and culture. And this is the point of freedom.

The Provincial Relief Commissioner did not consider it a matter of "belief" that God caused the earthquake, he considered it a matter of "fact". To this day I do not consider tectonic plates to be a matter of "belief". Like the Provincial Relief Commissioner I hold the view that my opinion represents "fact". It is simply not possible to negotiate between different views of "fact". Until the day he dies, the Provincial Relief Commissioner will consider it "fact" that earthquakes are caused by God.

That view should not seem unusual to many Jews, Christians or Muslims. At the heart of those religions is the same belief in the same all-powerful but benevolent God, whose actions are mysterious and sometimes confusing. When one starts to put one's mind in the place of a fundamentalist Muslim, and recognise that the place is not too different from a fundamentalist Jew or a fundamentalist Christian, then one only begins to understand the difficulty of the battle some call 'war on terror'.

To my mind the war on terror is not between the West and Islam, or between the United States and Afghanistan, the war on terror is more accurately described by the question: how does General Nadeem persuade the Provincial Relief Commissioner that contingency planning is not against the will of God?

The fourth thing I learned in Pakistan was the strength and power of friendship. The two most important friendships I developed in Pakistan were with two army generals, both of whom were critical to the relief effort – Farooq and Nadeem. These two men are incredibly different and there were times when I was caught in the middle of disagreements between the two.

8.

Pakistani Military: Building Bridges With My Father

I got on particularly well with two of Farooq's children – his son Ibrahim and his daughter Rasti. I first met Rasti one Sunday. She was then a precocious 13-year-old who had accompanied her father into work that day.

The government of Pakistan had held a formal closing ceremony back in March 2006 to mark the end of the relief effort and shift the focus to recovery. President General Musharraf conducted the ceremony that took place at the same time as the Commonwealth Games were being held in my home town of Melbourne. Musharraf is a squash player and Pakistan has one of the world's best field hockey teams.

While we were at the ceremony I asked General Farooq to introduce me to the President.

I asked him "Are you watching the squash at the Commonwealth Games?"

"I was, and you Australians are winning too much," said the President.

"Then you won't be watching the hockey!" Australia had just defeated Pakistan 3-0.

While the other generals looked nervous, Musharraf laughed and asked, "Do you like sport?"

"Yes, I love it."

Musharraf said to Farooq, "you must make sure this man goes to the Shandur Festival". Held in the second week of July every year since 1936 and irregularly for centuries before that, the Shandur Festival pits the towns of Chitral against Gilgit in a game of old world polo on the highest polo ground in the world in the Shandur Pass.

Chitral and Gilgit are cut off from each other for much of the year as snow closes the Shandur Pass. Traditionally, during the summer months when the snow clears, these two towns fight it out just below 4000 metres, where the altitude takes its toll on both horse and rider. It takes two and a half days to get there from Islamabad and the journey takes one along some of the world's most remote but spectacular roads, in the far northwest of Pakistan just below the Afghanistan border.

At around the same time as the ceremony closing the relief effort in Pakistan, an earthquake hit Lorestan in Iran. There should be better collaboration between India, Pakistan, Afghanistan and Iran for natural disaster response. Each of the major earthquake fault lines runs east to west, often having an impact on those countries. Major weather patterns also run east to west. Jan Vandemoortele had asked me, on behalf of the United Nations, to look at a tri-nations natural disaster program to see if we could organise better collaboration between Iran, Afghanistan and Pakistan. India would be ideal to include in the mix, although politically impossible, given the state of tension between India and Pakistan.

Even though the Iranian government has a particularly good mechanism for earthquake preparedness and response, they are always willing to learn and invited Farooq and I to address an earthquake management conference to be held late in June. This allowed three things to happen. Firstly, Farooq and I got to know each other a lot better on long flights (there is no direct flight from Islamabad to Tehran let alone Lorestan, so one has to go via Dubai). Secondly, we had a fascinating evening in Tehran with my cousin's friends (my uncle Allan married an Iranian doctor named Zohreh) – and thirdly we could sound out the Iranians on a proposed tri-nations disaster management program.

In late June the two of us boarded the Emirates flight from Islamabad to Iran via Dubai. We travelled well together as he preferred the aisle and I the window. We had also worked out a very good routine. When travelling, the requirement to pray five times a day for a practising Muslim can be waived.

Farooq chooses to still conduct his prayers even when travelling. In the post 9/11 era to have a bearded Muslim man praying in a business class seat tends to make other travellers panic. My job was to calm people should they panic during his prayers. If the food service came during his prayers it was my job to ensure that there were no pork products in the meal.

Farooq, being on the aisle seat, had an altogether different role. If the drinks service came when he was not praying, he would first ask for his tonic water. Then pointing at me he would say, "But him, he starts with a champagne, he will then have a gin and tonic and he will have a red wine with his meal!"

Somehow this story always sums up for me the tolerance of a deeply religious Pakistani. Even though Farooq would pray, refuse to touch alcohol or eat pork products, he would have no problem with me not doing the same and he would even go as far as ordering alcohol for me!

After touching down in Tehran we took a connecting flight to Bam to observe how the reconstruction was progressing after the 2003 earthquake, which devastated that city. We took two very important lessons away from Bam to share with Nadeem on my return and have since included them into current thinking for reconstruction and recovery in Pakistan. Firstly, expectation management is one of the most difficult balancing acts in post-disaster recovery and reconstruction. There is always an expectation from the affected community that the government should respond quickly. However, if one is to rebuild a community so that its future is better than its past, then one needs to take time in planning. Expectation management is about balancing the needs of a community to see 'something' being done immediately, with a better future being planned slowly. I was able to apply this lesson not only to Pakistan but also to Australia, showing that lessons can be learned in natural disasters and applied to vastly different countries.

The second learning from Bam was to be careful of transitional housing, which has a habit of becoming permanent. In Bam many shops and houses were immediately reopened by temporarily locating shipping containers among the rubble in place of the destroyed home or shop. However, by the time the city was rebuilt, some of the shipping containers were too long, literally, to be removed from the now rebuilt streets.

From Bam we went to Lorestan to present a paper on natural disaster management. The long drive to Lorestan coincided with the Australia-Italy game in the 2006 World Cup football finals. We needed to find a place to watch the game even though we were halfway between Tehran and Lorestan in 'the middle of nowhere' Iran. We stopped at a roadside cafe where the owner is probably still telling the story about how an Australian and a Pakistan army general turned up in his café to watch the soccer. After plying us with mint tea for the entire game, the owner felt sorry for us because Australia lost and he refused to take any payment.

A little further down the road all that mint tea caught up with us. We pulled into a roadside fuel station to visit the washrooms. Inside the male washrooms were individual urinals along the walls. The uncommon thing, to my eye, was the roll of toilet paper next to the urinal. I had never seen a urinal with a toilet roll before. For ladies who may be reading this there is a golden rule in men's urinals all around the world. A man must never look at another man's willy. So, while we were both relieving ourselves I asked Farooq why there was toilet paper next to the urinal.

"You need to dry yourself after urinating," he said. Australian primary schoolboys used to say: "No matter how much you wiggle, wobble or dance, the last drop always stays in your pants!"

"You see," Farooq went on, "if you have a drop of urine left on you then God will not accept your prayers."

Ablutions and cleanliness is an essential part of the pre-prayer ritual in Islam. I clearly must have looked bemused as Farooq said, "Here, I'll show you." He then proceeded to wash and dry himself and instructed me on how to wash and dry after urination as a father would to a young son. This was yet another of my 'how the heck did I get here moments'!

When my uncle Allan married Zohreh, my extended family included Zohreh's nephew Arash and niece Shideh. Arash left Iran when he turned 15 to understandably avoid military service in that country and went to live with Allan and Zohreh. Arash grew up to be the captain of the Point Lonsdale Surf Life Saving Club, and also a designer for Holden, working on the Ute. Shideh, while living in Australia, kept in touch with many of her childhood friends from Iran. She organised for Farooq and I to have dinner with a number of her friends in Tehran. Shideh's friends had no idea that Farooq was an army general and just thought he was a friend of mine. What unfolded over dinner was a very frank but eye-opening discussion on the differences between the application of Islam in Iran and Pakistan.

In general, the law in Iran requires strict observance, so the culture, at least among the rebellious educated youth, was to avoid the observance as far as possible. Headscarves were pushed back as far on the hair as possible. In Pakistan, on the other hand, the law required little, but the culture demanded a lot, with observance varying greatly, depending on where in Pakistan one was.

Farooq found the discussion about Islam in Iran fascinating, as did I. Iranians found the discussion about Pakistan equally as fascinating. We also found it quite distressing to see how disillusioned many of the youth in Iran were. There was a general sense of hopelessness about the future and disillusionment in the direction the country was heading, particularly in the religious sense. People were in two minds, however, about the actions of the President when it came to nuclear weapons.

Few of the youths we spoke with agreed with Iranian President Mahmoud Ahmadinejad's tormenting of the West, but they held the view that if the United States was entitled to nuclear weaponry then so should Iran be. Many in the West misunderstand Iran, as the country is not Arab but Persian. In many ways Iranians perceive the Arabs as a greater threat than the West. Nuclear weaponry is as much about re-establishing the predominance of Persia in the minds of the Islamic world, particularly the Arabian world, as it is about threatening the United States.

Farooq and I left Iran and headed back to Pakistan via Dubai. I was to learn another thing about Farooq during the return trip. We were due to land at 9 am on June 30, 2006. This was the day that Pakistan was to confer national awards on people for their role in the earthquake relief. Farooq told me while we were waiting in Dubai that both he and I had been nominated for an award but that he, Farooq, had blocked both his award and mine as he thought 'we were only doing our duty'. This was to prove embarrassing to the government of Pakistan. If the general in charge of the Federal Relief Commission, Farooq, was refusing his award then how did it make all the other generals who were to receive an award look? While we were in transit in Dubai, Musharraf telephoned Farooq and insisted that he accept the award. Farooq refused.

We landed the next morning in Islamabad and as Farooq's staff car was driving us from the airport back to Farooq's home, Musharraf called again.

Musharraf again asked Farooq to take the award. Farooq again refused. While I admit to being disappointed that Farooq had blocked my award, I had to admire that he applied the same standard to himself, going so far as to refuse the direct request of President Musharraf.

I don't think that Farooq understood how unusual and exceptional the Pakistan earthquake relief really was. It wasn't until the massive floods in Pakistan and later natural disaster responses, which were not run anywhere near as smoothly, that Farooq understood that what we had done in Pakistan for the earthquake was unusual and exceptional, not just 'normal duty' Farooq and his family remain my friends. Farooq was proud of his eldest son Ibrahim but thought that he needed to improve his swimming. I agreed to coach Ibrahim and through that process was introduced to the Pakistan National Swimming Team. I also agreed to act as voluntary assistant coach to the team during my two years in the country. This connection with the national swimming team taught me two additional very strong lessons about Islam and developing country governments.

For the first time in the country's history we had the national female swimming team and national male team training in the same pool at the same time, albeit with the boys in lanes one and two and the girls in lanes seven and eight.

General Farooq was appointed by Musharraf to head up the new National Disaster Management Authority. It had been a weakness of the government of Pakistan that there had not been a pre-existing national disaster management authority that would have had the responsibility to respond to the 2005 earthquake. This was an error not to be repeated.

It struck me that there were a lot of constitutional similarities between Australia and Pakistan. Australia is a country of six states and two territories. Pakistan is a country of six provinces and two autonomous areas. Even though the constitutions of the two countries are applied in very different ways, there are enough similarities in the way the Federal government structures work in both countries, for Pakistan to look towards Australia to gain some ideas on setting up the National Disaster Management Authority.

Australia's natural disaster response mechanism works very well. Our states have principal responsibility for immediate response, with the federal government giving support when needed. There is a national organisation, Emergency Management Australia (EMA) that facilitates exchange of lessons learned and knowledge between the states. Most Australians have never heard of EMA as the organisation simply gets on with its job without much fanfare. I thought this could be a good model for Pakistan.

The Australian High Commissioner in Pakistan at the time was a woman named Zorica McCarthy, who coincidentally was the ex-wife of John McCarthy, the Australian Ambassador in Indonesia at the time I was in East Timor. John was by then the Australian High Commissioner in India. I always thought it funny that Australia would put a divorced couple as High Commissioners in India and Pakistan, two countries technically at war. Fortunately, John and Zorica remained friends and are both talented and capable diplomats.

I put a proposal to Zorica that the Australian government could fund a trip to Australia for Farooq and the UN could pay for me to accompany him, in order for Farooq to get ideas on the establishment of the National Disaster Management Authority. Zorica agreed. I took Farooq to Canberra to meet the relevant political leaders and visit EMA headquarters. We also decided to visit the main EMA training facilities located at Mount Macedon outside Melbourne. Farooq took many lessons to consider for Pakistan.

While in Melbourne we met my great friend Chris. We also went to see my Dad. Farooq was the first of the army generals to recognise my Achilles heel. The relationship between me and my father had broken down many years before. Dad didn't understand or accept my career choice.

Farooq and I went to my favourite hamburger place, Andrew's Hamburgers, a few hundred metres from my father's house.

"Andrew, we have been here two days now, and not met your father", said Farooq. The relationship between father and son is the most important in Pakistan and for Farooq it was unthinkable that we had not paid a visit. "Where does he live?"

"200 metres that way", I indicated.

"Let's go", he said. We went inside, but Farooq had laid the groundwork for Nadeem to build on.

General Nadeem: Love and Marriage

Nadeem and I had become very close. We had got on very well from that first 2005 meeting and had developed a stronger bond as the earthquake relief unfolded. We shared many good times and some truly fascinating and uplifting discussions. I believe that one of the reasons Nadeem kept me around was for our discussions, but also for the odd time when we would disagree. Our first disagreement was about two trees in Abbottabad.

If it was not for the fact that Osama bin Laden was killed in Abbottabad in early 2011 perhaps only those who had been to Pakistan would ever have heard of the town. It's a pretty location nestled in the foothills of the Himalayas. It's also the home of a number of Pakistan army training facilities including the medical corps. It is on the grounds of the medical corps and the local golf course that the United Nations helicopter hub was placed for the entire period of the earthquake relief. Yet it very nearly wasn't on account of two trees. One of General Nadeem's many strengths is a great passion for the environment. When he was a brigade commander in the northern parts of Pakistan-controlled Kashmir, he ensured the clearance of walking trails up toward K2, including the installation of environmentally-friendly latrines in some of the world's most remote locations.

After our meeting at General Headquarters in October 2005, the United Nations and the Pakistan army determined that Abbottabad would be a good location for the helicopter hub, if enough space could be found. The United Nations was to bring in quite a number of MI-8 helicopters, a Soviet-designed, rotary-wing workhorse. We were also going to bring in the MI-26, the world's largest helicopter. This helicopter fleet would move an enormous amount of food and non-food items as part of the relief effort. The army band school and Abbottabad golf course were chosen as the main hub for the United Nations helicopters; however, there were two large trees in the middle of the flight paths.

People assume that helicopters can take off vertically (i.e. straight up and down). While this is true, it puts far less stress on the airframe for a helicopter to take off horizontally, in a similar way to an aeroplane. When carrying cargo it is particularly important to take a horizontal take-off path, if possible. Two trees grew in the middle of the horizontal take-off path. To move around the trees would take extra time and decrease the number of flights the helicopters could take. Nadeem and I had one heck of an argument about the trees as he swore we could do as many flights as we planned and still leave the trees in place. Nadeem was a helicopter pilot and had a view about the flight paths. I was taking my advice from the United Na-

experts who insisted the trees needed to be removed. Nadeem won the argument. The trees remained and we still achieved the flights. Nadeem was right!

Nadeem and I did a lot of learning together, principally about gender planning, which led to the success of increasing girls' enrolments in schools in Kashmir. After Nadeem saw that success and understood the need for age and gender-desegregated data, he saw the issue as being one of effective planning. We both saw the 'mainstreaming' of gender as an issue throughout all parts of the relief and recovery operation.

We both learnt that the issue around 'gender' is not the same as issues about 'women and girls'. For example, many may look at the problems associated with female-only households when all the men of a family have been killed in a natural disaster. Yet few think of the problems of male-only households when all the women in the family have been killed. Regardless of what one may think of different cultures, when there are specific tasks in the family assigned to the different genders in different cultural environments, then a family unit becomes dysfunctional if one or other of the genders is removed from the equation. Those planning relief and recovery operations need to understand the various issues regarding gender and plan the response to those issues.

Both those who look at gender issues merely through a feminist lens and those who are straying down the path of male chauvinism, are equally as distracting to a comprehensive response. Nadeem learnt this very quickly.

At an emergency planners' conference in Geneva during 2006 I listened to a presentation given by a gender adviser (the vast majority of whom are female) speak on issues regarding women's evidence in rape trials in Islamic countries. In some Islamic countries women's evidence is not accepted as equal to that of a man's evidence.

At this conference the woman presenter outlined the program she had been running in Sudan to have women's evidence accepted as equal. She had persuaded approximately 100 women who had been raped, and two of whom had wished to put the episode behind them, to pursue a prosecution of the male perpetrators. This woman saw it as a great success that after 100 attempts she achieved the first prosecution of a man based on the equal acceptance of women's evidence. The majority of the people in the room applauded her.

I put my hand up to ask what had happened to the other 99 women. The presenter informed us that there had been no conviction in the previous 99 cases and the men had walked free. I again asked what happened to the women. After having admitted a sexual act took place in the course of a rape trial, the man was found not guilty and the women were then charged with adultery. They were convicted and stoned to death.

When one becomes too blinded to an ideological goal one can lose sight of their impact on people. This presenter thought it was a great success that after one hundred tries they received one conviction for rape, however I thought it a great tragedy that 99 women had been charged with adultery, convicted and stoned to death. This would not have happened to them if not for the neo-academic feminist wanting to prove a point.

In a similar way, when gender issues are confused with feminism in issues regarding sexual and gender-based violence in conflict environments, similar distortion can take place. Rape as a weapon of war is abhorrent. Yet if one looks at the issue of rape in war through a feminist lens then the result is the creation of a large number of programs supporting the victims of rape. When one looks at the issue of rape as a weapon of war through a gender lens then two things become apparent. Firstly, it is appropriate to put in place as many programs as you can to look after the victims of rape.

Secondly, however, when looking through a gender lens and analysing who the perpetrators of rape are in many conflict environments, often it is young boys and youths forced into the acts as part of an initiation program implemented by some of the world's worst warlords. Would it not be best to have a cohesive policy in place to respond to such violence rather than employ random people, each with their own agenda?

In many ways the boys who are kidnapped, enrolled into the guerrilla military forces and forced to perpetrate these heinous crimes are also victims. When understanding this dynamic, a lot of programs can be put in place to try and protect the boys from kidnapping and thereby reduce not only the number of child soldiers but also the number of perpetrators of crime.

When looking through a feminist lens one deals with the consequence of rape. When looking through a gender lens one can deal with both the consequence of rape and the causes of rape. It is always best to stop the event from happening than to deal with the consequence afterwards.

In March 2007 my younger brother Ben was to get married in Melbourne in the same week as the World Swimming Championships were also taking place in Melbourne. Four swimmers from Pakistan were going to go to Melbourne, including two of the girls whom I had been helping to coach. A day or two before I was due to leave I was in Nadeem's office to get three quick decisions on issues involving the recovery effort. As I was leaving the room I asked:

"Sir, you know how you always say I should get married and you know how I'm going to my brother's wedding next week? Tell me this, why should I get married? What am I missing out on?"

Nadeem picked up his phone and called in his assistant Major Mushtaq and asked for some food to be brought in. We had a very long conversation about the meaning of life and love. He shared with me some of his deeply personal thoughts and issues regarding his experience in life, marriage and love. At the end of the conversation he summed up his view.

"Andrew, if I have had a very bad day, when I go home my wife will put her arms around me and tell me that everything is okay. That's what you're missing out on. That's why you should get married."

This isn't the sort of advice that you expect from an army general in Pakistan.

When my time in Pakistan was drawing to an end, Nadeem told me that he thought I'd done a lot for his country and in return he was going to do something for me. He said he was going to try and fix the relationship between me and my father. I'd shared with Nadeem some of the problems of my childhood and the fact that part of the problem was that my father didn't really understand what it was that I did for a living and why.

"So let's show him," Nadeem said. "Bring him to Pakistan and I'll show him what you've done."

Dad took some persuading to come to Pakistan. I tried a number of times to convince my father on the telephone, but each time he was about to agree, a suicide bombing in Karachi, Lahore or Islamabad would make global headlines and Dad would reconsider.

"Well is your father coming or not?" Nadeem asked me in exasperation one time. I said to Nadeem that I'd tried to persuade him and that my father changed his mind each time a suicide bomb went off.

"Andrew, I'm the Vice Chief of General Staff of the Pakistan Army, I'll make sure he has protection," Nadeem said.

"I know that Sir, but Dad doesn't." I paused. "Heck, Dad was in the military, he understands generals. Just ring him up and order him to come won't you?"

"Give me his number?" said Nadeem.

I left Nadeem's office, giving him my father's phone number and after half an hour or so on the phone Nadeem had persuaded my father and my stepmother to come and visit. He was on a mission!

Nadeem had organised for VIP treatment for my father and stepmother when they arrived in Islamabad. When I went to the airport to meet my parents, an official from the Department of Foreign Affairs ensured that there was no wait at the customs queue and that another official would be responsible for collecting their bags. By the time we arrived at my accommodation Nadeem had delivered flowers for my stepmother. Next morning Nadeem personally flew us around the earthquake-affected zone as part of his regular inspections and took the time to explain not only the size of the challenge we were confronted with, but my role in helping meet the challenge. I have to say that, if anything, Nadeem oversold my role!

Landing in Chakothi was particularly meaningful. Nadeem had the local military detachment set up a picnic under an old parachute. We ate a beautiful lunch in sight of the Line of Control between Indian-controlled and Pakistani-controlled Kashmir. Given that Nadeem had been posted as a brigade commander in Chakothi, he shared with my father stories of life as a senior commander in the conflict zone.

We drove down to the primary school. On my first visit there we saw blood-stained school books, destroyed desks and chairs and evidence everywhere of innocent young lives that had been taken by the natural disaster. Nadeem shared these stories with Dad as we walked around the rebuilt school, with new equipment and evidence of happy children recovering from the disaster. We showed my father the first A-framed construction built after Matt George's idea which resulted in the building of 400,000 emergency shelters and saving countless lives.

We flew over Muzaffarabad. In 2005 I had huddled around a small gas heater on Christmas Eve. In 2008 it was a town well on the way to recovery with a brand-new luxury hotel opening. It was somehow fitting that my first night in Muzaffarabad was in a tent, and my last visit saw me inside a luxury hotel. If nothing else, it convinced me that we had completed a job well. After landing back in Islamabad and spending a night in the capital, we drove to Lahore. Outside Lahore is the Wagah Border. Each evening at sunset there is a formal military ceremony beautifully choreographed between the Indian and Pakistan military forces on duty. Flags are ceremoniously lowered as soldiers bid to outdo each other in the highest of high kicks, loudest orders and the most well coordinated act of defiance that you could ever see.

The Wagah Border crossing divides the Grand Trunk Road between India and Pakistan and was the only road link between these two countries before the opening of the Aman Setu in Kashmir in 1999. The ceremony starts with a blustering parade by the soldiers from both countries and ends in the perfectly coordinated lowering of the national flags, and a brutal slamming of the two sets of border gates. This ceremony was toned down in 2010, a shame since it provided great entertainment and an attraction for national and international tourists.

As it was a military ceremony, Nadeem was anxious for Dad to enjoy it. He had instructed the rangers in charge on the Pakistan side to treat Dad, 'not as a VIP, but as a V-V-VIP'. Not only did we have the military escort from Lahore out to the border area, complete with out-rider police motorcycles, but Dad received formal gifts and was asked to inspect the Pakistani troops. I began to nickname Dad 'the Governor General of Pakistan' because everywhere he went he seemed to inspect troops.

Nadeem's daughter was married in the week my father was visiting, so we were invited to the wedding. At most Pakistani weddings men and women are separated in different rooms. While my stepmother joined the women's room, my father and I joined the men. The guests were made up of the Who's Who of Pakistani military and government. While we were enjoying the ceremony, senior official after senior official all introduced themselves to my father and thanked him for allowing me to be in Pakistan. Each one finished off by asking why it was that I wasn't married.

In Pakistan most marriages are arranged by the parents. It is the father's duty to find an appropriate spouse for his son and for the father and mother to find an appropriate spouse for their daughter. This often seems unusual to Western eyes.

In the West, marriage is about joining individuals. In the East, marriage is about joining families. In that context it isn't unusual that families should be involved. Most of the people I met in Pakistan were in the middle or upper class. The process of arranged marriage is very different for the upper classes than it is for the lower classes. With the middle and upper classes, a proposal came about when the family of the son proposed their boy to the family of the daughter. More often than not it is the daughter who gets to choose more than the son. Far from being an attack on female independence, arranged marriages in that context are often a family discussion in which the girl gets more choice than the boy.

There is no doubt that this is different in some of the lower classes and it is the horror stories of young daughters being sold that often makes TV news, thereby creating an inaccurate perception of the practice in the West. In my entire time in Pakistan more often than not people didn't defend the arranged marriages as much as feel desperately sorry for me that I didn't have one. The fact that I was a bachelor in my early forties was, to them, proof that there was a role for parents to get involved. As one army officer told me, "After all, parents often know their children better than the child themselves."

In Pakistan I made incredibly strong friendships. Given that Pakistanis believed in arranged marriages and that they believed it was my father's responsibility to find me a wife, it was too big a temptation for them to let the opportunity pass without them telling my father what they thought of my single status.

After several iterations of the same story my father finally said to Brigadier Waqar, "I just haven't found the right woman yet." Waqar simply pointed to the women's room and said, "Pick one."

My father was later to say that it wasn't how much the Pakistanis had said about what I had done in the country, it was how far out of their way so many senior people went to explain what my role was. My Pakistani friends genuinely wanted to reconcile my father and I.

I can report back to my Pakistani friends 'mission accomplished'. What Farooq had started in Melbourne in 2007, Nadeem finished in Islamabad in 2008. Between the two of them, these two generals had fixed a broken relationship. They did so because they cared. I will forever hold in deep affection not only Nadeem and Farooq but the whole range of friendships made with some incredible people in very difficult circumstances.

Closing Thoughts on Pakistan

Despite what you may be led to believe, via the media, Pakistan is a country with many hidden pleasures and great treasures. It is, without doubt, let down by its politics. The political situation should not hide from the world the fact that Pakistan is a country with many great people. I have made stronger friendships in the two and a half years in that country than in any other. I found the honesty, compassion and interest of the people to be genuine and strong.

I will remember fondly the times with Major Mushtaq talking philosophy, comparative religious ideology and openly wondering about the future and learning from the past.

From everyday people in villages to people in power, I found Pakistani people were curious about others, and had a desire to learn and understand others' views, even if they didn't agree.

Pakistanis fondness for their friends is genuine. They are good people who feel let down by poor politics and the minority of radical extremists.

It is why I say that you will never see greater pain than that on the face of a moderate Muslim in Pakistan when talking about Al Qua'eda. As general Nadeem, a man who rarely swears, once said, "Andrew, these people are fucking our religion".

Pakistan also reinforced a key message: good people can make Aid work. We were lucky with the group of people who at the start of October 2005 came together to form the Cluster Coordination team. These people, often at the cost of their careers, put the relief operation before their agencies demands. They did great work and delivered phenomenally good service to the people. They often fought their own agencies and their own bureaucracies. The truth is that the 'system' works only when you have the right people in place. But the system often rejects the 'right' people. It is why aid still doesn't work as it should.

The Pakistan earthquake relief was a special operation. A series of unrepeatable events occurred to allow this exceptional operation. It was a massive earthquake, with a credible military not afraid to ask for help. A new system was being put in place to coordinate relief, so new that 'nay sayers' didn't know how to stop it. And above all we had a series of key personal relationships that worked.

Nadeem and Farooq both asked me after the event if this is how aid normally runs. I don't think the Pakistanis realised just how much risk key people such as Rachel Lavy, James Shephard-Barron, Brian Kelly, Fawad Hussein, Rania Dagash, Jemilah Mahmood, Matt Hollingworth, Bill Fellows, Maurice Robson and many others all took.

These people went above their 'normal' responsibilities and did more than could have been expected. For me, working with them and for them was a great honour.

9.

The Philippines: The End of My Faith in Aid?

O n September 27, 2006 The Philippines was severely hit by Typhoon Milenyo. Within one month super-typhoon Paeng extensively damaged homes, schools and health centres in the provinces of Isabela and Aurora. It was quickly followed on November 12, 2006 by Typhoon Queenie, which further affected the same areas as Paeng. The most destructive typhoon to follow was Reming, which struck the western coast on November 30, with sustained winds of 190 km per hour and gusts of up to 225 km per hour. It was followed by another lower-order typhoon Seniang on December 9. In total, five typhoons hit approximately the same region in only two and a half months.

Nearly 700,000 people became displaced, either from weather-related events or from the fighting. This was the tenth largest displaced population in the world in 2008.

The most dramatic impact was a massive mudflow caused by Typhoon Reming on the southern slopes of Mount Mayon Volcano, in Albay Province. Mount Mayon is an almost perfect symmetrically-shaped volcano which stands majestically and beautifully over the town and province of Albay. It is almost constantly emitting steam and is one of the most active volcanoes in the world, meaning mud and ash on its slopes are incredibly susceptible to tremors, eruptions and rain brought by typhoons. The mud-flow submerged entire villages, killed more than 1,000 people and caused a displacement of more than 13,000 families. As of May 2008 there were still 6144 families in transitional shelter settlements awaiting permanent relocation, and approximately 4,000 families in permanent settlement still awaiting water and electricity to be connected to their resettled homes.

An NGO and a UN agency had constructed one of these resettlement villages, including small houses and toilets, but forgot to put in water connections. Consequently many houses had dry unusable toilets, and no running water as there was no funding available to put in pipes.

I left Pakistan in mid-2008 for The Philippines with both trepidation and uncertainty for my longer-term future. I had doubts around my belief in the UN and its human resources system.

My role was to run an Early Recovery program with communities affected by typhoons that hit The Philippines in 2006. Who runs an early recovery program two years after an event? The Philippines is one of the most natural disaster-prone countries, with more than 22 typhoons, a couple of earthquakes and a volcano or two erupting every year. Even by Philippine standards, 2006 was a tough year.

I visited Bicol, the administrative region of The Philippines, almost immediately upon arrival in the country and was shocked by the lack of progress over the previous two years. The poor quality of transitional shelters and even more worrying the quality of construction in some permanent relocation villages, stood out.

In one reconstructed village hand-pressed bricks were being used to build walls holding concrete slab roofs above tiny homes. In Pakistan we had rejected hand-pressed bricks as being unsuitable for carrying heavy loads. There is also a danger that concrete roofs will collapse and kill people unless there is an enormous amount of reinforcing and very strong bricks or concrete walls. If people were allowed to live in these houses being built by International Organisation for Migration (IOM) and an earthquake struck at night, those people would almost certainly die.

When I asked the IOM focal point why he chose this construction, he said "because the concrete roofs won't blow away in the next typhoon".

This wasn't a surprising response as there is a tendency in the aid world to 'build for the last disaster'. The problem is that the next disaster may be of a different type, so one needs to consider that too.

I asked in reply "What happens in the next earthquake?"

This aid worker responded "there are no earthquakes in The Philippines". Here it was again: the well-meaning amateur inadvertently putting lives at risk.

Not only is The Philippines sitting on the Asian 'Ring of Fire', it's one of the most earthquake-prone regions in the world. The Bicol region sat on the slopes of one of the world's most active volcanoes. When volcanoes erupt, earthquakes happen. Any housing reconstruction had to take into account not just the prospect of future typhoons, but also earthquakes.

When I raised this problem in Manila, I was criticised by some for 'embarrassing the IOM', rather than being supported for preventing a potential major future problem. Problems like this arise when the system employs well-meaning amateurs. In my view the challenge is to employ professionals. Mistakes like the one with concrete roofs should not be made. In 2008 the aid world was perhaps at its worst in The Philippines.

A True Reformer

The Resident Coordinator (RC) is the most senior UN official in a country. Nileema Noble, the RC in Philippines, was of Indian extraction and a woman who held the concerns for the people uppermost in her mind. She cared about people more than the UN system. To me this was a great strength and highly admirable. In every meeting she would ask "but what about the people". This was rare in the UN.

When Nileema first arrived in The Philippines, she uncovered a number of practices within the United Nations' offices that were questionable at best, corrupt at worst. Within the national staff were a few people who worked hard, and many others who feathered their own nests. One of the more senior of the national staff fell asleep most afternoons and would snore very loudly and the sounds of his slumber would echo down the corridor. This didn't set a good example or show leadership in work practices. Nileema had made it clear to the national staff that she was going to stamp out some of the poor agency practices and refocus people on the need to work hard for the underprivileged. Rather than concentrating their energies on changing their work practices, these staff seemed to concentrate their energies on trying to remove Nileema from her role and there were suggestions of Nileema being 'racist'. Being accused of racism in the UN is one thing people find hard to disprove. I saw no evidence of Nileema being racist. However, I did see evidence that Nileema was starting to hold people accountable for their lack of effectiveness in their roles, and it seemed that it was this threat people were responding to.

While there was never any threat that Nileema would be forced out by the government of The Philippines, there was a strong indication that the government would not object if she was removed. In the early part of my appointment Nileema was called back to New York for consultations. Nileema was removed from The Philippines and sent to a small remote South Pacific state.

Other than Nileema, in my entire time in The Philippines, I never heard a single United Nations staff member worry about the impact of programs on the poorest as Nileema had. Nileema was a good person done over by a bad system.

A Self-serving Government

As in Pakistan, my work in The Philippines brought me into contact with a number of members of The Philippines government. I asked one senior finance minister why he was involved in politics. As in Pakistan his answer was "I'm here to protect my family's financial interest". The 21 ruling families of The Philippines control most things in that country. If you ask yourself 'is it in the 21 families' interest to economically, socially or educationally empower the poor'? Very quickly you see the answer is 'no'. If these families also control the government, and you ask yourself will government aid genuinely help the poor? Again the answer is, cynically and sadly, probably not.

Aid is given for a series of complicated reasons. It is part of the diplomatic game in asserting influence. Aid is often not about giving to the poor.

Many people said to me that the great problem in The Philippines is poverty. Actually it was one of the least poor countries my working life had taken me to. In fact, it is a mid-level economy, which might make you wonder why the United Nations Development Program (UNDP) was present to 'develop' the economy. In fact, UNDP is on the ground in 177 of approximately 200 countries in the world. Does the organisation really concentrate on bringing the poor out of poverty? Wouldn't it be more efficient to concentrate on, say, the least developed 25 or 30 countries in the world rather than be spread so thinly across 177? I began to ask whether the United Nations should even be doing development work in The Philippines at all. This legitimate question remains unanswered.

In 2008 a number of typhoons hit The Philippines, causing major flooding in the southern province of Mindanao.

Mindanao is split between Christian and Islamic communities and has suffered from an on-going insurgency for a number of decades. At the time the floods hit, the peace process had broken down and fighting had re-started. Surely this is where the UN would respond well?

The United Nations response was to offer a mild supplementation to World Food Program (WFP) deliveries, but no emergency workers were sent in and no special effort was put into finding a roadmap to peace. Why? The government of The Philippines did not want to 'internationalise' the problem in Mindanao and asked the UN to restrict its response. While senior international bureaucrats sat comfortably in Manila, with their children in the International School, their comfortable semi-diplomatic lifestyles, 700,000 people were displaced in the southern province.

The United Nations, still leaderless in the region, thought it was acceptable to comply with the government request to largely turn a blind eye. There was no large-scale call for assistance; no call for the government to work to restore the peace process; no discussion or analysis of alternative governance structures such as applying a model of federalism to The Philippines. In fact, none of the sort of thing a neutral international arbiter could do. The government didn't want the UN to respond, and the UN dutifully complied.

Nevertheless, I went to a crisis meeting in Davao, Mindanao, to discuss the collapse of the peace process and the flooding. Present were some members of the international aid community, the government, and The Philippines Armed Forces. Almost everyone, except the military, was playing down the situation and saying that things should continue as normal.

I had put a proposition forward that something radically different needed to happen in Mindanao to move the region on from the previous decades' attempts at peace and on-again-off-again natural disaster response. The Government of Philippines was deeply offended and formally complained about me to the United Nations. The army general on the ground, however, pulled me aside and said "someone had to say that". Dealing with the military in Mindanao was quite refreshing.

"We want peace," he said. "I spend half my nights writing condolence letters to parents explaining why their son or daughter has just died in a futile conflict. I want to stop writing these letters. Someone has to push us to do something differently."

Within the very senior ranks of professional military organisations around the world are people who are prepared for war, but who would prefer to fight for peace. Counter-intuitively, some of the most pacifist people are senior professional generals. This was the case with a Mindanao general in The Philippines. It was not the case with the civilian government. I ultimately wrote to the United Nations comparing Mindanao with Kosovo. Like Kosovo in the mid-1990s, here was an opportunity to establish peace between Islamic and Christian communities, but the central government wasn't taking that opportunity.

At that time Islamic terrorist groups Abu Sayyaf and Jemaah Islamiah were becoming more active in The Philippines. The youth were becoming radicalised and there were suggestions that bomb-making technology was becoming more detailed and shared between extremists in Kashmir and The Philippines. A heady mix indeed. In my memo to the UN I warned of a major escalation of the conflict unless something different was done.

When the major weather events hit in 2008, the government's reaction was to close many schools and use them as evacuation centres. This strategy works for events that require short-term housing where the school closures may only be for a matter of days or weeks until the weather event subsides. It doesn't work so well in conflict-related events that may require housing for longer periods of time – until the conflict ends, in fact.

Closing schools, even for a short time not only interrupts the education of children, but leaves them with nothing to do during the day – and teenagers get distracted easily. Abu Sayyaf and Jemaah Islamiah were aware that the young people were getting bored and used this break in education for a spike in recruitment to their terrorist cause.

I warned the United Nations that in my view the spike in recruitment would lead to an increase in capacity of terrorist groups and a reduction in the possibility of achieving a long-lasting peace. It left me feeling very pessimistic about the future for The Philippines. Naturally, some in the UN would have preferred that the memo had never been written.

Fortunately, a couple of years after my departure a new President came to power, took a different approach and by 2012 had negotiated a new peace. Let's hope it holds, yet remember the UN played no role in this. If it doesn't hold, then a major terrorist attack in Manila deriving from terrorist groups with their base in Mindanao or the Sulu Islands will in part trace their cause back to the inaction in response to the 2008 weather- and conflict-related displacement.

Catholicism, the UN and Paedophilia in The Philippines

The Philippines was nominally a former colony of Spain although for many years it was governed as a province of Mexico. As it was a remote province, Queen Sophia had allowed the Catholic Church rather than government to rule the colonial possession. Impacts of that decision are still felt today.

The Philippines is often known as the world's largest Catholic country, even with the substantive Islamic minority in Mindanao. The Catholic Church still exerts an unshakable influence in the country, particularly preventing any attempts to provide comprehensive sex education within Filipino schools.

The church actively discourages any discussion about condom usage and in many schools teaches that only prostitutes use condoms. As a result many teenagers engage in sex without condoms, resulting in extremely high teenage pregnancy and STD rates. The Philippine *Daily Inquirer* reported on June 14, 2008:

> *The sexual revolution has ushered in a period in which the average adolescent experiences tremendous pressures to have sexual experiences of all kinds. Filipino teens get a higher exposure to sex from the internet, magazines, TV shows, movies and other media than decades ago, yet without any corresponding increase in information on how to handle the input. So kids are pretty much left to other kids for opinions and value formation when*

it comes to sex.

Statistics in the United States show that each year, almost 1 million teenage women (10 per cent of all women aged 15–19 and 19 per cent of those who have had sexual intercourse) become pregnant and one-quarter of teenage mothers have a second child within two years of their first.

In The Philippines, according to the 2002 Young Adult Fertility and Sexuality Study by the University of the Philippines Population Institute (UPPI) and the Demographic Research and Development Foundation, 26 per cent of our Filipino youth nationwide from ages 15 to 25 admitted to having a premarital sex experience. What's worse is that 38 per cent of our youth are already in a live-in arrangement.

The 1998 National Demographic and Health Survey (NDHS) reveals that 3.6 million of our teenagers (that's a whopping 5.2 per cent of our population!) got pregnant. In 92 per cent of these teens, the pregnancy was unplanned, and the majority, 78 per cent, did not even use contraceptives the first time they had sex. Many of the youth are clueless that even on a single intercourse, they could wind up pregnant.

Without a shadow of a doubt lack of sex education is a major challenge facing The Philippines, particularly among the poor. Surely if the United Nations chose to turn a blind eye in Mindanao at least the organisation could tackle the Catholic Church? But naturally, it didn't.

The juxtaposition between religion and sex is quite astonishing in The Philippines. In the well-to-do suburb of Makati sits the Green Belt Mall. Here there is a church directly opposite the Havana Café. After the conclusion of the sunset church service, many mainly women of the congregation headed straight into the Havana Café, a place well-known for prostitution to foreigners, where many of the 'women' were clearly underage.

Part of UNICEFs work in The Philippines was to try and formally raise the age of consent, which for many years had been as low as 12 or 13. This is not a surprise when you consider that the age of consent in Spain is still 13, Iceland 14 and Italy 15. The US and Australia, which have the age of consent ranging from16 to 18 depending on the state law applying, are actually at the older end of the scale.

One 22-year-old friend explained to me how she part-funded her education through school as a teenager.

"I was a cam girl from 13 to 17," she said. A cam girl creates a profile on a site for 'dating' Asian girls. She would allow herself to be contacted by much older men, and in return for a small amount transferred through Western Union or similar services would perform requested acts to herself on camera.

According to my friend, it was common and often expected by mothers that daughters would help fund their educations this way.

In my view, one of the great perversities in The Philippines was that the lack of sex education imposed by the Catholic Church meant that girls didn't get the opportunity to discuss or learn about the dangers of the internet, the sex trade and sexual activity. Voilà, the high rate of pregnancy, STDs and the creation of 'cam girls'.

What was worse, until the age of consent was raised, it was legal under Philippines laws for Australian, German or American old men to suggest a 'visit in person' to The Philippines to meet the girl in exchange for a 'gift', a real-life visit to the cam girls. The sex trade was alive and well in The Philippines, very often with the encouragement of the mothers.

Much is known about the 'food for sex' scandals by UN peacekeepers in west Africa, the UN staff roles in child and teenage trafficking into Bosnia during the war, and the goings on in places such as the Havana Café. Peace-keeping abuses have only been revealed by news organisations. Such was the case in Cambodia in the early 1990s and later in Somalia, Bosnia and Ethiopia. "I am afraid there is clear evidence that acts of gross misconduct have taken place," said Kofi Annan when Secretary-General and on several occasions. "This is a shameful thing for the United Nations to have to say, and I am absolutely outraged by it." Yet no major public investigation took place.

The United Nations is not known for its forthrightness and candour in internal investigations. It has been criticised for ignoring evidence of wrongdoing in the past, including accusations of rape and murder by peace-keepers.

But this didn't end the surprise in The Philippines.

More astonishing is the juxtaposition between the towns of San Fernando and Angeles City north of Manila. Since 1962 in San Fernando on Easter Friday people have volunteered, or paid, to be crucified. People are hammered to real crosses with long brass nails and hung for a period of time. Blissfully, this re-enactment of Christ's death is not followed all the way through to the final moments. People are pulled down to seek medical treatment. On the way to the crucifixion site, hundreds of people flagellate themselves with wooden sticks until the skin is torn from their backs. This is all done in the name of religion.

In Angeles City, 15 km up the road, lies the den of prostitution that even the *Lonely Planet* guide calls 'the home of child prostitution in The Philippines'.

One has to ask why a travel guide knows where the child prostitution is, but local police seemingly do not. I found this contrast between Angeles City and San Fernando baffling and I am yet to fully understand the dynamics that have made The Philippines what it is today.

Given the inordinate influence of the Catholic Church, the threats of terrorism and the seeming lack of desire of the government to bring in programs to genuinely improve the lives of the people, the ineffectiveness of the United Nations and the international community in that country, I was very pessimistic about the future of The Philippines.

The only positive I took from The Philippines was the scuba diving. I was lucky enough to meet up with a group of underwater dive photographers who taught me their trade. Underwater photography is now one of my passions. But I didn't join the UN to become a photographer. As my contract was coming to an end I was glad to leave The Philippines, and glad to leave the UN.

∞

10.

Who Wants a Strong UN Anyway?

For many readers of this book it may come as a surprise that the United Nations is not already a single coherent organisation. What might come as a more of a disillusioning surprise is that the United Nations cannot become one either.

Think about it in this way: ask yourself in whose interest it is to have a strong and efficient United Nations? It is certainly in the interest of the poor and dispossessed people of the earth. But these people have no power and no say. Is it in the interests of a politician who is a member of his or her national parliament with the objective to 'protect his or her family's land interest' to economically, educationally or socially empower the poor? In the vast majority of cases the answer is 'no'. If it is not in that person's interest, will they do it? Probably not.

So then let's ask the question who decides on reforming the United Nations? It is the members of the Security Council and the General Assembly, that is governments, not people. So, in which government's interest that they reform United Nations?

The government of Zimbabwe would not appreciate a strong and effective United Nations to tell Robert Mugabe where his country is going wrong?

What about Libya? What about Iran? Is it in the interest of the government of the United States that a strong and efficient United Nations might start asking questions about the execution rate in Texas? Or in the interest of the government of Australia to have questions about Australia's treatment of either the indigenous population or of asylum seekers?

There are very few countries of which one could honestly say it was in that country's politicians' interest to have a strong and effective United Nations. Again, here I differentiate between a politician's interest and his or her country's interest. It is quite depressing to consider that the vast majority of governments do not run a foreign policy based on collective good.

It was slowly dawning on me that working in the UN was like working in one great big *Yes Minister* episode. While there are many staff of the United Nations who strive tirelessly to improve the world, in my subjective opinion, those staff members are in the minority.

Reflections on the UN

In the United Nations not all employees are equal. There are employees on permanent and temporary contracts and those who are employed as 'consultants'. Depending on the type of contract they were employed with, employees had very different rights, benefits, pay, and tax concessions.

There exists a very rigid ranking within the staff of the United Nations. The rank structure, starting lowest to highest, began at G (General) level, then P (Professional) level, followed by D (Director) level, then Assistant Secretary General, Undersecretary General and Secretary General. Within each of these ranks are a different number of grades, and within each grade are a differing number of steps.

The unexpected thing for me was that there was more discussion about level, step, rank and entitlements than there ever was about poverty, development, or the general state of the world. People tended to focus on a career path, and not on the people who need the organisation's assistance. There was a number of highly motivated, well-intentioned and effective staff within the UN system but these people seemed to be a minority.

When one understands the human resources system of the UN though, one can have sympathy for the focus on human resource issues. There were two main ways in which one could search for jobs within the UN system.

One was through the websites of the United Nations various agencies or through the collective system called Galaxy. The second way was to look for temporary or fixed-term appointments advertised on Relief Web.

The average time between advertising and filling a job on Relief Web was around 180 days, and the average time between advertising on Galaxy and filling a job was 230 days. Given that many of these contracts were for three or six months, it meant that many of the UN staff members on temporary or fixed-term contracts were constantly worrying about their next job, and the job after their next job.

The human resources systems didn't encourage long-term work efficiency from its short-term staff. It also created unintended and counter-productive consequences. Many UN employees originally from the developing world find themselves being paid much higher incomes than they would earn in their home country. In many cultures people overseas earning huge salaries are expected to pay for a large number of extended family back home. This is understandable.

In Geneva, a person's right to be in Switzerland is derived from their 'Carte de Légitimation' based on their work status with the United Nations. If one loses a job with the United Nations then the Swiss Foreign Affairs Ministry is informed immediately. The right to remain in Switzerland by virtue of the UN employment is withdrawn.

Picture this: you are from a developing country and have been working for the United Nations for a decade. You have two children both of whom are in the international school, receiving high quality and subsidised education. You are earning far more than you ever would in your home nation and you are sending money to your extended family back home, many of whom depend upon your income. If you lose your job, your right to remain in Switzerland would be forfeited. Your children would be taken out of school and your entire family would have to return to your home developing country. In those circumstances it would be understandable to live by the maxim 'above all, do not get fired'.

Within the United Nations the one way to guarantee that you don't get fired is to do nothing wrong. The easiest way to do nothing wrong, is to do nothing. Many who have worked in bureaucracies would recognise this trait and understand that the one thing people who do very little, know how to do well is to block other people from doing work that highlights their own inactivity.

The human resources system of the United Nations does not promote innovative risk-taking. To take innovative risks would be to accept occasional failure. If the cost of failure is the cost of your child's education and your family's livelihood, you can understand why for many people, that risk is simply too high. By serving time, people make their way higher up the ranks of the system. One can understand why the last thing a supervisor wants is a subordinate who wants to change things. Energetic, dashing young people embarrass lethargic bosses.

I don't criticise any individual from the developing world in making the decision to do very little once they have a job in the United Nations. Logic would dictate a safe course of action within the system. For many without alternative options the risk of losing a job is too high. However, I wouldn't excuse those from the developed world as the same dynamic does not apply to them.

This attitude permeates the whole system. The double standards, the perverse incentives all work against an effective delivery of humanitarian and development aid. It is this system that needs to be changed. But it is a system that is incapable of significant change.

I was disappointed by many of the development workers within UNDP. I had little faith in people in the 'development' side of the aid world. Conversely I found many in UNHCR to be highly dedicated and courageous people. There are a small number of 'desk warmers' in UNHCR, for the same reasons as in UNDP, but the emergency response teams of UNHCR are full of incredible people. By now the reader might be coming to the conclusion that the United Nations system is a lot more complicated and a long less synergistic that one would have expected or hoped. For me, the bureaucracy was my greatest source of frustration: I came to the UN wanting *The West Wing*, but what I got was *Yes Minister*.

11.

Does Aid Have to be 'Not For Profit'? Could the Private Sector be the Way Forward?

Is it right to call for the doubling of foreign aid? Should we instead ask to double its effectiveness?

Over the years, I became more senior within the United Nations system, yet it was almost as if each step upwards made me more aware of the lack of macro-level effectiveness and efficiency of the overall system of aid and development. The UN's lack of response to the situation in Mindanao was particularly grating. It is also ironic that the major reason the Pakistan earthquake response worked so well was because of authority, command and control of military dictatorship of the Pakistan Army and not the UN.

When one works in the aid world it is natural to want to see the results of how largely Western intervention could lift the world out of poverty. One finds that the world of aid is a complex one. Aid should be focused on people, but often it is more about the bureaucracy and money than it is about delivering aid to the people who need it. The measure of success in aid should not be how much money is spent or how honourably we try, rather we should be measured by how honourably we succeed.

Right: With Shirley Shackleton, widow of Greg, outside the house in which her husband was murdered by the Indonesian military in 1975. We were there on the first day of East Timor's independence, 2002.

Above: With Bill Clinton, Timor, 2002.

Above: First cluster meeting to coordinate the Pakistan earthquake response, 2005.

Above: With Gerhard in a helicopter early in the earthquake response, October 2005.

Above: Early 2006, far north Pakistan.

Above: 'Beware of the terrorist', fooling around with Rania Dagash, at Muzaffarabad Airport, 2006.

Above: Overseeing the construction of the first ever emergency A-frame to be built as part of Operation Winter Race, October 2005. General Nadeem is on the far left.

Above: Lyse Doucet interviewing Emergency Relief Coordinator Jan Egeleand, October 2005.

Above: Going live on CNN with Becky Anderson. Islamabad 2005.

Above: With General Farooq at the end of the relief period, Islamabad, March 2006. Cricket talk and cricket bats were a constant bond.

Above: With Major Farooq in Muzaffarabad, Pakistani Kashmir, Christmas Day, 2005.

Above: General Nadeem during our first field cluster visit to set the ground rules for Army/ NGO cooperation, October 2005.

Above: A Pakistani elder. He had lost everything in the earthquake, but still managed to smile.

Above: In the Allai Valley Pakistan with local kids, January 2006.

Above: An emergency food distribution, January 2006.

An amazing team. The first forward coordination team 'OSOCC' in Muzaffarabad, October 2005.

Above: General Nadeem overlooking the rubble of the Chakothi primary school.

Above: Food drop, winter 2005/2006.

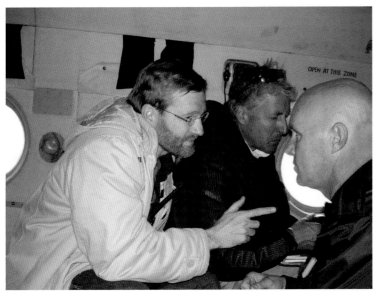

Left: Planning 'Operation Winter Race' aboard an Mi-8 Helicopter. Left to right: Me, James Shepherd-Barron and Matt George, October 2005.

Right: Hundreds of remote helipads had to be constructed for the delivery of aid supplies. This one was in the foothills of the Himalayas, early 2006.

Left: With a young girl, Allai Valley, 2006. Great people in Pakistan.

Above: Left to right – Me, my father, General Nadeem, my stepmother Caroline and co-pilot. Nadeem rebuilt the relationship between my father and me. Early 2008.

Above: With my father in ruins dating back to Alexander the Great, north of Islamabad, Pakistan, 2008.

Above: One of my favourite human beings in the world. Rania Dagash, in Islamabad, 2007.

Right: Housing reconstruction post typhoons, The Philippines, 2008. The hand-pressed bricks were potentially lethal.

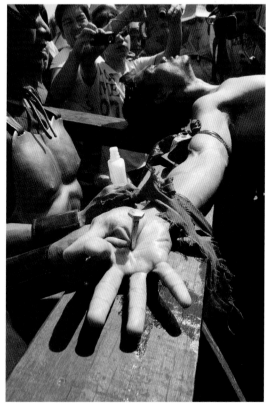

Above: Religious insanity, in my view. Easter crucifixion, The Philippines, 2009.

Above: As CEO of the Committee for
Melbourne, 2011.

Above: With Committee for Melbourne
Chairman George Pappas.

Above: In my home city, Melbourne, Australia. Adjusting to coming home is tough for aid workers.
More should be done to help.

Exploring Private Sector Options

If Pakistan was a career high, The Philippines was the low that made me really ask the question: Is aid effective? What could possibly be an alternative? Was the public sector the best place to fulfil a strategy to do good? Could more be achieved through a well-meaning private-sector company than through the bureaucratic public-sector system? Did such a company exist?

For the last decade or so, some of the largest corporations have, contrary to what the public might believe, made incredible differences to some of the most impoverished communities. For example, mining giant BHP Billiton has introduced an anti-malaria program in Mozal, Mozambique. The effect of this program has reduced adult malaria infection in the community around their aluminium smelter from approximately 92 per cent of the population to 5.6 per cent. And why did they do this? Two reasons. Firstly: it's the right thing to do. Secondly, the reduction in malaria infection has reduced absenteeism in their workforce. This, in turn, makes the company's assets more profitable. The success represents a clear link between community improvement and corporate improvement.

Many may think that BHP Billiton is motivated to conduct the anti-malaria program because it affects their profitability, and that this is proof of corporate bad-will, but I disagree. The ideal is to find a mechanism to deliver aid that is in the interests of both the community and the corporation, while guaranteeing the long-term sustainability of the anti-malaria program. A philanthropic mind-set is not enough. Corporate philanthropy depends on on-going goodwill and good economic circumstances. Understanding the benefits to business in improving community health doesn't need convincing philanthropic arguments or good economic circumstances, it needs an awareness that programs can be done in both the best interests of communities and companies.

Michael Porter and Mark Kramer from Harvard Business School coined a term 'shared value' to encompass operating models like that of BHP Billiton in Mozal. The theory of shared value hypothesises that companies not only can, but should, seek out those circumstances in which community good and corporate good can be achieved from the same events. Rather than hiding from the link with profit, Porter and Kramer surmised that the link with profit is a good thing that should be celebrated.

In the early 1990s there was no 'shared value' in Mozal in Mozambique. By 2009 there was. Clearly the landscape of the private sector is changing. More options exist now for those who want to 'do good' than existed at the time I went into aid.

As faith in the public sector decreases, a growing belief, based on research and evidence that a well-meaning private-sector intervention could work in true partnership with the public sector, may be the better way to bring many people out of poverty in the most equitable way possible. Hollywood stars such as Angelina Jolie and Brad Pitt are well known for their calls for the world to double foreign aid. Yet if foreign aid is ineffective, surely doubling the aid won't change things? But what is the alternative? Should the private sector replace foreign aid as the largest catalyst to bring the world out of poverty? Is the premise wrong from the start? Is foreign aid even a big player in bringing the world out of poverty anyway?

When looking at the macro level, just over half of all the capital flowing from Organisation for Economic Co-operation and Development (OECD) countries to the developing world comes from the private sector, a third comes from foreign workers' remittances (sending money back home), and the rest comes through aid.

Aid is actually the smaller player. The larger player is the collective flow of capital through the private sector. If we want to bring the world out of poverty, and we think funding plays a part, then why focus only on aid, which makes up only 17 per cent of capital flows.

Surely any effective and efficient attempt to help develop an economy, make it more resilient to disasters and to bring their people out of poverty, must be done in partnership between the private sector, remittances and official development assistance through aid?

Perhaps we should be calling for better collaboration and knowledge-sharing rather than a doubling of foreign aid?

A great friend of mine who has influenced me is Brian Kelly. We met in Pakistan when he ran the IOM operation there. Brian is from Connecticut in the United States. He is married to a Japanese woman and has two small children who learned Urdu, the national language of Pakistan, before either English or Japanese. They are destined to become children that see the whole world as home.

Brian and I shared a number of frustrations and visions. In running the IOM operation in Pakistan, rather than looking to the traditional government donors, Brian persuaded both Dow Chemicals and AIG to donate money and expertise into rebuilding houses and schools in some of the most remote parts of Kashmir.

During 2006 and 2007 we became more and more disillusioned at the lack of effectiveness and efficiency in the public-sector delivery mechanisms for aid and development. We both felt a degree of frustration when dealing with some in the political classes in developing countries.

We began to think that it is too easy to call for the doubling of foreign aid, when that merely represents more of the same thing but with the expectation of a different result. Self-serving government ministers, the 'Paris Declaration' impact and the failure of genuine UN reform, are just three key indicators that there is something desperately wrong with the whole system. What's more, even if it were to reform and change, it is, to paraphrase the Bobby Kennedy quote at the front of this book, a system that yields most painfully to change.

For half a century the international community has pumped billions of dollars into many developing countries with negligible results in the quality of life improvement for the poorest of the poor. The Democratic Republic of the Congo (DRC) provides a very good example of this. If you cut off 100 per cent of foreign aid to the DRC tomorrow, what would happen to the poor people there? Given that the vast majority of aid goes through the government of that country, and that many officials in that country are there to protect their own land or financial interest, how much of that 100 per cent do you think really trickles down to the poor? The answer is very little. If you cut off all foreign aid tomorrow there would be very little negative impact on the poor.

What is worse, the government of DRC receives about 70 per cent of its revenue from foreign aid and uses much of that revenue for repression of the poor through the use of violence by the police and security forces. Cutting off that aid might, in fact, reduce the government's ability to repress their own poor people by reducing the amount of money used to fund police and army forces. In a perverse way, cutting off aid may, in fact, help in the short term.

That's not to say that we should cut foreign aid. We just need to find ways of making it work better by being ruthless in cutting the inefficient programs, and supporting the efficient. The same would go for countries. If at a national level the impact of aid was demonstrably a net negative, or incredibly ineffective, why would we not cut it off?

We should, in addition, look at channelling the goodwill and finance available in the private sector. Brian's experiments with AIG and Dow Chemicals proved that it can be done if the investment climate is right. Brian and I often spoke about Rwanda. In 2006 there were 21 tradable commodities on the infant stock exchange. The government seeks to transform Rwanda from a low-income agriculture-based economy to a knowledge-based, service-oriented economy by 2020. It also recognises the key role of the private sector in accelerating growth and reducing poverty, and is looking for innovative ways to finance its development beyond traditional partners and instruments. It has been undertaking reforms to improve the business environment and to reduce the cost of doing business. Rwanda's growth performance has been remarkably strong over the past two years. Real growth accelerated to about 7.2 per cent in 2010 and 8.6 per cent in 2011 from 4.1 per cent in 2009. Production of non-tradables, such as construction and other services took off. We need to be careful not to overstate the change though. Rwanda was ranked as one of the poorest countries in the world in 1990 with a Human Development Index score of 0.232. By 2011 that had nearly doubled to 0.429 moving Rwanda up in the rankings in a positive trend. It is, however, still among the lowest quartile countries.

The country is moving up the rankings in the transparency international indexes from one of the most corrupt in the mid-1990s, to a Transparency International ranking of 5 in 2011, putting Rwanda in the middle of the league table. Rwanda is in a process of creating the macro and micro-economic variables so business can thrive.

We often thought that one thing that made Rwanda different from the DRC, or even Pakistan, was Rwanda's framework for development. The critical differences between DRC and Rwanda included an approach that liberalised the exchange rate mechanism, allowed for the repatriation of profit, ensured enforceability of contracts under local laws to allow businesses to invest with certainty, and from fostering mind-set of 'development investment' rather than 'development aid'. Critically, Paul Kagame was the key difference because he worked for the benefit of his country not himself.

It was at the same time in our discussions about trying to create a better mechanism than pure aid, that we met two senior staff from BHP Billiton, the world's largest miner. The company had then and still has a number of gas assets in Pakistan, and readily offered assistance when floods struck that country. The senior staff in Pakistan put me in touch with Ian Wood who was head of BHP Billiton's community engagement programs worldwide, and based in their headquarters in Melbourne. When I went to Melbourne in 2007 for the World Swimming Championships and my brother's wedding I also met with the staff of BHP Billiton to get more of an idea of the company's approach.

I was deeply surprised, and perhaps a little shocked, when the company shared their internal documents (not their external marketing documents) stating why they invested in the community. The company listed four aims of its strategies:

- The key beneficiary of the investment is the host community, and the primary reason for supporting the program is to contribute to sustainable community development, including projects with environmental outcomes.
- Key benefits to the company can include the promotion of a good company reputation, community goodwill, and stronger, more stable and supportive communities.
- The area in which support is provided is generally an area of mutual interest between the community and the company.
- The investment should aim to make strategic and sustainable improvements to the livelihoods of the communities where (the company) operates or may operate.

Brian and I began to look further into the approach of some of the leading multinationals including AIG, Dow Chemicals, BHP Billiton, Rio Tinto and some of the banks. We had been sceptical, but clearly something was changing. Perhaps our scepticism was based on naïve populism. Why would a large multi-national list in their internal documents the principal reason for doing community investment was to contribute to the sustainable community development of a country? This is the sort of objective that you expect to see of a UN agency or an NGO.

We saw continued anecdotal evidence in country after country that the aid mechanism was not working. There were rare examples of countries such as Rwanda, and perhaps now China, India, Brazil, Mozambique and Botswana, all improving their Human Development Index rankings, that have taken private sector investment rather than the public sector aid to begin to pull themselves out of poverty. They may not have yet fully succeeded, but they are to differing degrees, on the right track. Surely, we could change our mind-set to think that maybe the future is about building collaborative partnerships between private and public sector?

I met an interesting person during this time by the name of Matthew Hornibrook. Matthew came from a very famous building and construction family in Australia and had come to Pakistan together with Australia's former Prime Minister Bob Hawke, so he came with a degree of authority and credibility. He had an idea to build lightweight, aerated, concrete prefabricated housing structures in part of the earthquake reconstruction. While his product wasn't cost-effective for the Pakistan environment, the idea of a private sector solution was an interesting one.

I first met Matthew in General Nadeem's office when he and former Prime Minister Hawke were making a pitch for their product. Later that same day Zorica McCarthy, the Australian High Commissioner, hosted a dinner at the High Commissioner's residence in honour of former Prime Minister Hawke. Matthew and I began to speak in more detail about one of the interesting shelter challenges in the post-disaster environment.

A family-sized tent, delivered to a post-conflict environment, once you take into account the cost of storage and transportation to remote environments, costs about US$1200 per unit. Within that cost paradigm the manufacturing of the tent is a small component, the storage and transportation being the larger cost. Tents usually last three to six months, and are followed by a transitional shelter solution for up to two years, which may cost between $1,500 and $2,500 per unit. What usually follows is a permanent housing construction solution that, in the case of Pakistan, cost about US $3,500 per unit.

The difficulty post-disaster then is that you have a three-stage shelter process costing approximately US $7,500, but the beneficiary family only receives a net long-term benefit of about US $3,500 in value. The challenge I threw to Matthew was to see if we could design some type of housing solution that would drop a three-stage process into a two-stage process. Would there be a way to drop the transitional shelter stage either by making an emergency shelter last longer or bring a permanent solution faster?

Matthew and I would spend the next couple of years discussing these issues of emergency and transitional shelter. I looked to Matthew with some degree of hope that perhaps the private sector did have some good people in it who could provide interesting solutions. Hornibrook would show me though that not all is rosy on the private sector side.

There were clear changes happening in the world and Brian and I wanted to be part of them. We just didn't know how.

A Private Sector Warning

While working in The Philippines in 2008 and 2009 I was offered a role with UNICEF in their headquarters in New York to oversee their Early Recovery work in global emergencies. I'd always wanted to work in New York, but I had come to a decision to leave the United Nations post 2009.

I had been continuing a dialogue with Matthew Hornibrook since our meeting in Pakistan during 2006. We were discussing some very interesting designs for stronger emergency shelters that could last right through the transition period. I was already thinking that it would be interesting to see if more 'good' could be done in a well-motivated and well-run private sector company. Hornibrook seemed like he may provide a viable option.

Matthew had invited me to attend the Hornibrook 2008 annual dinner in Jakarta with former Prime Minister Bob Hawke in attendance. I took a couple of days leave and flew to Jakarta and began to talk seriously with Matthew about joining his business when my time in The Philippines finished. If there was any naïveté at all that the private sector would always be better than the public sector, Matthew Hornibrook removed that from me. I was to start in his Dubai-based operation in July 2009, which would allow me to be home for my father's 75th birthday.

As my departure date approached Hornibrook stopped answering phone calls and didn't return emails. On the day I was due to fly out to Dubai, he finally returned one of my calls and told me he was not going ahead with the contract due to financial constraints.

By late 2009 I found myself in Melbourne without a job and with no real desire to return to the aid world.

Ian Wood from BHP Billiton asked me to conduct a global review of the company's community investment programs. He wanted me to look at two key questions: Was BHP Billiton holding itself accountable according to global best practice, and could 'quality of life' indicators be used as key performance measures in their community investments?

I found it interesting that a well-motivated company asked about the results of its community investment in a much more rigorous way than the UN ever did, rather than an evaluation of the 'process'. In reviewing the company's global programs, a number of things came to mind. Resource companies have a growing recognition that they will be present in an economy for many generations and it is in the company's best interest to help the economy develop.

The Olympic Dam mine reserves in South Australia are estimated to last more than 700 years. The world's second largest miner, Rio Tinto, has reserves in Mongolia that should last well over a century and BHP Billiton's aluminium smelter in Mozambique has a life expectancy of between 50 and 100 years. Long term, equitable and sustainable economic growth is in the interest of companies. Community development is now seen as an element necessary for the overall success of a business in the long term.

In reviewing internal documentation of the company I saw BHP Billiton was committed to do the best it could to help achieve the Millennium Development Goals (MDGs). I was genuinely surprised that the company knew of the MDGs and saw a role for the company in helping achieve them. In Mozambique BHP Billiton was also responsible for a number of primary school education programs. Programs are carried out in the company's best interest as there is recognition that the children will, in due course, be the company's second-generation workforce. The better educated the children are, the better the quality workforce they will make. Both the company and the people win in that scenario.

It is interesting that in the minds of some of the best business leaders there is a search for genuine 'shared value', where community returns and company returns can work in harmony. Community and company returns do not have to be mutually exclusive; in fact community return and commercial return can be mutually assisting objectives. A good community makes a better business environment.

Good corporate management are beginning to see themselves as a temporary custodian of the company's presence, brand and the employees. This is a radical change in corporate thinking. It is embryonic and a mindset that is yet to fully mature.

When I reported back to Ian Wood, I was able to give him a mix of good and bad news. Firstly, BHP Billiton far exceeded global best practice in the way the company held itself accountable. That was the good news. The bad news was that the company could not look to UN agencies and NGOs for guidance on how to measure the impact of community investment programs as BHP already did it better. I also reported that he could, in fact, use quality of life indicators as key performance measures for some of the company's programs, but that such measures are usually measured against 'baseline data' on the current situation of community well-being, provided that a government has that data.

The first step in using the quality of life indicator as a key performance measure for a community investment program might therefore be in the creation of that baseline data. This takes time to gather, often a number of years. When looking at a two-year UN program, it is not worth understanding the baseline or 'starting point' if it would take you two years to figure it out. If you are a mining company with a 50 to 100-year vision, spending a couple of years gathering data makes perfect sense.

The scale of community investment was also of interest and surprise to me. Companies like BHP Billiton set a target of 1 per cent of pre-tax profit to engage in community investment programs. For BHP Billiton that investment in the community equates to US $220 million a year. This makes BHP Billiton the world's largest miner, in the top 10 companies in the world but also the third largest international development agency in Australia. This measure, though, understates the full impact.

In the case of Rio Tinto, their 2011 global spend of US$294 million in discretionary community programs makes them one of the larger donors to developing communities. It would rank Rio Tinto fifth in Australia behind the Australian government, World Vision, BHP Billiton and just behind the Australian Red Cross, and have two of the top five being private companies, two being aid organisations and one being government. But this is measuring only their community spend.

Committee for Melbourne

As 2009 drew to a close, a friend, Sally Capp, let me know that she was leaving an organisation called Committee for Melbourne. She suggested that I should throw my hat in the ring for her role as CEO. Committee for Melbourne is a not-for-profit, non-partisan member network that unites Melbourne's corporate leaders and organisations, who work together to enhance Melbourne's economic, social and environmental future. For me this was an interesting challenge.

Committee for Melbourne (CfM), at a local level was, on the surface, a good example of the private sector coming together for the good of the community. Could it be a model for a 'Private Sector OCHA' aimed at coordinating private sector contributions to the community? In my two years in the role member companies put time and effort into encouraging government to think differently about housing density, social cohesion, infrastructure planning and financing: all without charging anybody for their time, energy and personnel. The motivation: a good community is good for business, and it is simply the right thing to do.

Critically though, I learnt it is common for business leaders to join Not-for-Profit Boards, such as CfM to 'give back' to their communities. There is a danger though, that in joining a board to 'do good', business leaders may not use their business skillsfor which they are employed. George Pappas, Chairman of CfM Board, once said to me 'Sometimes when business leaders join boards like this they leave their 'business brains at the door'.

George and I were having the discussion in the context of three very poor years of growing financial deficit at CfM. Governance had slipped. As part of the reform we needed to institute, business thinking needed to return. Establishment of standard board sub-committees such as nominations, audit and risk, and renewed focus on the business model began with visible results.

The critical lesson is this: if business leaders join not-for-profit boards, they must keep their business brains focused. Indeed, business focus on effectiveness and efficiency is what is needed in not-for-profit organisations and the aid industry as a whole. A business leader can 'do good' by maintaining financial ruthlessness.

12.

Aid Effectiveness

Effectiveness and efficiency are two words often incorrectly used synonymously. In reality they mean very different things. 'Effectiveness' looks to results and if you have achieved change. 'Efficiency' is all about how much that change costs and if the cost is worth the result. To achieve long-lasting change and bring the world out of poverty, one needs to develop programs that are both effective and efficient.

One of the widest programs in the world is Development Aid – child sponsorships promoted by many aid agencies and very popular in the West. Give a few dollars a month to rescue a child – or so the advertising goes. Does it work?

Since 1953 the top eight child sponsorship providers have seen nearly 3.5 million children pass through a sponsorship scheme. Surely one would expect to see a great deal of academic study and research on both the effectiveness and efficiency of these child sponsorship programs? If you don't have a measure, how do you know if you are making a difference? How do you improve?

Bruce Wydick conducted one of the few independent international studies. Over the last 20 years a combined US $30 billion has been spent through child sponsorship programs. Wydick asked has it made a difference?

Observers of the aid world usually concentrate more on the motivation of an organisation trying to bring about change, rather than the large-scale change itself. They pick individual stories and market them letting you assume they are representative of the work of the entire agency. All that's needed to gain a continuity of funding for an organisation or program is to create the perception that the organisation is well-meaning and trying to make a difference. For many years the aid world said it was simply too hard to measure the impact of a program so analysis was usually done on process. By this most agencies talk about how much money is spent. That is the process. Rarely do agencies promote the results.

My experience has been similar. For years the aid world said that it is too hard to measure outcomes, so reports measure process. If you pick up almost any United Nations agency report it will say something along the lines of "we were given $100 million to spend on a child literacy program. We spent $97 million. That is 97 per cent implemented and therefore the program is successful." Rarely will the report go on to say "with that $97 million we saw an increase in child literacy from 13 per cent of the population to 27 per cent of the population, with that 14 per cent change being more efficient than a similar program in country X, but less efficient than in country Y. The lessons that we take away to improve efficiency are..."

Failing to properly evaluate the program fails to measure the impact on the people that the program is intended to serve. Bruce Wydick's study did find improvements from child sponsorships, but the increase in school attendance as a result of the study was only two years. But is the measurement of time in school the right indicator of success?

It would make a more interesting study to determine the long-term impact of attending school on the future employability and economic well-being of the sponsored child and his or her later family. Surely if the objective of a sponsorship is to break the cycle of poverty, then the only true measure is to ask if the child is or is not now out of poverty? How many children who have passed through child sponsorships are now doctors? How many are teachers? How many are government ministers or business leaders?

More damningly, how many recipients of current child sponsorships are the children of former recipients? We should ask if pumping funds into sponsorship alleviates a problem for only a short time but makes no real difference in the long term. The truth is this is rarely, if ever, measured.

The big question around child sponsorships should be 'have you lifted a child out of poverty?'

In over 50 years of aid has there been a macro change, or are the cynics right when they say 'the definition of aid is poor people in rich countries giving money to rich people in poor countries'?

Wydick's is the most optimistic study of effectiveness, but even his study finds that "we make no claims in this research that child sponsorship represents the most cost-effective path". Regarding efficiency, his study went on to say that: "...cost of these services (sponsorships) was about $28 per month to the sponsor, and the mean number of years of sponsorship in our sample was 11.33 years. Thus the total cost of sponsoring a single child to the average sponsor was approximately $3,806. Using our more conservative impact estimate of 2.88 additional years of schooling from child sponsorship, this puts the average cost of an additional year of schooling from the program at $1,321 per year, per sponsored child."

I raise an obvious question: Could you spend $3,806 (this is roughly 10 years average income in the DRC) in a way that achieves a better result than two additional years in school? Is this the optimum use of those funds?

Wydick goes on: "When addressing issues of cost efficiency it is important to understand that the development of international child sponsorship programs fundamentally arose from their usefulness as a marketing tool for mobilizing resources in rich countries to fight poverty in poor countries".

In academic language Wydick has hit on the elephant in the aid room: Child sponsorships are about marketing. The child is used as a marketing tool to tug at the heart strings of people in rich countries.

There is, in my mind, an inherent dishonesty in this. If an organisation intends to use the money for broader programs, then it should market programs as such.

Perhaps criticising either the effectiveness or efficiency of child sponsorships is a risky business. There is such a feeling of goodwill around child sponsorships that an assumption of a mean, Scrooge-like person is often thrown at anyone who dares raise questions. Hence criticism is rare.

I have another view. If child sponsorships are actually succeeding in bringing families out of poverty then it is a good thing to evaluate and show the success. But is it legitimate to show the opposite? It is legitimate to question if $1,321 is best spent to gain one additional year of schooling, or if that funding should be spent more effectively in another way to break the cycle of poverty?

One must question the sponsorship effectiveness because children are in need. If the child sponsorship doesn't break the cycle of poverty, then the sponsorship system is in reality a betrayal of those people to not question the system.

This is why it is best not to ask an agency 'what it is they will do for this generation'. It is better to ask 'what is it that you have done for previous generations?'

Unfortunately, the mentality of analysing effectiveness and efficiency does not exist within many organisations in the aid world. If one questions an aid agency about their effectiveness or efficiency from inside the system it can be career limiting. If criticising from outside the system one tends to be labelled 'right wing' and 'focused on capitalism and money'.

Until recently, no one has ever held the aid industry to account for its results. Only recently have reports, such as the Australian Government Aid Effectiveness Review, begun to ask 'what is the result for all our spending?'.

Aid: Is It the Only Choice?

Dambisa Moyo in her book *Dead Aid*, put the view that in many circumstances aid has entrenched not helped alleviate poverty. In the worst case scenario, she says, the provision of aid is redirected by host governments away from the funding of development programs and into the mechanism that allows repressive governments to continue to repress their populations.

In her book *The Crisis Caravan*, Linda Polman points out that "to warring parties as well, humanitarian funds and supplies represent a business opportunity; indeed, aid has become a permanent feature of military strategy". In his book *The End of Charity*, Nic Frances puts forward the thesis that charity can never deliver a just and sustainable world. He says that it is only through a value-centred market economy that we will ever see real social change.

When you look at the macro-level indicators between the DRC, a country with enormous resources and access to the ocean, and compare them with countries such as Rwanda, a country with no or few natural resources and no access to ports, the story becomes even more interesting. The Democratic Republic of Congo should be rich, Rwanda more likely to be poor. The reverse is true. While DRC still remains on the 'Aid Caravan',

Rwanda is pushing for a market-driven mechanism.

There is a clear narrative that the billions of dollars that have been spent on aid in many countries over many years have not worked. For countries to pull themselves out of poverty, they need to put in place mechanisms that break the cycle of aid and encourage a cycle of investment instead.

I remain hopelessly idealistic that we can bring the world out of poverty, but I am not wedded to the current process. We need well-meaning professionals and we need to encourage consolidation among the thousands of aid organisations that exist. We should look at professional systems, with accountability and a ruthless approach to those in employment in the aid industry who do not deliver that which the world needs delivering. For me, it is no longer good enough to be well meaning and to try, the international community must become well-meaning and succeed.

The Three Convergence Points Giving New Options

Today there is a growing awareness that foreign aid must be both effective and efficient. Secondly, there is a growing awareness among some leading private-sector corporations that it is in their interest to improve the lot of the community. Every business is run by people and most people want to leave the world in a better state. While there is a fundamental disparity in wealth across the world, we do have the power to change this. The answer is not to destroy capitalism. It is to continue to regulate and modify capitalism in appropriate ways. Australia just happens to do this very well. There is a growing awareness in corporate responsibility to strengthen the communities and markets that the corporation is part of.

Thirdly, Generation Y, those who are in their late teens to mid-thirties now, are demanding social outcomes as part of their work, not just financial outcomes. Generation Y is manifesting itself in Australia much more sharply now than it is in either North America or Europe. The best graduates in Australia are not hired and fired when they leave university, they hire and fire their employer. If their employer doesn't satisfy them, the best of them have the ability to fire the employer and get a new one. This dynamic only manifests itself in a market that has low unemployment. Australia's unemployment rate of around 5 per cent is among the lowest in the world.

Could the private sector really be a legitimate partner in trying to bring the world out of poverty?

Recently Australian resource companies have benefitted from improvements in health and education in the developing world and in Australian indigenous populations. Smarter and healthier people have led to better, more productive workforces.

Recently an indigenous group in the Pilbara region of Australia lacked clean drinking water, and the health of the group was so poor that they couldn't be employed. Once a water supply was built, health improved and the community could be prepared for work and the region was made ready for investment. This success story was initiated by Atlas Iron, a mining company.

Should such a program be implemented from a business perspective, a community perspective, or both? How should programs like this be planned and their success measured?

Companies realise that community investment is often met with public scepticism created by the assumption that corporate gain should not be a motivating factor in community investment. But why not? Why can't a program have both a community and a corporate benefit? How do we show that a link with profit is a positive and sustainable fact, rather than negative? If developing economy employment can be aligned with long-term corporate interests and positive returns to shareholders, doesn't this create the often sought after win-win scenario and a long-term sustainable partnership?

Rio Tinto recently signed a landmark deal in Australia to guarantee long-term investment in indigenous health, education and employment creation, in return for access to resources. Rio Tinto took a long-term view to convert an area's natural resource into a human resource for the benefit of the community, and yes, the shareholders. According to the United Nations, US $1 billion is spent per year through the core funding of the United Nations Development Program to attempt to alleviate global poverty.

Between BHP Billiton, ANZ, NAB and Rio Tinto nearly US $500 million per year is spent on community investment programs. This is half of the UNDP core budget from just four companies with community investment heads based in Melbourne, Australia.

When you add in the rest of the world, it is estimated that corporate community investment is worth in excess of $59 billion per annum. The entire UN system, including peace-keeping and political affairs has a budget of around US $15 billion.

Surely then we need to reassess the private sector role in development? We should look to synergies with private sector development investment not just public sector development aid that would improve both community benefit and return to shareholders?

Do we or don't we accept the profit motive as part of the development solution?

In the 50 countries in which the Australian government has an aid program, nearly US $5 billion is spent annually in aid, and nearly $90 billion is earned bilaterally in trade. Most of this trade is in resource-rich countries where Australian resource companies are among the leading players. Perhaps it is time to look at linking the aid and trade agendas for benefits to companies, communities and governments. In areas without natural resources, are there ways to tap other private sector skills for their development?

Is it possible to foster a culture that not only celebrates and encourages business involvement within social development? Why not look for social return on investment partnered with financial return on investment when planning corporate programs?

Given the breadth of resources and strength of dynamism wielded by the private sphere, there exists incredible potential for significant social impact in conjunction with enhanced shareholder returns. In many instances, social return may work in conjunction with achieving a commercial return when measured. This measurement is an innovative and emergent new space. Australian resource companies are among the global leaders in this space.

Do Australian companies that cut their teeth learning lessons of intercultural workings in indigenous communities have an unexploited comparative advantage in expanding work into developing economies? Have Australian companies maximised their advantage?

If good business is to engage development and environmental concerns in a productive manner, then there exists an enormous potential for positive action beyond what has so far been explored. The most successful companies are looking to align these win-win opportunities with their business models.

BHP Billiton, Rio Tinto, ANZ bank and National Australia Bank are four companies that the community at times likes to pillory in the press. They're often accused of making massive profits, particularly by the Occupy Movement. While I agree that we should kick someone when kicking is due, do we pat on the back when a patting is due?

When one analyses some major corporate approaches to community investment programs we see the desire to do programs well, measure their impact and justify that impact in both community and financial terms. One can see a change evolving in the corporate landscape. Australia is playing a significant role in the evolution.

BHP Billiton, Rio Tinto, ANZ and National Australia Bank have significant footprints in Australia. Surely the nature of the Australian economy and its position in the economic cycle gives this country a great opportunity to understand and maximise that three-way global convergence point before other economies. If Australia grasps the opportunity to understand how these three convergence points work, not only can the country create a new global leadership position, it can provide itself and those in need with a brighter future. Maybe Australia can lead the way in taking 'Shared Value' to the next level – to be a 'Grand Prix model' not a 'Billboard model'?

Maybe the key is in building new partnerships? Maybe we could create a new model for private-sector-based community development?

Drive down a typical highway and you'll see a succession of billboards, each one a stand-alone advertisement for a single brand. Watch a Grand Prix race, on the other hand, and you note a different approach: every car carries a multitude of brands. These complicated, high-performance machines are expensive to build and maintain. With just one sponsor, a car wouldn't amount to much.

Now think about how companies approach their community development and Corporate Social Responsibility programs. Much like billboards, today's community-oriented efforts are undertaken independently, and proudly associated with single company names. What if companies thought of community programs more like Grand Prix cars? What if they recognized the vast support communities often need, and partnered up to provide it? Presumably it would serve the communities better if CSR programs adopted the Grand Prix rather than the billboard model. Probably it would also be more profitable for the firms.

Rio Tinto and BHP Billiton are in the resource extraction business, and have learnt that communities and corporate interests can go hand in hand.

In some parts of the world government mismanagement of community development (deliberate or otherwise) has led to civil strife, sometimes resulting in armed conflict, creating a security scenario where business simply cannot continue to operate. Even when peace has returned, post-conflict nationalisation has been seen in many countries, with business losing billions in operational assets. Looking at history, business cannot afford to be not interested in community development. A company simply has too much to lose if things go wrong.

Increasingly, we've seen other companies recognise equitable community development as a critical business activity to reduce risk. This is a major change. In decades past, it would not have been uncommon for business leaders to say that it is a government's responsibility to ensure long-term sustainable economic growth for a community, and that a company's contribution would be through tax, employment, and royalties. Move forward to 2012, and those days are long gone. Most now recognise that business can't legitimately claim that socio-economic development is not a business concern.

At this point, some companies are looking beyond the risk-reduction argument, and seeing in equitable community development an opportunity to grow 'shared value'. This term coined by Michael Porter and Mark Kramer, reflects the view that business and community interests can be in sync. In particular, Porter and Kramer argue that businesses should search for those opportunities where value can be created for business by improving community well-being.

Like BHP's malaria example, the Australian-based bank ANZ, offers another case as it expands throughout the Asia Pacific. Its community development work in places such as Fiji, American Samoa and the Cook Islands focuses on financial literacy training programs. Cynics might well say that in educating people about the workings of small business loans or mortgages it is just expanding its market. On the other hand, who could deny that better informed people are more able to benefit from services we take for granted in the developed world? What is wrong with prospering along with a community empowered by greater skills in budgeting, saving and money management?

Neither of these cases should be viewed as corporate philanthropy; both are investments with returns to community and the business owners being measured and celebrated. The contribution that Porter and Kramer make with their 'shared value' concept is that it legitimises such investments—community work motivated by considerations of what is good for business, and not just the work motivated by philanthropic altruism.

Rio Tinto is now the majority shareholder in the development of the Oyu Tolgoi mine in Mongolia. When fully operational, this mine promises to account for between a quarter and a third of the GDP of Mongolia. The successful expansion of Rio Tinto Copper is intertwined with the economic development of Mongolia and its people. You can't have one without the other.

Back to the Grand Prix analogy. With so many companies now focused on community development, could we see more in the way of partnership? In other realms of economic activity, we see collaboration between non-competitor businesses as a path to improved shared profitability. Is there any reason we should not see it in community work?

Let's say a company is developing a new mine in a community that has seen little development. The resource company recognises that the huge boost to economic activity will raise many challenges. Towns need to be built, and the influx of workers needs to be managed. As money moves into an economy that had little reliable money supplies, let alone banks, people need to be equipped to handle it. Should a resource company try to engage with all these problems, relying on just itself and the government? It might think to partner with NGOs or UN agencies. But what about other companies?

The Grand Prix model might suggest to the resource company that it could contact a community-minded bank such as ANZ, point to the potential of the community, and encourage it to invest there, too. The community would then benefit from the first company employing and paying staff, and the second one accepting deposits, providing training, and extending credit as appropriate to those who could use it to build wealth. Why not then encourage a third company, a health company, to serve the growing healthcare needs of the community in a shared value model — that is, setting goals and measuring outcomes for the community as well as setting itself up to operate profitably?

If companies join forces to build communities, rather than trying to go it alone, communities are better served. When benefits are wholly dependent on one party's continuing commitment, they are at the mercy of any catastrophic event that damages that party. With more partners comes more stability. Communities grow healthier and more productive, and progress comes on many fronts. The companies on board benefit, too, from the faster progress that comes with shared commitment.

Do We Ditch Aid?

I'm not saying that we should ditch foreign aid and only look to the private sector. We need both. We need the private and public sectors to understand their role and hold themselves accountable. True partnerships and collaboration between public and private sectors and community organisations will need to be fostered in new ways if we are going to close the wealth disparity in the world.

When looking at the development of an undeveloped economy, we need to ask ourselves which part of economic development is best conducted by the public sector and which is best conducted by the private sector. While many may think it's not the role of the private sector to get involved, if 53 per cent of capital flows from OECD countries to the developing world pass through the private sector and if BHP Billiton is already the third largest development agency in Australia, then how can we deny collaboration with the private sector as a legitimate mechanism?

13.

Concluding Thoughts

"To accomplish great things, we must not only act but also dream, not only plan, but also believe." Anatole France

A Warning About Aid – It Will Change You

Many people approach me today asking for advice about whether they should or should not enter the Aid world. When one goes into Aid work, the things that you see and do will change you so much that they create a division between you and your family and friends. Returning home is not an easy transition and more needs to be done to prepare aid workers and their families for the departure but also, and more importantly, for the return. Aid work has many rewards, but one should not underestimate its costs either.

Psychological trauma is part of being an aid worker. It can come from a specific incident such as witnessing an atrocity, or it can build slowly over time. For me, the memories of the little girl, Maria, in Yugoslavia, or the feeling in Ntarama Church in Rwanda inspire emotion and sadness; they are scars on my soul. The experiences in the aid world change a person much in the same way that the horrific experiences of war changes a soldier, in both a negative and positive way. The need for ex-servicemen and women to come together collectively in clubs such as the Returned and Services League for mutual support is well known. Old soldiers need to gather together and tell old war stories in part to relieve themselves of tensions and experiences that stay with them their entire lives.

Aid workers are often like soldiers. They see some horrendous things, make some difficult decisions and often stay longer with communities they serve and can be just as strongly affected and traumatised by war and disaster. More needs to be done to help the transition home.

Knowledge and Moral Dilemmas – Tools of the Aid Trade

Effectiveness in aid comes down to personalities, judgements on moral dilemmas and politics. It shouldn't, but it does. When people get on well, collaborate and worry about the objective to bring the world out of poverty, an enormous amount can be achieved. Leadership is key and it all too often is lacking.

Life has a lot more 'grey' than 'black and white'. In life leaders often have to choose between the least bad of bad options. Rarely does one chose between good and bad. Choosing to follow a bad option because it is the 'least bad' of available alternatives, is often confused with, but is not the same as, thinking a chosen option is 'good'. One choses the least bad because it is a kind of utilitarianism: the least harm to the fewer people, as compared with the greatest good to the greatest number.

Take the war in Iraq. People forget that two choices available were to have a war and remove Saddam Hussein or to not have a war and keep him in place. The real choice wasn't between 'good' (peace) and 'bad' (war), it was a choice between Saddam in power (bad) and American-led invasion (bad). Both were bad options.

In 1994, during the height of the Bosnian conflict, aid workers often faced a staggering moral dilemma – and this story is true. Local militia (of ethnic group one) would approach an aid worker and say: "See that village down there (full of ethnic group two)? Well, we are going to 'ethnic cleanse' it. Will you bus the people out, please?" The aid worker could succumb to the request, become the tool of ethnic cleansing, lose the neutral status of the aid organisation in the eyes of ethnic group two and, consequently, be refused access to other areas where populations may die through lack of food and other aid. This is not a good choice.

Or, on the other hand, the aid worker could refuse to bus the people out. The result would be an immediate attack on the village and the aid worker may watch perhaps hundreds of people die. This is not a good choice either. And here lies the heart of a moral dilemma. With this dilemma there is no 'better option' to choose. On several occasions young delegates of aid organisations had to choose the 'least bad' option. In other words, they had to choose who would die.

In 1994, the world had advance warning of the Rwandan genocide. The world ignored the pleas of General Dallaire, the UN force commander, when he asked for a mere 2500 soldiers to stop genocide from happening. The world said 'this is not our war' and refused the request. Just 100 days later, up to one million people were dead. That is 10,000 a day, every day, for 100 days. That was the cost of non-intervention.

In 1992, the Europeans (especially the French and the Germans) said to the US that Bosnia was a European problem and that the US should keep out. 'We will fix it," they said. For three years, they tried and failed, and 250,000 people died before the US intervened. That was the cost of non-intervention.

The Verge of a New Choice?

We are on the verge of something new and interesting. When looking at a macroeconomic level, the countries that have effectively pulled themselves out of poverty have done so by putting a focus on development investment supplemented by development aid, not the countries that have put most of their focus on an aid-driven agenda.

There are clear comparative advantages with the private sector in some areas of economic development, and the public sector in other areas. There are particularly difficult issues that need to be examined in looking at the role of the collaborative sectors and the leadership that needs to be shown around the difficult issues.

What do you do if a government genuinely doesn't want to help its people? Do you continue pumping aid into a flawed system? While the United Nations is clearly needed for a political meeting place between nations, is it the best place for developmental assistance? For emergency assistance, how do we replicate the authority given to the UN cluster approach by the Pakistan Army, when the UN system itself doesn't wish to have that authority?

There is a lapse in leadership and a lapse in quality dialogue globally which is not manifesting itself in Australia alone. While we saw tremendous change in 2011 through the Arab Spring and other revolutionary uprisings, we have paralysis by analysis in many of the developed economies. The richest country in the world according to the International Monetary Fund, is Qatar with a per capita GDP of US $88,000 a year. The poorest is the Democratic Republic of the Congo, with a per capita GDP of US $329 per year. The wealthiest people in the world are 267 times better off than the poorest on a national basis. Yet, individual wealth disparity is even higher. Australia has a balance in the economy better than many other countries in the world. Would it not be good to ask what Australia is doing well rather than simply calling for the destruction of capitalism as many of the Occupy Movement protesters have asked for? Could we not make Australia even better? Could we then not provide a global model at which the Europeans and Americans seem to have failed?

I started my journey hoping to use my skills for the betterment of other people. I chose the public sector through the mechanisms of the Red Cross and the United Nations. This path has taken me to many countries, but as I gained seniority the realisation dawned that the world's generalisations of who are the good and bad guys are often wrong, or misguided. While many in the UN are good people, many others are bureaucrats in a system that protects itself, often at the cost of those it is intended to serve.

If we wish to break the cycle of poverty, then new partnerships are needed. A well-motivated private sector company can do more long-term good than a poorly trained but well motivated aid worker. Our task is to alter perceived stereotypes about private sector 'greed' and public sector and aid world altruism. We need to work harder at identifying the good players, be they public or private sector, and acknowledge them. We also need to remove those in the public sector who are just too inefficient or ineffective to justify the huge amounts of public money they spend. This will take time, dedication and skill. If you have the skills and desire to play a role in altering perceptions and changing thinking, then this would be using your skills for the betterment of other people. Are you up to that challenge?

About the Author

Andrew MacLeod was born and raised in Melbourne. He has a BA degree and LL.B degree from the University of Tasmania, and a LL.M degree (Shipping and Human Rights) from the University of Southampton. He worked as a Marine Litigation Attorney in Melbourne, Sydney and London before being recruited by the International Committee of the Red Cross (ICRC), for whom he worked as a Red Cross Delegate in the former Yugoslavia and later Rwanda during the 1990s. For his work he was awarded the Humanitarian Overseas Service Medal in the Balkans (plus bar for the Great Lakes), the Australian Defence Medal and the Silver Medal for Humanity from the Montenegrin Red Cross.

He later worked as a Senior Adviser on Disaster Response for the United Nations and was Chief of Operations in the United Nations Emergency Coordination Centre in the international response to the 2005 Kashmir earthquake. That earthquake response is recognised as one of the best-run natural disaster response operations in history, keeping 3.5 million people alive through a Himalayan winter, in some of the most difficult physical and political terrain.

Having coordinated massive relief campaigns, negotiated with military dictators and terrorists, Andrew MacLeod is often asked to speak about his experiences in Aid and draw lessons in leadership. Author, photographer and speaker, Andrew MacLeod was a Board Member and Foundation Chair of the Principles for Social Investment and a member of the United Nations Expert Group on Responsible Business and Investment in High Risk Areas. He remains a senior executive in the resource sector, a patron of the Australian charity Swags for Homeless, is on the advisory board to the *Big Issue* Australia, is an ambassador for the Victorian Youth Mentoring Alliance and an ambassador for 'Welcome to Australia'.

Committed to health and fitness, and in particular swimming, Andrew won a silver medal at the World Masters Games in 2002. He put his passion for swimming to good effect volunteering to help national swimming teams in the developing countries in which he has worked.

Email: Andrew@macleod.com
Web: www.andrew.macleod.com